Keto Instant Pot for Beginners

600 Quick and Delicious Keto Instant Pot Recipes to Reset Your Body and Live a Healthy Life – Lose up to 25 Pounds in 3 Weeks

Dr Ronda Wade

© Copyright 2019 Dr Ronda Wade - All Rights Reserved.

In no way is it legal to reproduce, duplicate, or transmit any part of this document by either electronic means or in printed format. Recording of this publication is strictly prohibited, and any storage of this material is not allowed unless with written permission from the publisher. All rights reserved.

The information provided herein is stated to be truthful and consistent, in that any liability, regarding inattention or otherwise, by any usage or abuse of any policies, processes, or directions contained within is the solitary and complete responsibility of the recipient reader. Under no circumstances will any legal liability or blame be held against the publisher for any reparation, damages, or monetary loss due to the information herein, either directly or indirectly. Respective authors own all copyrights not held by the publisher.

Legal Notice:

This book is copyright protected. This is only for personal use. You cannot amend, distribute, sell, use, quote or paraphrase any part of the content within this book without the consent of the author or copyright owner. Legal action will be pursued if this is breached.

Disclaimer Notice:

Please note the information contained within this document is for educational and entertainment purposes only. Every attempt has been made to provide accurate, up-to-date and reliable, complete information. No warranties of any kind are expressed or implied. Readers acknowledge that the author is not engaging in the rendering of legal, financial, medical or professional advice.

By reading this document, the reader agrees that under no circumstances are we responsible for any losses, direct or indirect, which are incurred as a result of the use of information contained within this document, including, but not limited to, errors, omissions, or inaccuracies.

Table of contents

Chapter1: Everything You Need to Know About the Ketogenic Diet 11

    What is the Difference between Keto and Atkins?................... 11

    Benefits of Ketogenic Diet................ 11

    Ketosis and Macros....................... 13

    How to Find That You are in Ketosis 14

Chapter2: Instant Pot Basic 15

    Instant Pot Benefits:........................ 15

    The Main Functions....................... 16

    How to Clean Your Instant Pot.......... 16

Chapter3: Food to Eat and Food to Avoid 18

Chapter4: Tips and Tricks..................... 19

Chapter5: Common Mistakes for Beginners 20

Chapter6: Breakfast Recipes................. 21

    Flavors Egg Cups 21

    Ham Broccoli Frittata..................... 21

    Spinach Ricotta Cheese Quiche 22

    Easy Egg Salad 22

    Simple Breakfast Egg Muffins........... 23

    Mini Mushroom Cheese Quiche 23

    Avocado Egg Bites 24

    Scrambled Eggs.............................. 24

    Easy Steamed Eggs 25

    Breakfast Egg in Marinara Sauce 25

    Healthy Breakfast Bowl 26

    Sausage Cheese Breakfast Casserole 26

    Tomato Egg Fritatta....................... 27

    Delicious Caprese Frittata................ 27

    Bacon Breakfast Casserole 28

    Feta Sausage Mushroom Frittata.............. 28

    Egg Sausage Tacos.......................... 29

    Cauliflower Mashed........................ 29

    Cheese Broccoli Frittata.................. 30

    Quick Mini Frittatas 30

    Korean Eggs 31

    Cheese Green Chilies Frittata.................. 31

    Spinach Pie.................................... 32

    Asparagus Frittata 32

    Garlic Tomato Frittata 33

    Breakfast Cheese Quiche 33

    Spinach Nutmeg Feta Pie................ 34

    Omelets in Jar............................... 35

    Basil Mozzarella Egg Cups 35

    Egg Salad Roll-Ups........................ 36

    Spinach Tomato Cups 36

    Simple Egg Cups............................ 37

    Bacon Frittata................................ 37

    Almond Pancake............................ 38

    Bacon Brussels sprouts................... 38

    Breakfast Quiche 39

    Mushroom Cheese Chive Omelet 39

    Kale Egg Cheese Breakfast............. 40

    Delicious Carrot Muffins................. 40

    Healthy Pumpkin Bread 41

    Cauliflower Cheese Egg Bake 41

Chia Breakfast Pudding 42

Eggs with scallions 42

Broccoli Cauliflower Mash 43

Healthy Almond Porridge 43

Chapter 7: Poultry Recipes 44

Quick BBQ Chicken Wings 44

Easy Chicken Adobo 44

Flavors Basil Chicken 44

Delicious Paprika Chicken 45

Tasty Parmesan Chicken 45

Mediterranean Chicken 46

Teriyaki Chicken 46

Garlicky Chicken 47

Tomato Onion Turkey 47

Orange Turkey Legs 48

Cauliflower Jalapeno Chicken 48

Thyme Duck Legs 49

Creamy Broccoli Turkey 49

Dijon Turkey Roast 50

Herb Lemon Chicken Wings 50

Whole Roasted Chicken 51

Chicken Wraps 51

Yummy Chicken Taco 52

Chicken Parmigiana 52

Italian Creamy Chicken 53

Delicious Pepper Cream Chicken 53

Thyme Dijon Chicken 53

Spicy Chicken 54

Indian Spiced Chicken Curry 54

Simple Salsa Chicken 55

Lime Garlic Chicken 55

Butter Chicken 56

Chicken Masala 56

Simple Chicken Curry 57

Stir Fried Chicken 57

Simple Moist Turkey Breast 58

Flavors Chicken Fajitas 58

Tasty Taco Chicken 58

Classic Chicken Shawarma 59

Rotisserie Chicken 59

Tasty Shredded Chicken 60

Creamy Garlic Pepper Chicken 60

Creamy Pepper Chicken 61

Simple Mexican Taco Wings 61

Salsa Verde Chicken 62

Thai Chicken 62

Ranch Chicken 62

Yummy Mexican Chicken 63

Buffalo Chicken 63

Artichoke Chicken 64

Chapter 8: Soup & Stew Recipes 65

Coconut Carrot Soup 65

Squash Cauliflower Soup 65

Creamy Squash Soup 66

Pork Soup 66

Mushroom Chicken Stew 67

Chicken Veggie Stew 67

Venison Stew 68

Creamy Taco Soup 68	Jalapeno Chicken Soup 82
Asparagus Soup 69	Chicken Curry Soup 83
Creamy Tomato Soup 69	Thyme Onion Soup 83
Thyme Asparagus Ham Soup 70	Chicken Poblano Soup 84
Beef Pork Soup 70	Ranch Chicken Soup 84
Tomato Coconut Soup 71	Tasty Tomato Cream Soup 85
Tomato Chicken Soup 71	Broccoli Soup 85
Italian Mushrooms Chicken Soup 72	Rosemary Lamb Stew 86
Garlic Kale Chicken Soup 72	Cauliflower Broccoli Chicken Stew 86
Artichoke Chicken Stew 72	**Chapter9: Beef Recipes 88**
Dijon Mushroom Stew 73	Flavorful Corned Beef 88
Thyme Basil Tomato Soup 73	Herb Meatloaf 88
Zesty Cabbage Soup 74	Italian Beef Roast 89
Tasty Asparagus Bacon Soup 74	Ginger Garlic Beef 89
Dill Celery Coconut Soup 75	Delicious Cajun Cheese Beef 90
Vegetable Soup 75	Lemon Chili Chuck Roast 90
Spinach Cheese Broccoli Soup 76	Easy Short Beef Ribs 91
Pumpkin Pepper Soup 76	Easy Bolognese Sauce 91
Cheese Soup 77	Tender & Juicy Chuck Roast 91
Zucchini Coconut Soup 77	Basil Cheese Beef 92
Thai Carrot Soup 78	Beef with Carrot & Cabbage 92
Curried Squash Soup 78	Paprika Corned Beef 93
Coconut Celery Chicken Soup 79	Flavorful Pepperoncini Roast 93
Mushroom Steak Soup 79	Ginger Garlic Broccoli Beef 94
Basil Parmesan Tomato Soup 80	Herb Vinegar Beef 94
Creamy Lemon Mushroom Soup 80	Spicy Beef Chili 95
Italian Cabbage Soup 81	Cajun Pepper Beef 95
Broccoli Carrot Soup 81	Spicy Taco Meat 96
Coconut Cauliflower Soup 82	Spicy Beef Chili 96

Delicious Beef Curry 97	Creamy Garlic Thyme Pork 110
Easy Taco Meat 97	Spicy Pork 110
Beef Brisket 98	Yummy Pork Carnitas 111
Apple Cider Beef 98	Easy Jamaican Pork 111
Lime Beef Tacos 98	Parmesan Pork Chops 112
Flavors Balsamic Beef Roast 99	Chili Garlic Pork 112
Spicy Texas Chili 99	Garlicky Pork Shoulder 113
Indian Beef Curry 100	Mushroom Pork Chops 113
Delicious Italian Beef 100	Cinnamon Ginger Pork Chops 114
Creamy Spicy Beef Curry 101	Creamy Spinach Pork 114
Tomatillo Beef Chili 101	Spiced Pork Ribs 115
Tasty Korean Beef 102	Easy Smoked Ribs 115
Jalapeno Cajun Beef 102	Chili Garlic Pork Roast 116
Chili Lime Shredded Beef 103	Yummy Pork Fajitas 116
Herb Almond Meatloaf 103	Tasty Ranch Pork Chops 116
Coconut Beef Brisket 104	Lemon Apple Pork Chops 117
Creamy Flank Steak 104	Thyme Pepper Shredded Pork 117
Tasty Beef Bourguignon 104	Cheesy Pork Chops 118
Ranch Roast 105	Country Style Pork Ribs 118
Thai Beef Roast 105	Onion Garlic Pork Loin 119
Ancho Chili Taco Meat 106	Delicious Butter Ranch Pork Chops .. 119
Pepper Rings Shredded Beef 106	Shredded Garlic BBQ Pork 120
Spicy Meatballs 107	Chipotle BBQ Pork Ribs 120
Flavorful Beef Shawarma 107	Flavors Pork Carnitas 121
Beef Stroganoff 108	Salsa Pork Chili Verde 121
Pepper Beef Chili 108	Cinnamon Spice Ham 122
Chapter10: Pork Recipes 109	Pork Chops with Apple Butter 122
Hawaiian Pork 109	Pork Chops in Garlic Sauce 123
Classic Pork & Cabbage 109	Cheese Butter Pork Chops 123

Shredded Pork Ragu 124
Asian Pork 124
Delicious Pork Chile Verde 125
Wine Rosemary Pork Belly 125
Butter Braised Pork Loin 126
Simple Creamy Pork Chops 126
Tasty Pork Butt 126
Tomatillo Sirloin Pork 127
Simple Jerk Pork 127
Tangy Pork 128
Shredded Asian Pork 128
Lime Pork Chops 129
Leek Pork 129
Olive Capers Pork 130

Chapter 11: Lamb Recipes 131
Quick Leg of Lamb 131
Classic Lamb Curry 131
Indian Lamb Korma 132
Simple Lamb Curry 132
Goat Curry 133
Tender Lamb Curry 133
Lamb with Gravy 134
Delicious Sage Lamb 134
Coconut Zucchini Lamb Curry 135
Flavorful Lamb Ragu 135
Thai Green Lamb Curry 136
Indian Lamb Rogan Josh 137
Cheese Herb Lamb Chops 137
Garlic Ginger Lamb Shanks 138

Ginger Apple Lamb 138
Almond Lamb Patties 139
Creamy Yogurt Lamb 139
Veggie Lamb Chops 140
Balsamic Lamb Shoulder 140
Zucchini Lamb Curry 141
Spinach Lamb Dish 141
Lamb Mushroom Stew 142
Mongolian Lamb 142
Mushroom Lamb Chops 143
Delicious Lamb Ribs 143
Asian Lamb Steaks 144
Red Wine Lamb 144
Spicy & Creamy Lamb 145
Delicious Italian Lamb 146
Tomato Thyme Lamb Shanks 146
Cauliflower Lamb Meatballs 147
Buttery Lamb 147
Coconut Ginger Lamb 148
Spicy Pepper Lamb Curry 148
Sprout with Lamb 149
Spicy Lamb Leg 150
Lemon Coconut Lamb 150
Lamb Garlic Eggplant Curry 151
Gluten-Free Lamb Curry 151
Squash Lamb Curry 152
Jamaican Goat Curry 152
Flavorful Indian Goat Curry 153
Perfect North-Indian Mutton Curry 154

Quick Lamb Rogan Josh 154

Delicious Jordanian Lamb 155

Chapter 12: Seafood & Fish Recipes 156

Lemon Butter Shrimp Scampi 156

Quick Shrimp Scampi 156

Flavorful Shrimp Curry 157

Thai Prawns 157

Garlic Butter Mussels 158

Lemon Garlic Shrimp Scampi 158

Wild-Caught Crab Legs 159

Shrimp Coconut Curry 159

Lemon Garlic Mussels 160

Crab Legs with Butter Sauce 160

Chili Herb Mussels 161

Garlic Tomato Swordfish 161

Salmon with Vegetable 161

Salmon with Sauce 162

Lemon Butter Crabs 162

Jerk Fish with Vegetable 163

Ginger Onion Haddock 163

Tomato Parsley Mussels 164

Lemon Garlic Steamed Tilapia 164

Garlic Cajun Fish Fillet 165

Lemon Salmon Fish Fillet 165

Quick & Simple Fish Fillet 166

Tomato Lemon Fish Fillet 166

Orange Ginger Fish Fillets 166

Simple 3 Ingredients Fish Fillets 167

Chili Lemon Fish Fillets 167

Butter Shrimp Grits 168

Frozen Shrimp 168

Coconut Cayenne Shrimp 169

Cajun Fish Fillet 169

Creamy Salmon Casserole 169

Orange Ginger Fish Fillets 170

Shrimp with Crumbled Cheese 170

Shrimp with Asparagus 171

Tomato Jalapeno Shrimp 171

Delicious Adobo Shrimp 172

Parmesan Salmon 172

Mussels with Asparagus 173

Bacon Lemon Pepper Shrimp 173

Teriyaki Shrimp 174

Ginger Garlic Fish Fillets 174

Cauliflower Shrimp Risotto 175

Cheese Thyme Mussels 175

Lemon Butter Scallops 176

Creamy Celery Crabmeat 176

Chapter 13: Vegan & Vegetarian Recipes 177

Cilantro Lime Cauliflower Rice 177

Fried Cabbage 177

Flavors Southern Cabbage 178

Parmesan Lemon Butter Brussel Sprouts 178

Creamy Cheese Brussels sprouts 179

Artichoke Spinach Dip 179

Spinach Cheese Dip 180

Creamy Ranch Cauliflower Mashed 180

Garlic Cheese Artichokes 181

Cheese Garlic Asparagus 181	Chili Turmeric Cauliflower 195
Delicious Cajun Zucchini 181	Yogurt Butter Cauliflower Mash 195
Perfect Herbed Carrots 182	Almond Cheese Broccoli 196
Cheese Zucchini Noodles 182	Tomato Garlic Bell Pepper 196
Lemon Garlic Kale 183	Sweet & Spicy Cinnamon Carrots 197
Garlicky Green Beans 183	Sweet Cinnamon Carrots 197
Coconut Green Beans 183	Italian Seasoned Carrots 198
Spicy Eggplant 184	**Chapter 14: Desserts Recipes** **199**
Balsamic Garlic Mushrooms 185	Creamy Chocolate Mousse 199
Easy Herbed Mushrooms 185	Mini Chocó Cake 199
Mushroom with Green Beans 185	Easy Pumpkin Pudding 200
Stir Fried Cabbage 186	Delicious Coconut Custard 200
Healthy Beets Salad 186	Vanilla Egg Custard 201
Broccoli Garlic Mash 187	Almond Coconut Cake 201
Asian Bok Choy 187	Perfect Carrot Almond Cake 202
Nutritious Beets with Cheese 188	Yummy Chocó Pudding Cake 202
Steamed Garlic Broccoli 188	Gluten-Free Chocó Lava Cake 203
Tomato Green Beans 189	Flavorful Vanilla Cheesecake 203
Delicious Parmesan Broccoli 189	Tasty Matcha Cheesecake 204
Healthy Butternut Squash 190	Yummy Chocó Layer Cheesecake 204
Healthy Sautéed Veggies 190	Delicious Peanut Butter Fudge 205
Spinach with Cheese 191	Choco Almond Cupcakes 205
Greens with Tofu 191	Cinnamon Pancakes 206
Creamy Basil Broccoli 192	Yummy Chocolate Mousse 207
Lime Sauce Mushrooms 192	Simple Chocolate Mug Cake 207
Stir Fried Leek Swiss chard 193	Chocolate Brownies 208
Stir Fried Broccoli Cauliflower 193	Almond Cheesecake 208
Asian Mushroom Curry 194	Hazelnuts Coconut Cake 209
Cauliflower Mac & Cheese 194	Hazelnuts Brownies 209

Almond Coconut Bars 210	Vanilla Coconut Custard 214
Choco Almond Pudding 210	Vanilla Berry Mousse 215
Choco Chip Orange Muffins 211	Lime Orange Pudding 215
Delicious Vanilla Pudding 212	Choco Coconut Truffles 216
Coconut Avocado Pudding 212	Delicious Almond Scones 216
Cinnamon Almond Cheese Cake 213	Blackberry Cinnamon Brownies 217
Yummy Chocolate Truffles 213	**Conclusion 218**
Walnut Pumpkin Mug Cake 214	

Chapter 1: Everything You Need to Know About the Ketogenic Diet

The ketogenic diet is nothing but a low-carb high fat and adequate protein diet. Ketogenic diet forces the body to burn the fats instead of carbohydrate. Normally carbohydrates in our meals are converted in the form of glucose. Excess glucose in our body is store into the form of glycogen. Human body stores these glycogens into the liver and muscles. when we are doing any hard work exercise or any physical activity our body uses glycogens as a fuel.

What is the Difference between Keto and Atkins?

- Dr. Russel Wilder was discovered ketogenic diet in 1921 for treatment of epilepsy where Atkins diet was introduced by a cardiologist named Robert Atkins in 1972.
- The ketogenic diet has protein limit about 20 percent of your daily calories intake was as Atkins diet has no limit for protein daily protein intake.
- The ketogenic diet is the way of eating changes your metabolism and fuel your body was an Atkins diet is easy to follow it provides both health benefits and weight loss.
- Atkins diet helps to provide short-term health benefits and weight loss benefits were as ketogenic diet is providing long-term health benefits such as effective and fast weight loss.
- Atkins diet is high in fat, high in protein and low in carb were as ketogenic diet is high in fat, moderate in protein and low in carb diet.
- Atkins diet uses net carbohydrate monitoring method to calculate carbohydrate intake were as in ketogenic diet uses total carbohydrate method.
- The ketogenic diet is more restrictive compared to Atkin diet regards to carbohydrates. Atkin diet has a higher consumption of carbohydrates after the induction phase was as ketogenic diet restricts less than 20 g of carbohydrate.
- The ketogenic diet is higher in fiber were as Atkins diet is lower in fiber compare to a ketogenic diet.
- Emphasis on macronutrient ratios are depending on diet goals in ketogenic diet were as Atkins diet emphasis on diet phase instead of macronutrient ratios.
- The ketogenic diet is very effective for treatment for epilepsy now recently it has adopted as a weight loss diet were as Atkins diet is specially designed for weight loss.

Benefits of Ketogenic Diet

- **Improves Metabolic Flexibility:** Metabolic flexibility is one of the energy sources which are needed to run our body cells. When you follow other diets, body uses glucose (carbs) as a fuel but in the ketogenic diet, you use ketones (fats) instead of glucose. This energy source changes will allow your cell to become metabolically flexible.
  Ketones serve one of the good alternative fuels for the Brain. Metabolic Flexibility helps to switch in between carbs and fats.

- Helps to maintain stable blood sugar levels: when your body uses ketones as a primary fuel instead of glucose which will help to keep your sugar level stable throughout the day. This will happen because of glucose needed insulin to transport into the cells where glucose can be used as energy. It will also help to increase insulin sensitivity.
  Ketones don't require insulin to be transported to cells, it means that ketogenic diet reduces and prevent insulin resistance which will help you to keep your fuel level steady all day long.

- Effectively Burns stored body fat: Ketogenic diet helps to burn body fats because it breaks down body fats and uses these fats as an energy source. When glucose level is high in body extra glucose is stored in the form of glycogens. Glycogens are glucose stored in the liver and muscles. When intakes of glycogens are increased in the body these extra glycogens are store in the form of fats.
  When carbohydrate intake is low in body our body breaks fats for energy known as ketones bodies. Many studies show that a ketogenic diet is very effective for weight loss in the long term compared to other diet plans.

- Boosts physical exercise performance: Research shows that a ketogenic diet helps to reduce fats faster than compared to other diet and effect of ketogenic diet is long term.ATP comes from glucose which provides energy to your body cells. Ketones produce more total energy than ATP. A recent study shows that the ketogenic diet boosts 20 times fast intramuscular fat burning
  If you are endurance athlete ketones are very beneficial for you where you only lose fats and not muscles during resistance training. It will help to maintain muscle mass and increase their performance.

- Help to improve brain health: Ketones can improve your brain function and mental health. It improves learning, memory, focus, and attention. Research study shows that ketosis is very helpful to prevent long-term neurological damage also reduces the risk of Alzheimer's, epilepsy, neurodegeneration, and Parkinson's disease. Ketones are providing up to 70 percent of brain energy needs.
  When insulin and glucose levels are low your liver produces ketones from fatty acids

- Improves heart function: Ketones have antioxidant properties which protect the lining of your blood vessels, boosts circulation and improves your heart functions and lower the risk of heart disease.
  One of the researches found that using ketogenic diet improves heart efficiency by 30 percent and blood flow by 75 percent.

- Helps to increase your lifespan: Ketosis triggers are one of the mechanisms helps to live longer. Ketosis unlocking genes that regulate metabolism and fight oxidative stress. Due to many health conditions causes damage inflammation to cells.
  Ketones trigger antioxidant effects are having an amazing effect on your brain. One of the studies shows that ketones help to prevent oxidative damage in neurons.

- Prevents various diseases: Ketones has anti-inflammatory and antioxidant properties which will help to prevent various diseases. Ketosis is helpful in Parkinson's disease, Alzheimer disease, cancer, obesity, heart disease, Huntington's and type-2 diabetes. Research shows that the classic ketogenic diet improves 50 percent epilepsy patients.

Ketosis and Macros

Ketosis and macros are playing the most important role in a ketogenic diet. They break down three main nutrients which are protein, fat, and carbohydrates needed in large amounts. The easiest way to calculate keto macros is used keto calculator.

Macros

Macros are macronutrients which are needed to your body in large quantities for tissue building and metabolic process. There are five macronutrients.

- Proteins
- Carbohydrates
- Fats
- Fiber
- Water

Among these five macronutrients, most of the people refer three main macronutrients which are carbohydrates, proteins, and fats. Macros play important role in the ketogenic diet they provide essential body energy which is calculated in the form of calories.

Research shows that if your intake too many wrong macros which will lead to obesity, diabetes and heart diseases. Therefore, balancing of essential macros helps you stay healthy. Macronutrients are essential for your body but besides these macronutrients, your body needs micronutrients which are needed in a smaller amount which are minerals and vitamins. A perfect planned ketogenic diet provides both micro and macronutrients to your body. Recommended energy from macronutrient is 45 to 65 percent from carbs, 20 to 35 percent from fats and 10 to 35 percent from protein

- Carbohydrates: Carbohydrates are made up of starch and sugar. To achieve successful ketosis, you should limit your carbohydrate intake. Fibers are also counted in carb you can't really digest fibers, so it has a minimal impact of your blood sugar because they just pass through your body. To limit your carb successfully you should identify food which is low in carbohydrate. You should find out carb values in the food that you have to eat which helps you to take allotted amount of carb per day.
- Proteins: Proteins play an important role in your body it is essential for preserving of lean muscles and also help to repair that muscle which is broken down during the ketogenic diet. It also helps to preserve lean muscles mass. Losing muscles mass is not a good sign which means you are loose muscles strength. During a ketogenic diet, you need to intake enough amount of protein to maintain your lean body mass. You should avoid too much

amount of protein intake during a ketogenic diet because protein has the potential to damage your kidney and also affect ketosis.
- **Fats:** Fats are important in ketogenic diet for energy, growth, and development by absorbing certain vitamins it provides protective cushioning for organs and also helps to maintain cell membrane. There are some healthy fats used in ketogenic diets such as butter, oils, heavy cream, avocados, and nuts. Consuming these type of healthy fat helps to push your body into ketosis and burning more unwanted fats from your body.

How to Find That You are in Ketosis

There are several methods to find out you are in ketosis or not are as follows

- Keto breath: During the ketosis, fatty acids are broken down for energy in kidney and liver during this process acetone released, due to acetone the smell of breath changes. These changes would happen in the first few days due to changing of diet. It means that you are entered in the ketosis.
- Dry mouth and increased thirst: When you start ketogenic diet insulin level decrease, your body starts expelling water and excess sodium. If you follow extremely low carb plan keto recommended taking 2 to 4 grams of sodium per day in your diet for balancing electrolytes. When your body shifts into ketogenic state your body use excess glycogens. This affects increase the need for urination due to this thirst increases. It means that you are in ketosis.
- Ketones detect in urine: you have to check the ketones in the urine with the help of Ketostix. It is one of the strip brands which is an inexpensive and accurate way to check for ketosis. Ketostix comes with a guide to check how deep the level of ketosis in your body. You just dip the strip in your urine collected in a clean and dry container. After that shake strip to remove excess and wait for 15 seconds the strip colors are changes, with the help of guide check your ketosis level. If the strip is shown deeper purple, it indicates ketones levels are higher.
- Blood test: Blood test is an expensive but most accurate method to measure your body is in ketosis. This method is used by diabetic people to measure blood ketones levels. To measure blood ketones, you need ketone meter and ketone test strips with lancet pen. If your ketone meter measures 0.5 and 3mml/L then you are in ketosis.

Chapter2: Instant Pot Basic

Instant Pot is a third-generation multi-cooker. It is small electric appliances using various types of cooking such as pressure cooking, rice cooker, slow cooker, steamer, sauté, yogurt maker, warmer and many more. It is a pre-programmed electric appliance

The device has many settings such as cook food on low, medium, high and keeps warm. There are more than 20 types of instant pots available in the market. Some instant pot has Bluetooth connectivity which allows you to monitor and control your instant pot with the help of a tablet or Smartphone.

Instant Pot is fast in cooking it generates more heat and pressure cooking is twice fast than the conventional cooking. Instant pot can help you to create easy fast and delicious recipes in the lowest time period it already has programmed buttons. Instant pot helps to cook your food quicker and safer compared to other cooking devices in your kitchen

Instant Pot Benefits:

1. **Saving your time and energy:**
   Instant Pot is a help to cook foods faster than other traditional methods of cooking. It is an electric pressure cooker which helps to reduce cooking time by 70 percent compare to another non-electric cooker. Instant pot requires less water for cooking and it saves up to 70 percent of energy. After microwave instant pot is the most energy efficient appliance. Using instant pot, you can cook a whole chicken in half an hour and veggies in just 5 minutes, so it saves your lots of timing and energy.

2. **Eliminate harmful micro-organisms in food:**
   Instant pot cooks food under high pressure which creates temperature above the boiling point of water, this may result in kills almost all living harmful micro-organisms such as bacteria, viruses, and fungi. Wheat, corn, rice, and beans are those foods which may carry fungal poisons called as aflatoxins. Researchers prove that the aflatoxins have a potent trigger of liver cancer and it may play a host role in another type of cancer as well. Just cooking foods to its boiling point is insufficient to destroy aflatoxins. Pressure cooking is the way to destroy aflatoxins. Kidney bean also contains a phytohaemagglutinin which is only destroying over pressure cooking.

3. **Cook tasty food and preserving nutrients:**
   When you pressure cook any food heat is even, quickly and deeply distributed in the pressure cooking. It doesn't require immersing food into the water. Enough water is required to pressure cooker filled with steam. Instant pot requires less water for pressure cooking due to this they save vitamins and minerals are dissolved in water. When steam equally distributed surround the food foods are not oxidized so it helps to maintain natural color and flavor of food.

4. Clean and Pleasant cooking experience:
Instant Pot has a fully sealed mechanism so there is no smell spread in the kitchen. This makes instant pot is an ideal convenient pressure-cooking appliance. During the cooking process, instant pot is quiet, and no steam is escaping from the pot this will help to keep aromas and flavor in the food. As per name multi-cooker, it cooks multiple foods, so it helps to reduce the cooking appliances in the kitchen. Instant pot heats only inner pot foods it not heating the surrounding atmosphere. So, it helps to keep your kitchen atmosphere cool.

The Main Functions

- **Keep warm / cancel:** This function is used to turn off your instant pot or keeps warm mode is used to maintain the temperature in between 145 F to 172 F. It helps to keep food warm.
- **Soup:** This button is used to make soup, broth or stock. Cooking time under this setting is in between 20 to 40 minutes and pressure are either high or low.
- **Sauté:** sauté is the most used button in instant pot. Using sauté, you can cook anything as you would in pan or skillet. You need to add just cooking oil or any fat into the inner pot and cook like a pan or skillet. In sauté mode you can adjust the temperature in three modes which are the normal mode, more mode, and less mode.
- **Meat/stew:** This function is used to make meat or stew in instant pot. It has 35 minutes default high pressure. You can adjust Less for high pressure 20 minutes of time and More for high pressure for 45 minutes of time.
- **Manual / Pressure:** This function is used to adjust the pressure in between high to low. This function is used for pressure cooking purpose. We can adjust pressure, time and temperature using + / - buttons
- **Slow cook:** Using this function you can use your instant pot in to slow cooker. You can also use glass lid comes with your instant pot for the slow cooking mode. A default time of slow cook function is 4 hours by pressing + / - buttons you can change slow cooking time in between 30 minutes to 20 hours.
- **Adjust:** This function is used to adjust the temperature of slow cooking and sauté functions in between Normal More and fewer settings.
- **Timer:** This function is used to delay the cooking start time. Press the timer button for 10 seconds by pressing slow cook button. It works for both slow cooking and pressure-cooking functions.

How to Clean Your Instant Pot

Cleaning instant pot needed Dish soap, vinegar, cotton or microfiber cloth and small scrub brush please follow the following instructions to clean your instant pot.

- Always keep in mind first unplug any appliance before cleaning. Check the cable has any damage.
- The separate lid then also separates interior pot from the housing.
- To clean the pot outside wipe outer portion of the housing to remove tough stains. Housing has electronic component so never immersed in water.
- Properly clean the housing area use small brush for removing dried food residue.
- Use soapy water to clean lid with hand-wash.
- Remove steam release handle to check for food particles.
- Remove the anti-block shield from under the lid to clean the steam valve after cleaning reattach the anti-block shield by tightening with hands.
- Remove the silicone ring and float valve and clean both and reattach both portions. Ensure the float valve moves up and down easily.
- Remove and clean the sealing ring check crack, leak over sealing ring if the ring is damage please replace the ring.
- Wash inner pot and steam rack properly. Wash it using the dishwasher
- To remove discoloring on the stainless-steel portion of the instant pot wipe or soak with vinegar.
- Finally, make sure that all parts are reattached securely check the silicon rings are properly fitted check anti-block shield now your instant pot is ready for cooking.

Chapter 3: Food to Eat and Food to Avoid

Eat freely

- Use only Grass-fed meat comes from a goat, lamb, beef etc. seafood and wild-caught fish, pastured eggs and pork, butter, ghee are high in omega 3 fatty acids
- Use healthy fats such as saturated fats like duck fat, chicken fat, goose fats MCT oils and coconut oils. Monosaturated fats like olive oil, macadamia oil, and avocado oil etc. Omega 3 fatty acids come from seafood and fatty fish. Omega 3 comes under polyunsaturated fats.
- Always use non-starchy vegetables such as leafy greens vegetables spinach, chives, radicchio, Swiss chard, lettuce, bok choy etc. Cruciferous vegetables like radishes, kale, kohlrabi. Cucumber, celery stalk, summer squash, asparagus etc.
- In fruits, the only avocado is allowed.
- Beverages and condiments coffee, tea, water. Pickles, bone broth, mayonnaise, fermented food, mustard. All herbs and spices, lime zest, lime juice. Eggs white protein and whey protein.

Avoid completely

- Completely avoid added sugar, sweeteners which causes the rise of blood sugars also causes insulin spikes.
- All grains sprouted grains, wheat, bulgur, rice, corn, oats. Also avoid all that products which are made from grains like pizza, cookies, bread, pasta. Sweets and sugar such as ice cream, table sugar, sweet puddings, cake, and agave syrup etc.
- Completely avoid factory formed fish and pork which are high in omega 6 fatty acids, avoid those fish which are high in mercury.
- Avoid Processed Foods like almond milk products, MSG some of the whey protein products. Sulfites like dried fruits.
- Artificial sweeteners should be avoided such as Acesulfame, saccharin, sucralose etc. This may lead to your carvings.
- Completely avoid refined oils and fats such as canola, sunflower, corn oil, soybean oil and Trans fats like margarine.
- Dairy products should be avoided in a ketogenic diet. Milk is difficult to digest so that you should avoid milk. Due to the lack of good bacteria, you should avoid milk during a ketogenic diet.
- Avoid Tropical fruits such as papaya, pineapple, banana, mango etc. high carb fruits like grapes and tangerine. Also avoid fruit juices completely.
- Avoid wheat gluten and soy products, should aware of BPA lined cans because BPA has some of the negative effects on your health it may cause cancer and impaired thyroid function.
- Avoid Legumes like lentil, beans, peanuts and chickpeas which are high in carb. Legumes are hard to digest because it contains phytates and lectins.

Chapter 4: Tips and Tricks

1. **Stay Hydrated:** This is one of the most important things in keto diet you should hydrate your body every day because water plays important role in body processes. You can consume keto coffee, tea, and smoothies in the morning. Drink lots of water when you wake up
2. **Exercise:** During the keto diet, regular exercise helps you to boost your ketones levels. Regular exercise during keto diet gives you weight loss. At the time of exercise, body depletes its glycogen store. Regular exercise will help you to balance your blood sugar levels. Regular exercise increases the level of protein in the liver and muscles.
3. **Increase Healthy Fat Intake:** Regularly consume plenty of fats will help you to boost your ketones level and also help you to reach ketosis. Ketogenic diet for metabolic health, weight loss provides 6 to 80 percent of calories from fat. Good fats include coconut oil, tallow, lard, avocado oil, and olive oil. If you consume at least 60 percent of calories from fat will help you to boost your ketone levels.
4. **Eat Fermented Foods:** Eat fermented foods like kimchi, pickles, kefir, sauerkraut and coconut water to improve digestion. It will also keep you hydrated.
5. **Count Carbs Intake:** Counting daily carb intake is very important when you are in keto diet. Certain foods have hidden carbohydrate which is keto friendly but has loaded with sugar. Such foods are milk, yogurt, chicken wings with barbecue sauce, breaded meats and most fruits. During the ketogenic diet, you should consume a maximum of 50 grams of carbohydrates.
6. **Use MCT oils:** MCT oils have more protein and carbs that are used to maintain ketosis. It provides quick energy to your body because MCT oils are immediately metabolized into ketone bodies.
7. **Measure your ketones:** you can measure the ketones using a glucose meter and keto sticks. Glucose meter provides the most accurate results, but it is expensive alternatives because most of the people are deterred from using them daily. Another way use keto sticks are a cheap way to measure ketones. Keto sticks results are not as accurate as a glucose meter.
8. **Improve your sleep:** Sleep is very important in ketosis if you are sleeping poorly will evaluate stress hormones which causes blood sugar dysregulation problems. Always sleep in a dark room and recommended sleep is 7 to 9 hours.
9. **Use Exogenous ketones:** Exogenous ketones are most popular supplement available in the market.it is a shortcut to getting into ketosis.it helps during the initial phase of ketosis where your body uses ketones for energy instead of carbohydrate.

Chapter5: Common Mistakes for Beginners

1. Not enough fats: In keto, if you want to lose fat you should consume enough amounts of fats. You need to spend money to earn money, same will happen here if you lose fats then you should intake enough amount of fats to getting into ketosis.
2. Consumes too much protein: In a ketogenic diet, your body gets energy from breaking down fats proteins are needed only to maintain muscle mass. If you consume more protein than your body it converts excess protein into glucose. Which may cause raise your blood sugar levels.
3. Stop comparing to others: Stop comparing yourself to others because your body reacts differently than someone else. The ketogenic diet is very useful in weight loss but if someone loses 8 lbs in 7 days, it doesn't mean that you also get the same result. There are many different factors will affect your results.
4. Not enough water: Many people are not consistently drinking enough water throughout a day during ketosis its advice that drinks a gallon of water throughout a day. This will help your body organs can function properly.
5. Too much dairy: In ketogenic diet, you use full-fat dairy, if you consume too much then it is very difficult to lose weight. Dairy products have full of calories if you eat too much then the body doesn't burns extra fat for energy. Normally your body burns 2000 calories throughout a day. If you consume 1500 calories your body just burn remaining 500 calories from fat. That's why you should avoid too much dairy products during a keto diet.
6. Consume enough good salt: Due to higher carbohydrate diet, many people face higher sodium ratio. During low carb ketogenic diet, you need to get additional 3 to 5 grams of sodium from natural foods and through the use of Himalayan sea salt and pink salt. You can consume additional sodium from drinking organic broth, consuming sea vegetables like dulse, nori, and kelp, also consume celery, cucumber, sprouted and salted pumpkin seeds.
7. Keep stress down: Chronic stress badly affects your ability to stay in ketosis. Stress raises up stress hormones in your body functions to evaluate blood sugar. Using some strategies will help you to reduce your stress and create more peace and relaxation in your life.

Chapter 6: Breakfast Recipes

Flavors Egg Cups

Preparation Time: 10 minutes; Cooking Time: 10 minutes; Serve: 4
Ingredients:
- 4 eggs
- 2 tbsp fresh cilantro, chopped
- ¼ cup half and half
- ½ cup cheddar cheese, shredded
- ½ cup tomatoes, diced
- ½ cup mushrooms, diced
- Pepper
- Salt

Directions:
1. In a bowl, mix together eggs, half and half, cheese, vegetables, cilantro, pepper, and salt.
2. Divide egg mixture into the four ramekins and cover ramekins with foil pieces.
3. Pour two cups of water into the instant pot then place trivet into the pot.
4. Place ramekins on top of the trivet.
5. Seal pot with lid and cook on high for 5 minutes.
6. Release pressure using quick release method than open the lid.
7. Serve and enjoy.

Nutritional Value (Amount per Serving):
Calories 146; Fat 10.9 g; Carbohydrates 2.4 g; Sugar 1.2 g; Protein 10 g

Ham Broccoli Frittata

Preparation Time: 10 minutes; Cooking Time: 30 minutes; Serve: 4
Ingredients:
- 4 eggs
- 1 cup cheddar cheese, shredded
- 1 cup half and half
- 2 cups frozen broccoli
- 1 cup sweet peppers, sliced
- 8 oz ham, diced
- 1 tsp pepper
- 1 tsp salt

Directions:
1. Spray 6*3 baking pan with cooking spray and set aside.
2. Place sliced peppers in the bottom of prepared pan.
3. Spread ham on top of sliced peppers and broccoli.
4. In a bowl, whisk half and half, eggs, pepper, and salt. Add cheese and stir well.
5. Pour bowl mixture on top of veggies mixture and cover dish with foil.
6. Pour 2 cups of water into the instant pot then place a trivet in the pot.
7. Place pan on top of the trivet.
8. Seal pot with lid and cook on high for 20 minutes.
9. Allow to release pressure naturally then open the lid.
10. Serve and enjoy.

Nutritional Value (Amount per Serving):

Calories 374; Fat 25.8 g; Carbohydrates 11.1 g; Sugar 2.9 g; Protein 25.4 g

Spinach Ricotta Cheese Quiche

Preparation Time: 10 minutes; Cooking Time: 10 minutes; Serve: 4
Ingredients:
- 4 eggs
- ½ cup cheddar cheese, shredded
- 2 tbsp ricotta cheese
- 2 tbsp unsweetened almond milk
- ¼ cup ham, diced
- ¼ cup onion, diced
- ½ cup mushrooms, diced
- ½ cup spinach, chopped
- 1 tbsp butter
- ¼ tsp sea salt

Directions:
1. Spray four ramekins with cooking spray and set aside.
2. Melt butter in a large pan over medium heat.
3. Add ham and vegetables to the pan and sauté for 5 minutes.
4. Meanwhile, in a mixing bowl, whisk together remaining ingredients.
5. Add cooked veggies into the egg mixture and stir well.
6. Pour 1 cup water into the instant pot then place trivet into the pot.
7. Pour mixture into the prepared ramekins and place on top of the trivet.
8. Seal pot with lid and cook on high for 6 hours.
9. Release pressure using quick release method than open the lid.
10. Serve and enjoy.

Nutritional Value (Amount per Serving):
Calories 177; Fat 13.4 g; Carbohydrates 2.4 g; Sugar 0.9 g; Protein 11.9 g

Easy Egg Salad

Preparation Time: 5 minutes; Cooking Time: 5 minutes; Serve: 6
Ingredients:
- 8 eggs
- ½ cup mayonnaise
- Pepper
- Salt

Directions:
1. Spray baking dish with cooking spray.
2. Break the eggs into the prepared baking dish. Season with pepper and salt.
3. Pour 1 cup water into the instant pot and place trivet into the pot.
4. Place dish on top of the trivet.
5. Seal pot with lid and cook on high pressure for 5 minutes.
6. Allow to release pressure naturally then open the lid.
7. Mash eggs with a masher.
8. Add mayonnaise and stir well.
9. Serve and enjoy.

Nutritional Value (Amount per Serving):

Calories 160; Fat 12.4 g; Carbohydrates 5.1 g; Sugar 1.7 g; Protein 7.6 g

Simple Breakfast Egg Muffins

Preparation Time: 10 minutes; Cooking Time: 5 minutes; Serve: 2
Ingredients:
- 1 egg
- 1 tbsp cheddar cheese, shredded
- 4 cherry tomatoes, cut in half
- Pepper
- Salt

Directions:
1. Spray small ramekin dish with cooking spray.
2. Break egg into the prepared dish and top with cheese, tomatoes, pepper, and salt.
3. Pour one cup water into the instant pot then place trivet into the pot.
4. Place ramekin dish on top of the trivet.
5. Seal pot with lid and cook on high for 5 minutes.
6. Release pressure using quick release method than open the lid.
7. Serve and enjoy.

Nutritional Value (Amount per Serving):
Calories 90; Fat 3.9 g; Carbohydrates 9.8 g; Sugar 6.7 g; Protein 5.8 g

Mini Mushroom Cheese Quiche

Preparation Time: 10 minutes; Cooking Time: 5 minutes; Serve: 6
Ingredients:
- 4 eggs
- 1 cup water
- ¼ cup heavy cream
- 1 scallion, chopped
- 2 oz cremini mushrooms, chopped
- 3 oz cheddar cheese, shredded
- Pepper
- Salt

Directions:
1. Add cheddar cheese into the bottom of the silicone mold.
2. Add mushrooms and scallions on top of the cheese.
3. Add eggs, cream, and salt into the blender and blend well.
4. Pour egg mixture over the mushrooms and scallions.
5. Pour 1 cup water into the instant pot and place trivet into the pot.
6. Place silicone muffin tray on top of the trivet.
7. Seal pot with lid and cook on high for 5 minutes.
8. Release pressure using quick release method than open the lid.
9. Remove quiche from silicon muffin tray and serve.

Nutritional Value (Amount per Serving):
Calories 120; Fat 9.5 g; Carbohydrates 1.1 g; Sugar 0.5 g; Protein 7.6 g

Avocado Egg Bites

Preparation Time: 10 minutes; Cooking Time: 10 minutes; Serve: 7

Ingredients:
- 4 eggs
- ½ cup avocado pico de gallo
- ¼ tsp cumin
- ¼ tsp garlic powder
- ¼ tsp chili powder
- ¼ cup heavy cream
- ½ cup cottage cheese
- ½ cup cheddar cheese, shredded
- Pepper
- Salt

Directions:
1. Pour 1 cup of water into the instant pot then place trivet into the pot.
2. Add all ingredients except avocado pico de gallo into the blender and blend until smooth.
3. Add 1 tablespoon of avocado pico de gallo into each muffin cup.
4. Divide the egg mixture into the muffin cups and place muffin cups on top of the trivet.
5. Seal pot with lid and select steam mode and set timer for 10 minutes.
6. Allow to release pressure naturally then open the lid.
7. Serve and enjoy.

Nutritional Value (Amount per Serving):
Calories 135; Fat 8.3 g; Carbohydrates 6.6 g; Sugar 0.7 g; Protein 8.5 g

Scrambled Eggs

Preparation Time: 5 minutes; Cooking Time: 7 minutes; Serve: 2

Ingredients:
- 2 eggs
- ½ tbsp butter
- 1 tbsp coconut milk
- Pepper
- Salt

Directions:
1. Spray small ramekin dish with cooking spray.
2. Crack eggs into the bowl. Add coconut milk, pepper and salt and beat with a fork.
3. Add butter and stir well.
4. Pour 1 cup of water into the instant pot and place trivet into the pot.
5. Place bowl on top of the trivet.
6. Seal pot with lid and select steam mode and set timer for 7 minutes.
7. Release pressure using quick release method than open the lid.
8. Remove dish from the instant pot and stir eggs with a fork until it scrambled.
9. Serve and enjoy.

Nutritional Value (Amount per Serving):
Calories 106; Fat 9 g; Carbohydrates 0.8 g; Sugar 0.6 g; Protein 5.8 g

Easy Steamed Eggs

Preparation Time: 5 minutes; Cooking Time: 10 minutes; Serve: 2
Ingredients:
- 1 cup water
- 2 large eggs
- 2 tbsp fresh coriander, chopped

Directions:
1. In a bowl, whisk eggs with 1 cup of water.
2. Sift egg mixture through a sieve. Pour egg mixture into the baking dish and cover with foil.
3. Pour 1 cup of water into the instant pot and place trivet in the pot.
4. Place dish on top of the trivet.
5. Seal pot with lid and select steam mode and set timer for 10 minutes.
6. Release pressure using quick release method than open the lid.
7. Garnish with coriander and serve.

Nutritional Value (Amount per Serving):
Calories 72; Fat 5 g; Carbohydrates 0.4 g; Sugar 0.4 g; Protein 6.3 g

Breakfast Egg in Marinara Sauce

Preparation Time: 10 minutes; Cooking Time: 11 minutes; Serve: 6
Ingredients:
- 6 eggs
- 1 ½ cup marinara sauce, sugar-free
- ½ tsp ground cumin
- ½ tsp paprika
- 1 tsp chili powder
- 1 bell pepper, diced
- ½ onion, diced
- 2 garlic cloves, minced
- 1 tbsp olive oil
- Pepper
- Salt

Directions:
1. Add oil into the instant pot and set the pot on sauté mode.
2. Add garlic, cumin, paprika, chili powder, bell pepper, and onion to the pot and stir well. Season with pepper and salt and cook for 5 minutes.
3. Add marinara sauce and stir well.
4. Break the eggs into the sauce and spread evenly.
5. Seal pot with lid and cook on low for 10 minutes.
6. Release pressure using quick release method than open the lid.
7. Garnish with parsley and serve.

Nutritional Value (Amount per Serving):
Calories 151; Fat 8.5 g; Carbohydrates 12.1 g; Sugar 7.3 g; Protein 7.1 g

Healthy Breakfast Bowl

Preparation Time: 10 minutes; Cooking Time: 30 minutes; Serve: 4
Ingredients:
- 3 eggs
- 3 tbsp olive oil
- 2 tbsp fresh basil
- 1 ½ cups almond milk
- 5 garlic cloves, sliced
- 2/3 cup mushrooms, sliced
- 1/3 cup onion, sliced
- 4 cups fresh spinach
- Pepper
- Salt

Directions:
1. Add oil into the instant pot and set the pot on sauté mode.
2. Add garlic, onion, and mushrooms to the pot and sauté until onion is softened.
3. Take one bowl which fits into your instant pot and sprays with cooking spray.
4. Add spinach into the bowl.
5. In another bowl, whisk together eggs, almond milk, pepper, and salt.
6. Pour egg mixture into the spinach bowl with vegetables.
7. Add basil and stir well.
8. Pour 1 cup water into the pot and place trivet in the pot.
9. Place bowl on top of the trivet.
10. Seal pot with lid and cook on high for 30 minutes.
11. Allow to release pressure naturally then open the lid.
12. Serve and enjoy.

Nutritional Value (Amount per Serving):
Calories 363; Fat 35.4 g; Carbohydrates 8.9 g; Sugar 4 g; Protein 7.8 g

Sausage Cheese Breakfast Casserole

Preparation Time: 10 minutes; Cooking Time: 25 minutes; Serve: 4
Ingredients:
- 10 eggs, lightly beaten
- 2 cups water
- ½ cup almond milk
- 1 ½ cups cheddar cheese, shredded
- ½ cup onion, diced
- ½ cup bell pepper, diced
- 16 oz breakfast sausage

Directions:
1. Add sausage into the instant pot and sauté until browned.
2. Add onion and bell pepper to the pot and sauté for 2-3 minutes.
3. Transfer sausage mixture into the 7" dish.
4. Sprinkle cheese on top of sausage mixture.
5. In a bowl, whisk together eggs and almond milk and pour over sausage and cheese mixture. Cover dish with foil.
6. Pour 2 cups of water into the instant pot and place trivet into the pot.

7. Place dish on top of the trivet.
8. Seal pot with lid and cook on high for 25 minutes.
9. Release pressure using quick release method than open the lid.
10. Serve and enjoy.

Nutritional Value (Amount per Serving):
Calories 792; Fat 64.3 g; Carbohydrates 5.5 g; Sugar 3.4 g; Protein 47.4 g

Tomato Egg Fritatta

Preparation Time: 10 minutes; Cooking Time: 23 minutes; Serve: 6

Ingredients:
- 6 eggs
- 10 oz can Rotel tomatoes, drained
- ½ cup cheddar cheese, grated
- 2 tbsp sour cream
- ¼ cup almond milk
- Pepper
- Salt

Directions:
1. In a bowl, whisk eggs with sour cream and almond milk.
2. Add tomatoes and cheese and stir well.
3. Spray 7-inch spring-form baking pan with cooking spray.
4. Pour egg mixture into the prepared baking pan.
5. Pour 1 ½ cups of water into the instant pot and place trivet into the pot.
6. Place baking pan on top of the trivet.
7. Seal pot with lid and cook on high for 23 minutes.
8. Release pressure using quick release method than open the lid.
9. Serve and enjoy.

Nutritional Value (Amount per Serving):
Calories 140; Fat 10.7 g; Carbohydrates 2.7 g; Sugar 1.9 g; Protein 8.6 g

Delicious Caprese Frittata

Preparation Time: 10 minutes; Cooking Time: 35 minutes; Serve: 4

Ingredients:
- 6 eggs
- 1 tbsp basil, chopped
- ¼ cup parmesan cheese
- ½ cup mozzarella cheese
- ½ cup cherry tomatoes, cut in half
- ½ cup almond milk
- Pepper
- Salt

Directions:
1. Pour 1 cup of water into the instant pot and place trivet in the pot.
2. Spray 8" baking pan with cooking spray and set aside.
3. In a bowl, whisk together eggs, with almond milk, pepper, and salt.
4. Add cherry tomatoes, parmesan cheese, basil, and mozzarella cheese and stir well.
5. Pour bowl mixture into the prepared baking pan.

6. Seal pot with lid and cook on high for 25 minutes.
7. Allow to release pressure naturally for 10 minutes then release using quick release method.
8. Serve and enjoy.

Nutritional Value (Amount per Serving):
Calories 261; Fat 19.9 g; Carbohydrates 3.9 g; Sugar 2.1 g; Protein 17.8 g

Bacon Breakfast Casserole

Preparation Time: 10 minutes; Cooking Time: 15 minutes; Serve: 4
Ingredients:
- 6 eggs
- 1 cup water
- ½ tsp garlic powder
- ½ bell pepper, diced
- ½ onion, diced
- 1 cup cheddar cheese, shredded
- 6 bacon pieces, cooked and crumbled
- 1 tsp pepper
- 1 tsp salt

Directions:
1. In a bowl, whisk together eggs, garlic powder, pepper, and salt until combined.
2. Add bell pepper, onion, cheese, and bacon and stir well.
3. Pour egg mixture into the casserole dish.
4. Pour 1 cup of water into the instant pot and place trivet in the pot.
5. Place casserole dish on top of the trivet.
6. Seal pot with lid and cook on high for 13 minutes.
7. Allow to release pressure naturally then open the lid.
8. Serve and enjoy.

Nutritional Value (Amount per Serving):
Calories 375; Fat 27.9 g; Carbohydrates 4.3 g; Sugar 2.1 g; Protein 26.3 g

Feta Sausage Mushroom Frittata

Preparation Time: 10 minutes; Cooking Time: 45 minutes; Serve: 6
Ingredients:
- 12 eggs
- 4 oz feta cheese, crumbled
- 5 oz baby spinach
- ½ cup bell peppers, diced
- 4 oz mushrooms, sliced
- ½ cup almond milk
- 4 oz ground sausage
- 1 tsp sea salt

Directions:
1. Add sausage into the instant pot and sauté until browned.
2. In a bowl, whisk together egg, milk, and salt.
3. Once sausage is browned then add bell pepper and mushrooms into the pot and sauté for 3-4 minutes.
4. Turn off the instant pot. Add spinach and stir until spinach is wilted.
5. Spray 7" baking pan with cooking spray.

6. Add sausage mixture to the prepared pan.
7. Pour egg mixture on top of sausage mixture. Add feta cheese on top of egg mixture.
8. Pour 1 ½ cups of water into the instant pot then place a trivet in the pot.
9. Place dish on top of the trivet.
10. Seal pot with lid and cook on high for 45 minutes.
11. Release pressure using quick release method than open the lid.
12. Serve and enjoy.

Nutritional Value (Amount per Serving):
Calories 298; Fat 23.1 g; Carbohydrates 4.8 g; Sugar 3 g; Protein 19.3 g

Egg Sausage Tacos

Preparation Time: 10 minutes; Cooking Time: 15 minutes; Serve: 6
Ingredients:
- 6 eggs
- 2 tbsp salsa
- ½ cup tomatoes, diced
- 1 avocado, diced
- ¼ cup onion, diced
- 1 cup sausage
- ¼ tsp pepper
- ½ tsp salt

Directions:
1. In a bowl, whisk eggs with sausage, onion, pepper, and salt.
2. Pour 1 cup water into the instant pot and set the pot on sauté mode.
3. Pour egg mixture into the baking dish and place on top of the trivet.
4. Seal pot with lid and cook on high for 10 minutes.
5. Allow to release pressure naturally for 10 minutes then release using quick release method.
6. Top with salsa, tomatoes, and avocado. Stir until egg and sausage break into the pieces.
7. Serve and enjoy.

Nutritional Value (Amount per Serving):
Calories 179; Fat 13.3 g; Carbohydrates 5.2 g; Sugar 1.3 g; Protein 11 g

Cauliflower Mashed

Preparation Time: 10 minutes; Cooking Time: 10 minutes; Serve: 8
Ingredients:
- 3 medium cauliflower heads, cut into florets
- 1 tbsp garlic, minced
- 1/2 cup chicken stock
- 4 tbsp butter
- 1 tsp dried rosemary
- 1 tsp sea salt

Directions:
1. Add all ingredients except butter into the instant pot and stir well.
2. Seal pot with lid and cook on high for 10 minutes.
3. Allow to release pressure naturally then open the lid.
4. Add butter and stir until it melted.

5. Blend the cauliflower using a blender until you smooth.
6. Serve and enjoy.

Nutritional Value (Amount per Serving):
Calories 109; Fat 6.1 g; Carbohydrates 11 g; Sugar 5.2 g; Protein 4.7 g

Cheese Broccoli Frittata

Preparation Time: 10 minutes; Cooking Time: 33 minutes; Serve: 6

Ingredients:
- 4 eggs
- 1/4 cup coconut milk
- 1 cup broccoli florets, cut into pieces
- 4 garlic cloves, minced
- 1 small onion, diced
- 1 1/2 cups cheddar cheese, shredded
- 1 tsp fresh thyme, chopped
- 1 tbsp parsley, chopped
- 1 lemon zest
- 2 tbsp butter
- 1 tsp sea salt

Directions:
1. Add butter into the instant pot and select sauté.
2. Add onion and garlic and sauté for 5 minutes.
3. Add broccoli and sauté for another 5 minutes.
4. Grease casserole dish with butter and set aside.
5. In a large bowl, whisk together eggs and milk until well combined.
6. Add thyme, parsley, lemon zest, and salt, stir well to combine.
7. Add onion broccoli mixture and cheddar cheese and stir to combine.
8. Pour mixture into the prepared casserole dish.
9. Pour 1 cup water into the instant pot then place trivet into the pot.
10. Place casserole dish on a trivet. Seal pot with lid and select manual and set timer for 23 minutes.
11. Allow to release pressure naturally then open the lid.
12. Serve warm and enjoy.

Nutritional Value (Amount per Serving):
Calories 226; Fat 18.6 g; Carbohydrates 4 g; Sugar 1.5 g; Protein 11.7 g

Quick Mini Frittatas

Preparation Time: 5 minutes; Cooking Time: 5 minutes; Serve: 6

Ingredients:
- 5 eggs
- Splash of almond milk
- Pepper
- Salt

Directions:
1. Whisk together all ingredients in a bowl.
2. Pour egg mixture into the mini silicone molds.
3. Pour 1 cup water into the instant pot then place trivet into the pot.

4. Carefully place silicone molds on a trivet.
5. Seal pot with lid and cook on manual high pressure for 5 minutes.
6. Release pressure using quick release method than open the lid carefully.
7. Serve and enjoy.

Nutritional Value (Amount per Serving):
Calories 52; Fat 3.6 g; Carbohydrates 0.3 g; Sugar 0.3 g; Protein 4.6 g

Korean Eggs

Preparation Time: 5 minutes; Cooking Time: 5 minutes; Serve: 1

Ingredients:
- 1 egg
- 1/3 cup water
- 1/8 tsp garlic powder
- 1/8 tsp sesame seeds
- 1 tsp scallions, chopped
- Pepper
- Salt

Directions:
1. Whisk together egg and water in a small bowl.
2. Strain egg mixture over a fine strainer into a heat safe bowl.
3. Add remaining ingredients and mix well. Set aside.
4. Pour 1 cup water into the instant pot and then place trivet into the pot.
5. Place egg bowl on a trivet. Seal pot with lid and cook on high pressure for 5 minutes.
6. Release pressure using quick release method than open the lid carefully.
7. Serve hot and enjoy.

Nutritional Value (Amount per Serving):
Calories 67; Fat 4.6 g; Carbohydrates 0.9 g; Sugar 0.5 g; Protein 5.7 g

Cheese Green Chilies Frittata

Preparation Time: 10 minutes; Cooking Time: 25 minutes; Serve: 4

Ingredients:
- 4 eggs
- 1/2 tsp ground cumin
- 10 oz can green chiles, drained and chopped
- 1 cup half and half
- 1/4 cup cilantro, chopped
- 1 cup Mexican cheese, shredded
- 1/2 tsp salt

Directions:
1. Whisk together eggs, 1/2 cup cheese, cumin, half and half, and salt.
2. Pour egg mixture into the oven-safe dish and cover with foil.
3. Pour 2 cups water into the instant pot and place trivet into the pot.
4. Place egg mixture dish on top of the trivet.
5. Seal pot with lid and cook on high pressure for 20 minutes.
6. Allow to release pressure naturally then open the lid.
7. Top with remaining cheese and broil for 5 minutes.

8. Serve and enjoy.

Nutritional Value (Amount per Serving):
Calories 268; Fat 20.6 g; Carbohydrates 8.4 g; Sugar 0.5 g; Protein 13.6 g

Spinach Pie

Preparation Time: 15 minutes; Cooking Time: 25 minutes; Serve: 6

Ingredients:
- 3 eggs
- 1 1/2 cup feta cheese, crumbled
- 1/4 cup parsley, chopped
- 1 lemon zest
- 1/2 cup cream
- 1 1/2 lbs spinach, chopped
- 4 garlic cloves, grated
- 1 small onion, diced
- 1/2 cup parmesan cheese, shredded
- 1/4 tsp nutmeg, grated
- 2 tbsp fresh dill, chopped
- 2 tbsp butter
- 1 tsp sea salt

Directions:
1. Add butter into the instant pot and set the pot on sauté mode.
2. Add garlic and onion into the pot and sauté for 5 minutes or until lightly brown.
3. Add spinach and sauté until wilted.
4. Grease casserole dish with butter and set aside.
5. In a large bowl, whisk together cream and eggs until well combined.
6. Add nutmeg, dill, parsley, lemon zest, and sea salt. Stir to combine.
7. Add onion-spinach mixture and parmesan cheese and stir well to combine. Pour mixture into the casserole dish.
8. Add crumbled feta into the mixture and place lid on the casserole dish.
9. Pour 1 cup water into the instant pot then place trivet into the pot.
10. Place casserole dish on a trivet. Seal pot with lid and select manual and set timer for 20 minutes.
11. Allow to release pressure naturally then open the lid.
12. Serve and enjoy.

Nutritional Value (Amount per Serving):
Calories 243; Fat 17 g; Carbohydrates 9 g; Sugar 3.1 g; Protein 14.6 g

Asparagus Frittata

Preparation Time: 10 minutes; Cooking Time: 25 minutes; Serve: 4

Ingredients:
- 6 large eggs
- 1/2 cup almond milk
- 1/8 tsp black pepper
- 1 cup asparagus, cut into pieces and cooked
- 2 tbsp chives, chopped
- 1 cup cheddar cheese, shredded
- 1/4 tsp salt

Directions:
1. Spray baking dish with cooking spray and set aside.
2. Add all ingredients into the bowl and whisk well.
3. Pour egg mixture into the prepared dish and cover the pan with aluminum foil.
4. Pour 1 cup water into the instant pot then place trivet into the pot.
5. Place dish on top of the trivet.
6. Seal pot with lid and cook on high for 25 minutes.
7. Allow to release pressure naturally then open the lid.
8. Serve and enjoy.

Nutritional Value (Amount per Serving):
Calories 297; Fat 24 g; Carbohydrates 4 g; Sugar 2.4 g; Protein 18 g

Garlic Tomato Frittata

Preparation Time: 10 minutes; Cooking Time: 5 minutes; Serve: 4
Ingredients:
- 6 eggs, beaten
- 1/2 cup fresh spinach, chopped
- 1/4 tsp black pepper
- 1/2 tsp garlic powder
- 1/2 tsp garlic powder
- 1 tsp onion, minced
- 1/4 cup tomato, diced

Directions:
1. Take one pan which fits into your instant pot and sprays with cooking spray. Set aside.
2. Add all ingredients into the large mixing bowl and whisk well to combine.
3. Pour egg mixture into the prepared pan.
4. Pour 1 cup water into the instant pot then place trivet into the pot.
5. Place pan on a trivet and seal instant pot with lid.
6. Select manual high pressure for 5 minutes.
7. Allow to release pressure naturally then open the lid.
8. Serve and enjoy.

Nutritional Value (Amount per Serving):
Calories 99; Fat 6 g; Carbohydrates 1.5 g; Sugar 1 g; Protein 8 g

Breakfast Cheese Quiche

Preparation Time: 10 minutes; Cooking Time: 11 minutes; Serve: 4
Ingredients:
- 4 eggs
- 1/2 cup mozzarella cheese, shredded
- 2 tbsp ricotta cheese
- 1/2 cup mushrooms, diced
- 1/2 cup spinach
- 2 tbsp almond milk, unsweetened
- 1/4 cup ham, diced
- 1/4 cup onion, diced
- 1 tbsp coconut oil
- 1/4 tsp sea salt

Directions:

1. Grease four ramekins with butter and set aside.
2. Heat coconut oil in a large pan over medium heat.
3. Add ham and vegetables and cook for 5 minutes or until vegetables are softened.
4. Meanwhile, in a bowl, whisk remaining ingredients until well mix.
5. Stir cooked ham and vegetables into the egg mixture.
6. Pour 1 cup water into the instant pot then place trivet into the pot.
7. Pour egg mixture into the prepared ramekins and place on a trivet.
8. Seal pot with lid and cook on high for 6 minutes.
9. Release pressure using quick release method than open the lid.
10. Serve and enjoy.

Nutritional Value (Amount per Serving):
Calories 150; Fat 11 g; Carbohydrates 2 g; Sugar 1 g; Protein 9 g

Spinach Nutmeg Feta Pie

Preparation Time: 10 minutes; Cooking Time: 30 minutes; Serve: 6
Ingredients:
- 3 eggs
- 1/4 tsp nutmeg, grated
- 2 tbsp fresh dill, chopped
- 1/4 cup parsley, chopped
- 1 lemon zest
- 1/2 cup cream
- 1 cup water
- 1 1/2 cups feta cheese, crumbled
- 1/2 cup parmesan cheese, shredded
- 1 1/2 lbs spinach, chopped
- 4 garlic cloves, minced
- 1 small onion, diced
- 2 tbsp butter
- 1 tsp sea salt

Directions:
1. Set instant pot on sauté mode then add butter into the pot.
2. Add garlic and onion and sauté for 7 minutes.
3. Add spinach and sauté for 3 minutes.
4. Take one casserole dish which fits into your instant pot and grease with butter. Set aside.
5. In a bowl, whisk together eggs and cream until well combined.
6. Add nutmeg, dill, parsley, lemon zest, and sea salt and stir well to combine.
7. Add onion garlic and spinach mixture and parmesan cheese. Stir well to combine.
8. Pour mixture into the prepared casserole dish.
9. Spread crumble feta cheese on egg mixture. Cover casserole dish.
10. Pour 1 cup water into the instant pot then place trivet into the pot.
11. Place casserole dish on a trivet. Seal pot with lid and select manual and set timer for 20 minutes.
12. Release pressure using quick release method than open the lid.
13. Serve and enjoy.

Nutritional Value (Amount per Serving):
Calories 243; Fat 17.5 g; Carbohydrates 9.2 g; Sugar 3.1 g; Protein 14.6 g

Omelets in Jar

Preparation Time: 10 minutes; Cooking Time: 10 minutes; Serve: 4
Ingredients:
- 12 eggs, beaten
- 4 medium jalapeno peppers, seeded and chopped
- 8 bacon slices
- 1/4 cup heavy cream
- 1 cup cheddar cheese, shredded
- 1/8 tsp ground black pepper
- 1/4 tsp sea salt

Directions:
1. Spray jars from inside with cooking spray.
2. In a pan, cook bacon slices over medium heat until crispy.
3. Remove bacon slices from pan make crumble and set aside.
4. Add jalapeno in the same pan and cook for 2 minutes or until softened.
5. In a bowl, beat eggs, pepper, heavy cream, and salt. Fold in shredded cheese, jalapeno peppers, and bacon.
6. Divide egg mixture evenly between the 4 jars.
7. Pour 2 cups water into the instant pot then place a trivet in the pot.
8. Place jars on a trivet. Seal pot with lid and cook on high pressure for 7 minutes.
9. Allow to release pressure naturally then open the lid.
10. Serve and enjoy.

Nutritional Value (Amount per Serving):
Calories 540; Fat 41.4 g; Carbohydrates 3.2 g; Sugar 1.7 g; Protein 38.1 g

Basil Mozzarella Egg Cups

Preparation Time: 10 minutes; Cooking Time: 5 minutes; Serve: 3
Ingredients:
- 6 eggs
- 3 tsp heavy cream
- 3 oz tomatoes, chopped
- 6 oz mozzarella, chopped
- 3 turkey slices
- 10 basil leaves, chopped

Directions:
1. Spray 3 ramekins with cooking spray.
2. Divide chopped tomatoes evenly into the three ramekins.
3. Divide half mozzarella into the ramekins then divide basil leaves.
4. Crack 2 eggs in each ramekin. Top with remaining cheese.
5. Add 1 tsp cream to each ramekin.
6. Pour 1 cup water into the instant pot then place trivet into the pot.
7. Place ramekins on top of trivet and seal pot with lid and cook on manual high pressure for 5 minutes.
8. Release pressure using quick release method than open the lid.
9. Allow to cool for 5 minutes then serve.

Nutritional Value (Amount per Serving):
Calories 662; Fat 31.1 g; Carbohydrates 4 g; Sugar 1.5 g; Protein 88.4 g

Egg Salad Roll-Ups

Preparation Time: 10 minutes; Cooking Time: 2 minutes; Serve: 3
Ingredients:
- 6 eggs
- 1/8 cup scallions, diced
- 1/4 cup celery, diced
- 1/2 cup mayonnaise
- 1 tsp Dijon mustard
- 1/4 tsp black pepper
- 2 tbsp dill pickles, diced
- 3 cabbage leaves
- 1 tsp kosher salt

Directions:
1. Spray a loaf pan with cooking spray and set aside.
2. Crack eggs into the loaf pan. Season eggs with pepper and salt.
3. Pour 1 cup water into the instant pot then place trivet into the pot.
4. Place egg loaf pan on a trivet.
5. Seal pot with lid and cook on high pressure for 2 minutes.
6. Allow to release pressure naturally for 10 minutes then release using quick release method than open the lid.
7. Transfer eggs into the bowl and place in refrigerator to chill.
8. Once eggs are chilled then grate into the mixing bowl.
9. Whisk together remaining ingredients except for cabbage leaves and fold in grated eggs.
10. Add a scoop of egg salad on a cabbage leaf and make a roll.
11. Serve and enjoy.

Nutritional Value (Amount per Serving):
Calories 287; Fat 22 g; Carbohydrates 11.8 g; Sugar 4 g; Protein 11.9 g

Spinach Tomato Cups

Preparation Time: 10 minutes; Cooking Time: 8 minutes; Serve: 2
Ingredients:
- 6 eggs
- 1 tomato, chopped
- 1/4 cup feta cheese
- 1 cup baby spinach, chopped
- 1 cup water
- 1/2 cup mozzarella cheese
- 1 tsp pepper
- 1/2 tsp salt

Directions:
1. Pour water into the instant pot then place trivet.
2. Divide spinach between two cups.
3. In a bowl, whisk together all remaining ingredients and pour into the spinach cups. Place cups on a trivet.
4. Seal pot with lid and cook on high pressure for 8 minutes.

    5. Release pressure using quick release method than open the lid.
    6. Serve and enjoy.

Nutritional Value (Amount per Serving):
    Calories 270; Fat 18.5 g; Carbohydrates 4.5 g; Sugar 2.7 g; Protein 22.1 g

Simple Egg Cups

Preparation Time: 10 minutes; Cooking Time: 5 minutes; Serve: 4
Ingredients:
- 4 eggs
- 1/2 cup cheddar cheese, shredded
- 1 cup mix vegetables, diced
- 1/2 cup mozzarella cheese, shredded
- 2 tbsp cilantro, chopped
- 1/4 cup half and half
- Pepper
- Salt

Directions:
1. Add all ingredients except mozzarella cheese into the mixing bowl and mix well.
2. Pour egg mixture into the four half-pint wide mouth jars. Place lids on top but do not seal.
3. Pour 2 cups water into the instant pot then place trivet into the pot.
4. Place egg jars on a trivet.
5. Seal pot with lid and cook on high pressure for 5 minutes.
6. Release pressure using quick release method than open the lid carefully.
7. Carefully remove egg jars from instant pot and top with shredded mozzarella cheese and broil until cheese melted.
8. Serve and enjoy.

Nutritional Value (Amount per Serving):
    Calories 165; Fat 11.4 g; Carbohydrates 4.1 g; Sugar 1.2 g; Protein 11.3 g

Bacon Frittata

Preparation Time: 10 minutes; Cooking Time: 15 minutes; Serve: 4
Ingredients:
- 6 eggs
- 1/2 tsp Italian seasoning
- 2 1/2 tbsp heavy cream
- 1/4 cup bacon, cooked and chopped
- 1/2 cup tomato, chopped
- 1 cup fresh spinach
- 1/4 tsp pepper
- 1/4 tsp salt

Directions:
1. In a bowl, whisk eggs with spices and heavy cream.
2. Spray 7" baking pan with cooking spray.
3. Add bacon, tomato, and spinach to the pan. Pour egg mixture over the bacon mixture.
4. Cover pan with aluminum foil piece.
5. Pour 1 ½ cups of water into the instant pot then place trivet to the pot.
6. Place baking pan on top of the trivet. Seal instant pot with lid and cook on manual high pressure for 15 minutes.

7. Release pressure using quick release method than open the lid.
8. Serve and enjoy.

Nutritional Value (Amount per Serving):
Calories 120; Fat 8.5 g; Carbohydrates 1.9 g; Sugar 1.2 g; Protein 9.2 g

Almond Pancake

Preparation Time: 10 minutes; Cooking Time: 17 minutes; Serve: 2
Ingredients:
- 1 egg
- 1 1/2 tbsp olive oil
- 3/4 tsp baking powder
- 3 tbsp swerve
- 1 cup almond flour
- 1 1/4 cups coconut milk
- 3/4 tsp baking soda

Directions:
1. In a large mixing bowl, mix together flour, baking soda, baking powder, and swerve.
2. Add buttermilk, oil, and eggs and whisk until well combined.
3. Spray 7" spring-form pan with cooking spray. Pour batter into the prepared pan.
4. Pour 1 cup water into the instant pot then place a trivet in the pot.
5. Place pan on top of the trivet.
6. Seal pot with lid and cook on low pressure for 17 minutes.
7. Release pressure using quick release method than open the lid carefully.
8. Remove pan from the pot and set aside to cool completely.
9. Slice and serve.

Nutritional Value (Amount per Serving):
Calories 289; Fat 27.2 g; Carbohydrates 8.8 g; Sugar 0.7 g; Protein 6.7 g

Bacon Brussels sprouts

Preparation Time: 10 minutes; Cooking Time: 6 minutes; Serve: 4
Ingredients:
- 1 lb Brussels sprouts, trimmed and halved
- 1/2 cup orange juice
- 2 bacon slices, diced
- 1 tbsp olive oil
- 2 tsp orange zest
- 1/2 cup water

Directions:
1. Add olive oil to the instant pot and set the pot on sauté mode.
2. Add bacon and sauté for 3-5 minutes or until crisp.
3. Add water and orange juice and deglaze the instant pot.
4. Add Brussels sprouts and stir well.
5. Seal pot with lid and cook on manual high pressure for 3 minutes.
6. Release pressure using quick release method than open the lid.
7. Top with orange zest and serve.

Nutritional Value (Amount per Serving):
Calories 145; Fat 7.9 g; Carbohydrates 13.9 g; Sugar 5.1 g; Protein 7.6 g

Breakfast Quiche

Preparation Time: 10 minutes; Cooking Time: 30 minutes; Serve: 6
Ingredients:
- 8 eggs
- 1 1/2 cup mozzarella cheese, shredded
- 1/2 cup almond flour
- 1/2 cup almond milk
- 1/4 tsp pepper
- 2 green onions, chopped
- 1 cup tomatoes, chopped
- 1 red pepper, chopped
- 1/4 tsp salt

Directions:
1. Place trivet into the bottom of the instant pot.
2. Pour 1 cup water into the instant pot.
3. In a large bowl, whisk eggs, flour, milk, pepper, and salt.
4. Add vegetables and cheese and stir until combined.
5. Pour egg mixture into the dish that will fit inside your instant pot.
6. Cover dish with foil and place on the trivet.
7. Seal instant pot with lid and select manual high pressure for 30 minutes.
8. Allow to release pressure naturally for 10 minutes then release using quick release method.
9. Carefully remove the dish from the instant pot.
10. Serve and enjoy.

Nutritional Value (Amount per Serving):
Calories 177; Fat 13.1 g; Carbohydrates 5.4 g; Sugar 3.1 g; Protein 10.9 g

Mushroom Cheese Chive Omelet

Preparation Time: 10 minutes; Cooking Time: 10 minutes; Serve: 4
Ingredients:
- 5 eggs, lightly beaten
- 1/2 tbsp cheddar cheese
- 2 tbsp butter
- 1 onion, chopped
- 2 tbsp chives, minced
- 1 bell pepper, chopped
- 1 1/2 cups mushrooms, sliced
- 1/2 cup coconut milk

Directions:
1. Add butter into the instant pot and set the pot on sauté mode.
2. In a bowl, whisk eggs until well combined.
3. Add remaining ingredients and mix well. Pour egg mixture into the instant pot and cook for 2 minutes.
4. Seal pot with lid and select manual high pressure for 8 minutes.
5. Release pressure using quick release method than open the lid.
6. Serve and enjoy.

Nutritional Value (Amount per Serving):
Calories 229; Fat 18.9 g; Carbohydrates 7.8 g; Sugar 4.6 g; Protein 9.4 g

Kale Egg Cheese Breakfast

Preparation Time: 10 minutes; Cooking Time: 20 minutes; Serve: 3
Ingredients:
- 3 eggs
- 1 tsp herb de Provence
- 1/2 cup cheddar cheese, shredded
- 1/2 cup kale, chopped
- 1/4 cup heavy cream
- 1/2 cup bacon slices, chopped
- 1/2 small onion, chopped
- Pepper
- Salt

Directions:
1. In a large bowl, whisk together egg and heavy cream.
2. Add kale, bacon, cheddar cheese, herb de Provence, pepper, and salt. Stir well.
3. Pour egg mixture into the baking dish.
4. Pour 1 cup of water into the instant pot and place trivet in the pot.
5. Place baking dish on top of the trivet.
6. Seal pot with lid and cook on high for 20 minutes.
7. Allow to release pressure naturally then open the lid.
8. Serve and enjoy.

Nutritional Value (Amount per Serving):
Calories 197; Fat 15.5 g; Carbohydrates 3.1 g; Sugar 0.9 g; Protein 11.7 g

Delicious Carrot Muffins

Preparation Time: 10 minutes; Cooking Time: 20 minutes; Serve: 8
Ingredients:
- 3 eggs
- 1 1/2 cups water
- 1/2 cup heavy cream
- 1 tsp apple pie spice
- 1 cup shredded carrot
- 1/3 cup Truvia
- 1 tsp baking powder
- 1/4 cup coconut oil, melted
- 1 cup almond flour
- 1/2 cup pecans, chopped

Directions:
1. Pour water into the instant pot then place a trivet in the pot.
2. Add all ingredients except pecans and carrots into the large bowl and using electric mixer blend until fluffy.
3. Add carrots and pecans and fold well.
4. Pour batter into the silicone muffin cups and place on top of the trivet.
5. Seal pot with lid and cook on high for 20 minutes.
6. Release pressure using quick release method than open the lid.
7. Serve and enjoy.

Nutritional Value (Amount per Serving):
Calories 183; Fat 18 g; Carbohydrates 7 g; Sugar 4.3; Protein 3.9 g

Healthy Pumpkin Bread

Preparation Time: 10 minutes; Cooking Time: 25 minutes; Serve: 4
Ingredients:
- 2 eggs, lightly beaten
- 1 tbsp almond butter, melted
- 1/4 cup almond milk
- 1 cup almond flour
- 1/2 cup pumpkin puree
- 1/4 tsp turmeric powder
- 1/2 tsp pumpkin pie spice
- 1/4 tsp nutmeg
- 1/2 tsp salt

Directions:
1. In a large bowl, combine together almond flour, pumpkin pie spice, turmeric, nutmeg, baking powder, and salt.
2. Add pumpkin puree, eggs, and almond milk into the almond flour mixture and stir until well combined.
3. Spray spring-form pan with cooking spray.
4. Pour bread batter into the prepared pan and cover with foil.
5. Pour 1 cup of water into the instant pot then place a trivet in the pot.
6. Place pan on top of the trivet.
7. Seal pot with lid and cook on low for 25 minutes.
8. Allow to release pressure naturally then open the lid.
9. Cut bread into the slices and serve.

Nutritional Value (Amount per Serving):
Calories 143; Fat 11.7 g; Carbohydrates 6 g; Sugar 2.2 g; Protein 5.8 g

Cauliflower Cheese Egg Bake

Preparation Time: 10 minutes; Cooking Time: 7 minutes; Serve: 4
Ingredients:
- 8 eggs
- 1/4 cup green onions, chopped
- 2 cups cauliflower, chopped
- 8 bacon slices, chopped
- 1 cup mozzarella cheese, shredded
- 1/2 cup coconut milk
- 1/2 tsp salt

Directions:
1. Spray instant pot from inside with cooking spray and set on sauté mode.
2. Add bacon to the pot and sauté until lightly browned.
3. Add chopped cauliflower on top on bacon and spread evenly.
4. In a bowl, whisk eggs, pepper, salt, and milk and pour over cauliflower.
5. Top with mozzarella cheese.
6. Seal pot with lid and cook on high for 7 minutes.

7. Release pressure using quick release method than open the lid.
8. Garnish with green onions and serve.

Nutritional Value (Amount per Serving):
Calories 435; Fat 33.1 g; Carbohydrates 6.2 g; Sugar 3 g; Protein 28.9 g

Chia Breakfast Pudding

Preparation Time: 10 minutes; Cooking Time: 10 minutes; Serve: 3
Ingredients:
- 1/2 cup chia seeds
- 1/2 tsp cinnamon
- 1/2 tsp agar powder
- 1 tsp vanilla
- 1 cup water
- 1/2 cup coconut milk
- 2 tbsp swerve
- 1 cup raspberries
- 1/4 tsp salt

Directions:
1. Add water, chia, cinnamon, vanilla, swerve, and salt into the instant pot and stir well. Cook on sauté mode for 3-4 minutes.
2. Add raspberries and cook for 5 minutes.
3. Add agar and milk. Stir well and cook for 5 minutes. Stir constantly.
4. Transfer pudding in serving bowl and place in refrigerator for 1-2 hours.
5. Serve chilled and enjoy.

Nutritional Value (Amount per Serving):
Calories 214; Fat 15.9 g; Carbohydrates 13 g; Sugar 3.3 g; Protein 5.6 g

Eggs with scallions

Preparation Time: 10 minutes; Cooking Time: 5 minutes; Serve: 1
Ingredients:
- 2 eggs
- 1/2 tsp garlic powder
- 1/2 tsp black pepper
- 1/2 cup water
- 1 tbsp sesame seeds
- 2 tbsp scallions, chopped
- 1 tsp sea salt

Directions:
1. Pour 1 cup of water into the instant pot then place a trivet in the pot.
2. In a small bowl, whisk eggs and water.
3. Sift egg mixture through a sieve into the baking dish.
4. Add scallions and stir well. Season with garlic powder, pepper, and salt.
5. Sprinkle sesame seeds and mix well.
6. Place dish on top of the trivet.
7. Seal pot with lid and cook on high for 5 minutes.
8. Release pressure using quick release method than open the lid.
9. Serve and enjoy.

Nutritional Value (Amount per Serving):
Calories 189; Fat 13.3 g; Carbohydrates 5.4 g; Sugar 1.3 g; Protein 13.2 g

Broccoli Cauliflower Mash

Preparation Time: 10 minutes; Cooking Time: 22 minutes; Serve: 3

Ingredients:
- 2 cups broccoli, chopped
- 1 lb cauliflower, chopped
- 1 tsp dried rosemary
- 1/4 cup olive oil
- 2 garlic cloves, minced
- 1 tsp salt

Directions:
1. Add cauliflower and broccoli into the instant pot and pour water in the pot until veggies cover completely.
2. Seal pot with lid and cook on high for 12 minutes.
3. Allow to release pressure naturally then open the lid. Drain veggies well and back in instant pot.
4. Set pot on sauté mode.
5. Add oil, rosemary, garlic, and salt. Stir well and cook for 10 minutes.
6. Turn off the instant pot and mash veggies mixture using a potato masher. Season with pepper and salt.
7. Serve and enjoy.

Nutritional Value (Amount per Serving):
Calories 207; Fat 17.2 g; Carbohydrates 13 g; Sugar 4.7 g; Protein 4.8 g

Healthy Almond Porridge

Preparation Time: 10 minutes; Cooking Time: 10 minutes; Serve: 2

Ingredients:
- 2 tbsp chia seeds
- 1 tsp vanilla
- 1 tsp swerve
- 3 tbsp hemp seeds
- 3 tbsp coconut oil
- 1 cup unsweetened almond milk
- 1/4 tsp salt

Directions:
1. Add coconut oil into the instant pot and set the pot on sauté mode.
2. Add chia and hemp seeds and stir well.
3. Pour 1/2 cup of water into the pot and stir well and cook for 5 minutes.
4. Add almond milk, swerve, vanilla, and salt. Stir well and cook for 5 minutes.
5. Serve and enjoy.

Nutritional Value (Amount per Serving):
Calories 302; Fat 29.6 g; Carbohydrates 4.5 g; Sugar 0.3 g; Protein 5.8 g

Chapter 7: Poultry Recipes

Quick BBQ Chicken Wings

Preparation Time: 5 minutes; Cooking Time: 5 minutes; Serve: 6
Ingredients:
- 2 lbs chicken wings
- ½ cup BBQ sauce, sugar-free
- 1 cup water

Directions:
1. Pour water into the instant pot.
2. Add chicken wings into the instant pot steamer basket.
3. Seal pot with lid and cook on high for 5 minutes.
4. Allow to release pressure naturally for 10 minutes then release using quick release method.
5. Preheat the oven 232 C/ 450 F.
6. Spray a baking tray with cooking spray.
7. In a bowl, add chicken wings and BBQ sauce. Toss well.
8. Spread chicken wings onto a baking tray and bake in preheated oven for 10 minutes.
9. Serve and enjoy.

Nutritional Value (Amount per Serving):
Calories 319; Fat 11.3 g; Carbohydrates 7.6 g; Sugar 5.4 g; Protein 43.7 g

Easy Chicken Adobo

Preparation Time: 10 minutes; Cooking Time: 20 minutes; Serve: 6
Ingredients:
- 2 lb chicken breasts, boneless and skinless
- ¼ cup soy sauce, low-sodium
- ¼ cup vinegar
- 8 garlic cloves, pressed
- 1 onion, chopped
- 1 tsp pepper
- 2 bay leaves

Directions:
1. Add all ingredients into the instant pot and stir well.
2. Seal pot with lid and select poultry mode and set timer for 10 minutes.
3. Release pressure using quick release method than open the lid.
4. Set pot on sauté mode and cook for 10 minutes.
5. Serve and enjoy.

Nutritional Value (Amount per Serving):
Calories 309; Fat 11.3 g; Carbohydrates 4.2 g; Sugar 1 g; Protein 44.9 g

Flavors Basil Chicken

Preparation Time: 10 minutes; Cooking Time: 10 minutes; Serve: 3

Ingredients:
- 3 chicken breasts, boneless and skinless
- 1 tbsp olive oil
- ¼ tsp garlic salt
- 1/8 tsp dried oregano
- 1/8 tsp dried basil
- 1 cup water
- Pepper

Directions:
1. Add oil into the instant pot and set the pot on sauté mode.
2. Season chicken with basil, oregano, pepper, and garlic salt.
3. Add chicken to the pot and sauté for 4 minutes on each side.
4. Seal pot with lid and cook on high for 5 minutes.
5. Allow to release pressure naturally for 10 minutes then release using quick release method. Open the lid.
6. Serve and enjoy.

Nutritional Value (Amount per Serving):
Calories 318; Fat 15.5 g; Carbohydrates 0.2 g; Sugar 0.1 g; Protein 42.3 g

Delicious Paprika Chicken

Preparation Time: 10 minutes; Cooking Time: 10 minutes; Serve: 4

Ingredients:
- 2 ½ lbs chicken thighs, skinless
- ½ cup chicken stock
- ½ cup can tomatoes, pureed
- 2 tbsp sweet paprika
- 1 bell pepper, chopped
- 1 onion, chopped
- 1 tbsp olive oil
- Pepper
- Salt

Directions:
1. Season chicken with pepper and salt.
2. Add oil into the instant pot and set the pot on sauté mode.
3. Add bell pepper and onion to the pot and sauté for 3-4 minutes.
4. Add paprika and sauté for a minute.
5. Add seasoned chicken to the pot with stock, salt, and tomatoes.
6. Seal pot with lid and cook on high for 10 minutes.
7. Release pressure using quick release method than open the lid.
8. Serve and enjoy.

Nutritional Value (Amount per Serving):
Calories 607; Fat 25.1 g; Carbohydrates 8.4 g; Sugar 4.1 g; Protein 83.5 g

Tasty Parmesan Chicken

Preparation Time: 10 minutes; Cooking Time: 8 minutes; Serve: 4

Ingredients:

- 4 chicken breasts, skinless and boneless
- ¼ cup parmesan cheese, grated
- 1 cup mozzarella cheese, shredded
- ¼ cup fresh basil, sliced
- 3 cups marinara sauce, sugar-free
- Pepper
- Salt

Directions:
1. Season chicken with pepper and salt.
2. Add the marinara sauce into the instant pot. Place chicken on top of sauce.
3. Seal pot with lid and cook on high for 8 minutes.
4. Release pressure using quick release method than open the lid.
5. Top chicken with parmesan cheese and mozzarella cheese.
6. Place lid on the instant pot until cheese is melted.
7. Serve and enjoy.

Nutritional Value (Amount per Serving):
Calories 350; Fat 14.3 g; Carbohydrates 3.3 g; Sugar 2 g; Protein 48.3 g

Mediterranean Chicken

Preparation Time: 10 minutes; Cooking Time: 10 minutes; Serve: 4
Ingredients:
- 3 lbs chicken thighs, skinless and bone-in
- 2 tbsp parsley, chopped
- 1 tbsp fresh lemon juice
- 1 cup chicken broth
- ½ cup black olives, pitted
- ½ tsp oregano
- 2 tomatoes, chopped
- 1 small garlic head, sliced in half
- 1 onion, chopped
- 1 bell pepper, chopped
- 1 tbsp olive oil
- Pepper
- Salt

Directions:
1. Season chicken with pepper and salt and set aside.
2. Add oil into the instant pot and set the pot on sauté mode.
3. Add garlic, onion, ad bell pepper to the pot and sauté for 3 minutes.
4. Add chicken, broth, olives, oregano, tomatoes, and salt. Stir to combine.
5. Seal pot with lid and cook on high for 10 minutes.
6. Release pressure using quick release method than open the lid.
7. Add parsley and lemon juice. Stir well.
8. Serve and enjoy.

Nutritional Value (Amount per Serving):
Calories 739; Fat 31.1 g; Carbohydrates 8.8 g; Sugar 4.6 g; Protein 101 g

Teriyaki Chicken

Preparation Time: 10 minutes; Cooking Time: 8 minutes; Serve: 6
Ingredients:

- 2 ½ lbs chicken thighs, skinless and boneless
- 4 scallions, sliced
- 1 tbsp ginger, minced
- 1 tbsp garlic, minced
- ½ cup mirin
- ½ cup soy sauce

Directions:
1. Add chicken, garlic, ginger, mirin, and soy sauce into the instant pot and stir well.
2. Seal pot with lid and cook on high for 8 minutes.
3. Allow to release pressure naturally for 5 minutes then release using quick release method. Open the lid.
4. Garnish with scallions and serve.

Nutritional Value (Amount per Serving):
Calories 412; Fat 14.1 g; Carbohydrates 12.8 g; Sugar 6 g; Protein 56.4 g

Garlicky Chicken

Preparation Time: 10 minutes; Cooking Time: 10 minutes; Serve: 6
Ingredients:
- 3 lbs chicken thighs, bone-in
- 1 cup chicken stock
- 1/8 tsp nutmeg
- 1 tsp dried thyme
- 1 celery rib, sliced
- 35 garlic cloves, peeled
- 1 tbsp olive oil
- Pepper
- Salt

Directions:
1. Season chicken with pepper and salt and set aside.
2. Add oil into the instant pot and set the pot on sauté mode.
3. Add garlic to the pot and sauté until lightly brown.
4. Add chicken, stock, nutmeg, thyme, celery, pepper, and salt. Stir well.
5. Seal pot with lid and cook on high for 10 minutes.
6. Release pressure using quick release method than open the lid.
7. Serve and enjoy.

Nutritional Value (Amount per Serving):
Calories 480; Fat 19.4 g; Carbohydrates 6.1 g; Sugar 0.4 g; Protein 66.9 g

Tomato Onion Turkey

Preparation Time: 10 minutes; Cooking Time: 20 minutes; Serve: 4
Ingredients:
- 2 lbs ground turkey breast
- 2 garlic cloves, chopped
- 15 oz can tomato, diced
- 2 bell peppers, chopped
- 1 tbsp butter
- 1 cup chicken broth
- 1 onion, sliced

Directions:

1. Add butter into the instant pot and set the pot on sauté mode.
2. Add ground turkey into the pot and sauté for 5 minutes.
3. Add tomatoes, bell peppers, garlic, and broth into the pot and stir well.
4. Seal pot with lid and cook on high for 15 minutes.
5. Release pressure using quick release method than open the lid.
6. Stir well and serve.

Nutritional Value (Amount per Serving):
Calories 506; Fat 20.1 g; Carbohydrates 10.1 g; Sugar 5.7 g; Protein 68 g

Orange Turkey Legs

Preparation Time: 10 minutes; Cooking Time: 25 minutes; Serve: 4
Ingredients:
- 2 turkey legs
- ½ tsp pepper
- 1 cup chicken stock
- 1 green chili, chopped
- 2 green onions, chopped
- 2 tbsp orange zest
- 2 tbsp chili sauce
- ½ cup soy sauce
- 1 tsp sea salt

Directions:
1. Season turkey legs with pepper and salt and place into the instant pot.
2. Pour stock in the pot.
3. Seal pot with lid and cook on high for 15 minutes.
4. Release pressure using quick release method than open the lid.
5. Set pot on sauté mode. Add chili sauce and soy sauce. Stir well.
6. Add onion, orange zest, and green chili. Stir well and cook for 10 minutes,
7. Serve and enjoy.

Nutritional Value (Amount per Serving):
Calories 594; Fat 27 g; Carbohydrates 4.2 g; Sugar 1 g; Protein 78.5 g

Cauliflower Jalapeno Chicken

Preparation Time: 10 minutes; Cooking Time: 20 minutes; Serve: 5
Ingredients:
- 5 chicken thighs
- 2 bay leaves
- 1 tsp dried thyme
- 1 tsp peppercorn
- 5 cups chicken stock
- 1 tbsp swerve
- 3 tbsp fish sauce
- 1 chili pepper, chopped
- 3 jalapeno peppers, chopped
- 1 onion, chopped
- 2 tbsp olive oil
- ¾ cup cauliflower, chopped
- 1 ½ tsp salt

Directions:
1. Add all ingredients into the instant pot and stir well.

2. Seal pot with lid and select poultry mode and set timer for 20 minutes.
3. Allow to release pressure naturally then open the lid.
4. Stir well and serve.

Nutritional Value (Amount per Serving):
Calories 358; Fat 17.2 g; Carbohydrates 5.5 g; Sugar 2.7 g; Protein 44.2 g

Thyme Duck Legs

Preparation Time: 10 minutes; Cooking Time: 8 hours; Serve: 4

Ingredients:
- 2 lbs duck legs
- 1 tbsp thyme, chopped
- 3 thyme sprigs
- 2 bay leaves
- 1 tbsp peppercorn
- 2 celery stalks, chopped
- ¼ cup fresh parsley, chopped
- 5 cups chicken stock
- 3 tbsp butter
- 2 tsp salt

Directions:
1. In a small bowl, mix together all spices and rub over the meat.
2. Place meat into the instant pot along with remaining ingredients.
3. Seal pot with lid and select slow cooker mode and set the timer for 8 hours.
4. Allow to release pressure naturally then open the lid.
5. Serve and enjoy.

Nutritional Value (Amount per Serving):
Calories 501; Fat 23 g; Carbohydrates 2.9 g; Sugar 1.1 g; Protein 67.4 g

Creamy Broccoli Turkey

Preparation Time: 10 minutes; Cooking Time: 35 minutes; Serve: 3

Ingredients:
- 10 oz ground turkey
- ½ tsp dried oregano
- ½ tsp dried thyme
- ½ tsp pepper
- ¼ cup parmesan cheese, grated
- 3 tbsp sour cream
- 1 cup mozzarella cheese, shredded
- ¼ cup chicken broth
- 1 green onion, chopped
- 2 tbsp olive oil
- 1 cup broccoli, chopped
- ½ tsp salt

Directions:
1. Add oil into the instant pot and set the pot on sauté mode.
2. Add onion and sauté for a minute.
3. Add broccoli, broth, and turkey and stir well.
4. Seal pot with lid and cook for 15 minutes.
5. Release pressure using quick release method than open the lid.
6. Season with oregano, thyme, pepper, cheese, and salt. Stir well.
7. Transfer instant pot mixture to a baking dish.

8. Preheat the oven to 176 C/ 350 F.
9. Place baking dish in preheated oven and bake for 20 minutes.
10. Top with cream and serve.

Nutritional Value (Amount per Serving):
Calories 384; Fat 27.2 g; Carbohydrates 3.8 g; Sugar 0.7 g; Protein 34.4 g

Dijon Turkey Roast

Preparation Time: 10 minutes; Cooking Time: 55 minutes; Serve: 5
Ingredients:
- 2 lbs turkey breast, skinless and boneless
- 4 cups chicken stock
- 3 tbsp Dijon mustard
- ¼ cup olive oil
- 1 tsp pepper
- 2 tsp sea salt

Directions:
1. Place turkey breast into the instant pot then pour chicken stock into the pot.
2. Seal pot with lid and cook on high for 25 minutes.
3. Release pressure using quick release method than open the lid.
4. Remove turkey breast from the pot and set aside.
5. Preheat the oven to 218 C/ 425 F.
6. In a small bowl, whisk together Dijon, pepper, olive oil, and salt. Brush turkey breast with Dijon mixture and place onto a baking tray.
7. Roast meat in the preheated oven for 15 minutes on each side.
8. Serve and enjoy.

Nutritional Value (Amount per Serving):
Calories 290; Fat 13.9 g; Carbohydrates 9 g; Sugar 7 g; Protein 32 g

Herb Lemon Chicken Wings

Preparation Time: 10 minutes; Cooking Time: 15 minutes; Serve: 2
Ingredients:
- 4 chicken wings
- 2 rosemary sprigs
- ½ tsp black pepper
- ½ lemon, sliced
- 2 garlic cloves, minced
- ½ onion, chopped
- 1 cup chicken stock
- 3 tbsp olive oil
- 1 tsp sea salt

Directions:
1. Rub chicken wings with oil and season with pepper and salt. Set aside.
2. Set instant pot on sauté mode.
3. Add chicken wings to the pot and cook for 3-4 minutes on each side. Remove chicken wings from the pot and set aside.
4. Add garlic and onion to the pot and sauté until softened.

5. Add stock, lemon slices, chicken wings, and rosemary to the pot and stir well.
6. Seal pot with lid and select steam mode and cook on high for 15 minutes.
7. Release pressure using quick release method than open the lid.
8. Serve and enjoy.

Nutritional Value (Amount per Serving):
Calories 761; Fat 43 g; Carbohydrates 5.6 g; Sugar 1.9 g; Protein 85.5 g

Whole Roasted Chicken

Preparation Time: 10 minutes; Cooking Time: 25 minutes; Serve: 8
Ingredients:
- 4 lbs whole chicken
- 1/4 tsp pepper
- 1/4 tsp poultry seasoning
- 1/4 tsp dried thyme
- 1 1/2 cup chicken stock
- 1 tbsp olive oil
- 1 tsp paprika
- 1/2 tsp salt

Directions:
1. Add oil into the instant pot and set the pot on sauté mode.
2. Place chicken in a pot and cook on sauté mode until lightly brown.
3. In a small bowl, mix together pepper, poultry seasoning, dried thyme, paprika, and salt.
4. Once the chicken is brown from all the sides then add mix seasoning and chicken stock.
5. Seal pot with lid and select manual high pressure for 25 minutes.
6. Allow to release pressure naturally then open the lid.
7. Transfer chicken to the plate.
8. Drizzle pot juices over the chicken and serve.

Nutritional Value (Amount per Serving):
Calories 449; Fat 18.7 g; Carbohydrates 0.4 g; Sugar 0.2 g; Protein 65.8 g

Chicken Wraps

Preparation Time: 10 minutes; Cooking Time: 10 minutes; Serve: 4
Ingredients:
- 1 lb ground chicken
- 1/2 cups can chestnuts sliced, drain
- 1/8 tsp allspice, ground
- 1/2 tsp ginger, ground
- 2 tbsp balsamic vinegar
- 1/4 cup chicken stock
- 1/4 cups coconut aminos
- 5 garlic cloves, minced
- 3/4 cup onion, diced
- Green onion, chopped
- Romaine lettuce leaves

Directions:
1. Add all ingredients in instant pot except green onion and lettuce leaves.
2. Seal pot with lid and select high pressure for 10 minutes.
3. Release pressure using quick release method than open the lid.
4. Using fork break the meat into the chunks.

5. Arrange lettuce leaves on serving the dish.
6. Spoon the meat into the lettuce leaves and sprinkle with green onions.
7. Serve and enjoy.

Nutritional Value (Amount per Serving):
Calories 233; Fat 8.5 g; Carbohydrates 3.6 g; Sugar 1.0 g; Protein 33.4 g

Yummy Chicken Taco

Preparation Time: 10 minutes; Cooking Time: 15 minutes; Serve: 6
Ingredients:
- 1 1/2 lbs chicken breasts, boneless
- 1 1/2 tomato puree
- 1/4 tsp chipotle powder
- 2 tsp garlic cloves, minced
- 1/2 ancho chile, dried and soaked
- 1/2 cup onion, diced
- 1/2 tsp sea salt
- 1/2 tbsp cumin

Directions:
1. Add soaked ancho chile, cumin, garlic, chipotle powder, salt and 1/2 cup water in a blender and blend until pureed.
2. Add puree mixture into the instant pot.
3. Add tomato puree, onions, and chicken into the pot and stir well.
4. Seal pot with lid and cook on high for 15 minutes.
5. Release pressure using quick release method than open the lid.
6. Serve and enjoy.

Nutritional Value (Amount per Serving):
Calories 275; Fat 9.2 g; Carbohydrates 12.1 g; Sugar 0.6 g; Protein 34.4 g

Chicken Parmigiana

Preparation Time: 10 minutes; Cooking Time: 15 minutes; Serve: 6
Ingredients:
- 1 1/2 lbs chicken tenders
- 1/2 cup olive oil
- 24 oz tomato sauce
- 2 tbsp butter, salted
- 1/4 tsp garlic powder
- 1/2 cup parmesan cheese, grated
- 2 cups mozzarella cheese, shredded

Directions:
1. Add olive oil in instant pot and select saute once oil heats up then add chicken pieces.
2. Brown both sides of chicken.
3. Add garlic powder, tomato sauce, butter, and parmesan cheese over the chicken.
4. Seal pot with lid and cook on high pressure for 15 minutes.
5. Release the pressure using quick release method than open the lid.
6. Sprinkle mozzarella cheese on top and place lid on the pot until cheese is melted.
7. Serve and enjoy.

Nutritional Value (Amount per Serving):

Calories 528; Fat 35.9 g; Carbohydrates 7.5 g; Sugar 4.9 g; Protein 45.0 g

Italian Creamy Chicken

Preparation Time: 10 minutes; Cooking Time: 12 minutes; Serve: 4
Ingredients:
- 1 lb chicken breasts, boneless
- 5 oz cream chicken soup
- 2 tbsp Italian dressing, dry mix
- 8 tbsp cream cheese

Directions:
1. Place chicken breasts into the instant pot.
2. In a small bowl mix together cream chicken soup, cream cheese, and Italian dressing.
3. Pour bowl mixture over the top of chicken breasts and seal pot with lid.
4. Select poultry mode and cook on high pressure for 12 minutes.
5. Release pressure using quick release method than open the lid carefully.
6. Serve and enjoy.

Nutritional Value (Amount per Serving):
Calories 307; Fat 17.5 g; Carbohydrates 1.3 g; Sugar 0.7 g; Protein 34.4 g

Delicious Pepper Cream Chicken

Preparation Time: 10 minutes; Cooking Time: 8 minutes; Serve: 3
Ingredients:
- 8 oz chicken breasts, skinless and boneless, cut into pieces
- 1 medium onion, sliced
- 1 red pepper, sliced
- 1 green pepper, sliced
- 1/2 cup sour cream
- 2 cups chicken broth
- 2 tbsp garlic powder

Directions:
1. Add all ingredients into the instant pot and stir well.
2. Seal pot with lid and cook on manual high pressure for 8 minutes.
3. Allow to release pressure naturally then open the lid.
4. Serve and enjoy.

Nutritional Value (Amount per Serving):
Calories 305; Fat 14 g; Carbohydrates 14 g; Sugar 6.4 g; Protein 28 g

Thyme Dijon Chicken

Preparation Time: 10 minutes; Cooking Time: 13 minutes; Serve: 4
Ingredients:
- 2 lbs chicken breasts, skinless and boneless
- 1 tsp sage, dried
- 1 tbsp rosemary, dried
- 1 tsp thyme, dried
- 1 cup almond milk
- 1/2 tsp pepper
- 1 tbsp Dijon mustard

- 1/2 tsp salt

Directions:
1. In a bowl, add all ingredients and mix until chicken is well coated.
2. Place marinated chicken in the fridge for 1 hour.
3. Pour marinated chicken into the instant pot.
4. Seal pot with lid and cook on high for 13 minutes.
5. Release pressure using quick release method than open lid carefully.
6. Serve and enjoy.

Nutritional Value (Amount per Serving):
Calories 463; Fat 17.7 g; Carbohydrates 4.1 g; Protein 67.9 g; Sugar 3 g

Spicy Chicken

Preparation Time: 10 minutes; Cooking Time: 25 minutes; Serve: 2
Ingredients:
- 2 chicken breasts
- 3 bacon slices, cooked and crumbled
- 2 jalapeno peppers, chopped
- 1 1/2 tbsp chili powder
- 1 cup chicken broth
- 1 cup sour cream

Directions:
1. Add chili powder, jalapeno peppers, and chicken broth in instant pot and stir well.
2. Place chicken into the pot and seal pot with lid and cook on high for 25 minutes.
3. Release pressure using quick release method than open lid carefully.
4. Add sour cream and bacon, stir well.
5. Serve and enjoy.

Nutritional Value (Amount per Serving):
Calories 721; Fat 48 g; Carbohydrates 9 g; Sugar 1.4 g; Protein 59 g

Indian Spiced Chicken Curry

Preparation Time: 10 minutes; Cooking Time: 15 minutes; Serve: 6
Ingredients:
- 2 lbs chicken breasts, boneless, skinless, and cut into cubed
- 1 tbsp ginger, grated
- 1 tbsp garlic, minced
- 1/2 cup onion, sliced
- 2 tbsp curry powder
- 8 oz can tomato sauce
- 14 oz can coconut milk
- 2 cups Roma tomatoes, chopped
- 1 tbsp ginger, grated
- 1 tbsp garlic, minced
- 1/2 cup onion, sliced
- 1 tbsp olive oil
- 1 tsp salt

Directions:
1. Add olive oil into the instant pot and set the pot on sauté mode.
2. Add ginger, garlic, and onion into the pot and sauté for 1 minute.
3. Add tomatoes, sugar, tomato sauce, coconut milk, pepper, and salt and stir well.

4. Seal pot with lid and select manual and set timer for 12 minutes.
   5. Release pressure using quick release method than open the lid.
   6. Season chicken with pepper and salt.
   7. Place chicken into the instant pot and seal pot with lid and cook on high pressure for 3 minutes.
   8. Allow to release pressure naturally then open the lid.
   9. Serve and enjoy.

Nutritional Value (Amount per Serving):
   Calories 473; Fat 28.2 g; Carbohydrates 9.4 g; Sugar 3.7 g; Protein 46.7 g

Simple Salsa Chicken

Preparation Time: 10 minutes; Cooking Time: 15 minutes; Serve: 8
Ingredients:
- 2 lbs chicken breasts, skinless and boneless
- 1 1/2 cup salsa
- Salt

Directions:
   1. Add all ingredients into the instant pot and stir well.
   2. Seal pot with lid and select poultry setting and set timer for 15 minutes.
   3. Release pressure using quick release method than open the lid.
   4. Remove chicken from pot and shred using a fork.
   5. Return shredded chicken into the pot and stir well.
   6. Serve and enjoy.

Nutritional Value (Amount per Serving):
   Calories 229; Fat 8.5 g; Carbohydrates 3.1 g; Sugar 1.5 g; Protein 33.6 g

Lime Garlic Chicken

Preparation Time: 10 minutes; Cooking Time: 10 minutes; Serve: 2
Ingredients:
- 1 lb chicken thighs, skinless and boneless
- 1 tbsp chili powder
- 1 1/2 lime juice
- 1/2 cup chicken broth
- 6 garlic cloves, minced
- 1 tsp cumin
- 1/4 tsp black pepper
- 1 tsp kosher salt

Directions:
   1. Add all ingredients into the instant pot and stir well.
   2. Seal pot with lid and cook on high pressure for 10 minutes.
   3. Allow to release pressure naturally then open the lid.
   4. Remove chicken from pot and shred using a fork.
   5. Return shredded chicken into the pot and stir well.
   6. Serve and enjoy.

Nutritional Value (Amount per Serving):
Calories 470; Fat 18.1 g; Carbohydrates 5.9 g; Sugar 0.6 g; Protein 68.1 g

Butter Chicken

Preparation Time: 10 minutes; Cooking Time: 25 minutes; Serve: 4
Ingredients:
- 1 3/4 lbs chicken thighs, skinless, boneless, and cut into pieces
- 1 tsp turmeric
- 1 tsp ground coriander
- 1 tsp paprika
- 1 tsp garam masala
- 1 tsp ginger, minced
- 1 cup coconut milk
- 15 oz tomato sauce
- 1 red bell pepper, chopped
- 1/4 tsp ground cumin
- 1/4 tsp cayenne pepper
- 1/2 large onion, diced
- 2 tbsp butter
- 1/4 tsp black pepper
- 1 tsp salt

Directions:
1. Add butter into the instant pot and set the pot on sauté mode.
2. Add onion and sauté for 5-8 minutes or until lightly brown.
3. Add ginger and garlic and sauté for 30 seconds.
4. Add spices and stir for another 30 seconds.
5. Add chicken and stir well and cook for 5 minutes.
6. Add red pepper and tomato sauce and stir well.
7. Seal pot with lid and cook on high for 15 minutes.
8. Allow to release pressure naturally then open the lid.
9. Add coconut milk and stir well.
10. Serve and enjoy.

Nutritional Value (Amount per Serving):
Calories 508; Fat 24 g; Carbohydrates 11.6 g; Sugar 6.9 g; Protein 60 g

Chicken Masala

Preparation Time: 10 minutes; Cooking Time: 15 minutes; Serve: 4
Ingredients:
- 8 chicken thighs, boneless and cut into pieces
- 28 oz can tomato, crushed
- 1 tsp fresh ginger, sliced
- 1 small onion, diced
- 1 cup plain yogurt
- 2 tsp garam masala
- 3 tsp garlic, minced
- 1/2 cup water
- Pepper
- Salt

Directions:
1. Place chicken thighs into the instant pot.
2. Add remaining ingredients except for yogurt into the instant pot and stir well.

3. Seal pot with lid and cook on manual high pressure for 15 minutes.
4. Release pressure using quick release method than open the lid.
5. Add yogurt and stir well and leave for 5 minutes.
6. Season with pepper and salt.
7. Serve and enjoy.

Nutritional Value (Amount per Serving):
Calories 435; Fat 15 g; Carbohydrates 11.4 g; Sugar 7.9 g; Protein 60.1 g

Simple Chicken Curry

Preparation Time: 10 minutes; Cooking Time: 15 minutes; Serve: 6
Ingredients:
- 2 lbs chicken breast
- 16 oz can tomato sauce
- 1 cup onion, chopped
- 6 oz can coconut milk
- 2 tbsp curry powder
- 2 garlic cloves, minced
- 6 oz tomato paste
- 1 tsp salt

Directions:
1. Add all ingredients except chicken into the instant pot and stir well to combine.
2. Add chicken into the pot.
3. Seal pot with lid and select manual and set timer for 15 minutes.
4. Allow to release pressure naturally then open the lid.
5. Stir well and serve.

Nutritional Value (Amount per Serving):
Calories 286; Fat 10.4 g; Carbohydrates 13.6 g; Sugar 7.5 g; Protein 35.4 g

Stir Fried Chicken

Preparation Time: 10 minutes; Cooking Time: 2 minutes; Serve: 6
Ingredients:
- 3 chicken breasts, cubed
- 1 1/2 tbsp sesame seeds
- 1/2 cup coconut aminos
- 1 tsp garlic, minced
- 2 green onion, sliced
- 3 cups asparagus, cut into pieces
- 3 bell peppers, diced
- 1 onion, diced
- 1 tbsp sesame oil
- Pepper
- Salt

Directions:
1. Add sesame oil into the instant pot and select sauté.
2. Add chicken into the pot and sauté until chicken almost done.
3. Add remaining ingredients and stir well to combine.
4. Seal pot with lid and select steam for 2 minutes.
5. Release pressure using quick release then open the lid.
6. Stir and serve.

Nutritional Value (Amount per Serving):
Calories 214; Fat 9.1 g; Carbohydrates 9.9 g; Sugar 5.2 g; Protein 23.9 g

Simple Moist Turkey Breast

Preparation Time: 10 minutes; Cooking Time: 30 minutes; Serve: 8
Ingredients:
- 6 lbs turkey breast
- 1 celery rib, cut into 1-inch pieces
- 1 1/2 cups chicken stock
- 1 tsp thyme
- 1 onion, peeled and quartered
- Pepper
- Salt

Directions:
1. Pour chicken broth into the instant pot.
2. Add celery, onion, and thyme into the chicken broth.
3. Season turkey breast with pepper and salt.
4. Place trivet into the instant pot then places seasoned turkey breast on a trivet.
5. Seal pot with lid and cook on high for 30 minutes.
6. Allow to release pressure naturally then open the lid.
7. Transfer turkey breast on serving platter.
8. Cut turkey breast into the slices and serve.

Nutritional Value (Amount per Serving):
Calories 360; Fat 5.8 g; Carbohydrates 14 g; Sugar 12 g; Protein 58.3 g

Flavors Chicken Fajitas

Preparation Time: 10 minutes; Cooking Time: 12 minutes; Serve: 6
Ingredients:
- 2 lbs chicken tenders, boneless
- 1 onion, diced
- 3 bell peppers, sliced
- 1 package taco seasoning
- 13 oz can tomato with green chilies, diced

Directions:
1. Add all ingredients into the instant pot and stir well.
2. Seal pot with lid and cook on high pressure for 12 minutes.
3. Release pressure using quick release method than open the lid.
4. Serve in tortillas and enjoy.

Nutritional Value (Amount per Serving):
Calories 326; Fat 11.4 g; Carbohydrates 8.8 g; Sugar 5.3 g; Protein 45.1 g

Tasty Taco Chicken

Preparation Time: 10 minutes; Cooking Time: 15 minutes; Serve: 4
Ingredients:

- 1 lb chicken breasts, boneless
- 1/2 cup hot water
- 1 packet taco seasoning
- 6 oz can tomato paste
- 15 oz can tomato, diced
- 1 lb chicken thighs, boneless
- Pepper
- Salt

Directions:
1. Add all ingredients into the instant pot and mix well.
2. Seal pot with lid and cook on high pressure for 15 minutes.
3. Allow to release pressure naturally then open the lid.
4. Shred the chicken using a fork.
5. Serve and enjoy.

Nutritional Value (Amount per Serving):
Calories 321; Fat 11.2 g; Carbohydrates 13 g; Sugar 8 g; Protein 42.6 g

Classic Chicken Shawarma

Preparation Time: 10 minutes; Cooking Time: 15 minutes; Serve: 6

Ingredients:
- 1 1/2 lbs chicken breasts, skinless and boneless
- 1 cup chicken broth
- 1/8 tsp ground cinnamon
- 1/2 tsp turmeric
- 1 tsp paprika
- 1/2 lb chicken thighs, skinless and boneless
- 1/4 tsp chili powder
- 1 tsp ground allspice
- 1/4 tsp granulated garlic

Directions:
1. Slice chicken thighs and chicken breast into strips and place in instant pot.
2. In a small bowl, combine together all spices.
3. Sprinkle spice mix over the chicken strips. Mix well to coat chicken with spices.
4. Pour broth on top of chicken.
5. Seal pot with lid and select poultry mode and cook for 15 minutes.
6. Allow to release pressure naturally then open the lid.
7. Serve and enjoy.

Nutritional Value (Amount per Serving):
Calories 236; Fat 9.3 g; Carbohydrates 0.9 g; Sugar 0.2 g; Protein 35.3 g

Rotisserie Chicken

Preparation Time: 10 minutes; Cooking Time: 25 minutes; Serve: 6

Ingredients:
- 4 lbs whole chicken, remove all parts from chicken cavity
- 1 cup chicken broth
- 1 tsp paprika
- 1 tsp granulated garlic
- 1 lemon, halved
- 1 onion, quartered
- 1 tbsp olive oil

- 1/2 tsp pepper
- 1/2 tsp salt

Directions:
1. Rinsed chicken and pat dry with paper towel.
2. Place lemon and onion into the chicken cavity.
3. Mix together all spices then add olive oil into the spices. Mix well.
4. Rub spice mixture all over the chicken.
5. Place chicken into the instant pot and set the pot on sauté mode and cook for 3-4 minutes.
6. Pour broth into the instant pot.
7. Seal pot with lid and cook on manual high pressure for 25 minutes.
8. Allow to release pressure naturally then open the lid.
9. Serve and enjoy.

Nutritional Value (Amount per Serving):
Calories 614; Fat 25.1 g; Carbohydrates 3.4 g; Sugar 1.3 g; Protein 88.8 g

Tasty Shredded Chicken

Preparation Time: 10 minutes; Cooking Time: 27 minutes; Serve: 6
Ingredients:
- 2 lbs chicken breasts, skinless and boneless
- 1/2 cup salsa
- 1 tbsp olive oil
- 1/2 tsp oregano
- 1/2 tsp paprika
- 1 tsp garlic
- 1 tsp cumin
- 1 tbsp chili powder
- 14 oz can tomato, diced
- 7 oz can green chilies
- 1/2 tsp pepper
- 1/2 tsp salt

Directions:
1. Add chicken in instant pot and drizzle with olive oil.
2. Add remaining ingredients into the instant pot.
3. Seal pot with lid and cook on manual high pressure for 27 minutes.
4. Release pressure using quick release method then, open lid carefully.
5. Shred the chicken using a fork and serve.

Nutritional Value (Amount per Serving):
Calories 341; Fat 14 g; Carbohydrates 7.5 g; Sugar 3 g; Protein 45.2 g

Creamy Garlic Pepper Chicken

Preparation Time: 10 minutes; Cooking Time: 8 minutes; Serve: 3
Ingredients:
- 8 oz chicken breasts, skinless and boneless, cut into pieces
- 1/2 cup sour cream
- 2 cups chicken broth
- 2 tbsp garlic powder
- 1 medium onion, sliced
- 1 red pepper, sliced
- 1 green pepper, sliced

Directions:
1. Add all ingredients into the instant pot and stir well.
2. Seal pot with lid and cook on manual high pressure for 8 minutes.
3. Allow to release pressure naturally then open the lid.
4. Serve and enjoy.

Nutritional Value (Amount per Serving):
Calories 305; Fat 14 g; Carbohydrates 13 g; Sugar 6.4 g; Protein 28 g

Creamy Pepper Chicken

Preparation Time: 10 minutes; Cooking Time: 25 minutes; Serve: 2
Ingredients:
- 2 chicken breasts, skinless and boneless
- 1 cup chicken stock
- 1 cup sour cream
- 2 jalapeno peppers, chopped
- 1 1/2 tbsp chili powder
- 3 bacon slices, fried

Directions:
1. Add chili powder, jalapeno peppers, and chicken broth in instant pot and stir well.
2. Place chicken into the pot and seal pot with lid and cook on high for 25 minutes.
3. Release pressure using quick release method than open lid carefully.
4. Add sour cream and bacon, stir well.
5. Serve and enjoy.

Nutritional Value (Amount per Serving):
Calories 706; Fat 48.3 g; Carbohydrates 9.8 g; Sugar 1.4 g; Protein 57.7 g

Simple Mexican Taco Wings

Preparation Time: 10 minutes; Cooking Time: 20 minutes; Serve: 6
Ingredients:
- 1 1/3 lbs chicken wings
- 1/4 cup taco seasoning
- 1 1/2 tsp smoked salt

Directions:
1. Place chicken wings into the bowl and sprinkle with taco seasoning and salt. Rub seasoning over the wings.
2. Pour 1 cup water into the instant pot then place trivet into the pot.
3. Place chicken wings on top of the trivet. Seal pot with lid and cook on high pressure for 10 minutes.
4. Allow to release pressure naturally then open the lid.
5. Place chicken wings on a baking tray and broil for 10 minutes in preheated broiler.
6. Serve and enjoy.

Nutritional Value (Amount per Serving):
Calories 212; Fat 7.5 g; Carbohydrates 4 g; Sugar 1 g; Protein 29.2 g

Salsa Verde Chicken

Preparation Time: 5 minutes; Cooking Time: 12 minutes; Serve: 8
Ingredients:
- 2 lbs chicken breasts, skinless and boneless
- 1 cup salsa Verde
- 3/4 cup onion, sliced

Directions:
1. Add all ingredients into the instant pot and stir well.
2. Seal pot with lid and cook on high for 12 minutes.
3. Release pressure using quick release method than open the lid.
4. Shred the chicken using a fork and stir well.
5. Serve and enjoy.

Nutritional Value (Amount per Serving):
Calories 227; Fat 8 g; Carbohydrates 2.3 g; Sugar 0.9 g; Protein 33.3 g

Thai Chicken

Preparation Time: 10 minutes; Cooking Time: 12 minutes; Serve: 8
Ingredients:
- 2 lbs chicken breasts, skinless and boneless
- 1 cup Thai peanut sauce
- 1 tbsp sesame oil
- 1/2 bell pepper, diced
- 1/2 onion, chopped

Directions:
1. Add oil into the instant pot and select sauté.
2. Add bell pepper and onion and sauté for 2-4 minutes.
3. Add remaining ingredients and stir well.
4. Seal pot with lid and cook on manual high pressure for 12 minutes.
5. Release pressure using quick release method than open the lid.
6. Shred the chicken using a fork and serves.

Nutritional Value (Amount per Serving):
Calories 280; Fat 13.1 g; Carbohydrates 4.2 g; Sugar 1.7 g; Protein 35 g

Ranch Chicken

Preparation Time: 10 minutes; Cooking Time: 12 minutes; Serve: 8
Ingredients:
- 2 lbs chicken breasts, skinless and boneless
- 1 oz ranch packet seasoning
- 4 oz cream cheese, cubed
- 1 cup chicken broth
- 1/4 cup bacon, chopped

Directions:
1. Set the instant pot on sauté mode.

2. Add chopped bacon into the instant pot and sauté for 3-4 minutes or until crisp.
3. Add remaining ingredients into the instant pot and stir well.
4. Seal pot with lid and cook on manual high pressure for 12 minutes.
5. Release pressure using quick release method than open the lid.
6. Shred the chicken using a fork and stir well.
7. Serve and enjoy.

Nutritional Value (Amount per Serving):
Calories 273; Fat 13.8 g; Carbohydrates 0.5 g; Sugar 0.1 g; Protein 34 g

Yummy Mexican Chicken

Preparation Time: 10 minutes; Cooking Time: 12 minutes; Serve: 8
Ingredients:
- 2 lbs chicken breasts, skinless and boneless
- 4 oz can jalapenos, diced
- 10 oz can tomato, diced
- 1/2 cup green pepper
- 1/2 cup red pepper
- 1/2 cup onion
- 1 lime juice
- 2/3 cup chicken broth
- 1/2 tsp chili powder
- 2 tsp cumin
- 2 tsp garlic powder
- 1 tbsp olive oil
- 1/4 tsp salt

Directions:
1. Add olive oil into the instant pot and select sauté.
2. Add onion and bell peppers into the pot and sauté for 3-4 minutes.
3. Add tomatoes, chicken, broth, chili powder, cumin, garlic powder, and jalapenos. Stir well.
4. Seal pot with lid and cook on high pressure for 12 minutes.
5. Allow to release pressure naturally then open the lid.
6. Remove chicken from pot and place on cutting board. Using fork shred the chicken.
7. Return shredded chicken into the pot with lime juice.
8. Stir well and serve.

Nutritional Value (Amount per Serving):
Calories 252; Fat 10 g; Carbohydrates 4.2 g; Sugar 2.3 g; Protein 34 g

Buffalo Chicken

Preparation Time: 10 minutes; Cooking Time: 12 minutes; Serve: 8
Ingredients:
- 2 lbs chicken breasts, skinless and boneless
- 1/2 cup buffalo wing sauce
- 2/3 cup onion, chopped
- 1/2 cup celery, diced
- 1/4 cup bleu cheese, crumbles
- 1/2 cup chicken broth

Directions:
1. Add all ingredients except cheese into the instant pot and stir well.

2. Seal pot with lid and cook on high pressure for 12 minutes.
3. Allow to release pressure naturally then open the lid.
4. Remove chicken from pot and place on cutting board. Using fork shred the chicken.
5. Return shredded chicken into the pot with crumble cheese and stir well.
6. Serve and enjoy.

Nutritional Value (Amount per Serving):
Calories 229; Fat 9 g; Carbohydrates 1.2 g; Protein 33.6 g; Sugar 0.5 g

Artichoke Chicken

Preparation Time: 10 minutes; Cooking Time: 5 minutes; Serve: 4
Ingredients:
- 4 chicken breasts, skinless and boneless
- 14 oz chicken broth
- 1/4 cup butter
- 1/2 tsp smoked paprika
- 1/4 cup water
- 14 oz can artichoke hearts, drained
- 1/2 tsp dried thyme
- 1/2 tsp pepper
- 1 tsp salt

Directions:
1. Add all ingredients except artichoke into the instant pot and stir well.
2. Seal pot with lid and cook on high pressure for 5 minutes.
3. Release pressure using quick release method than open the lid.
4. Add artichoke hearts and stir well.
5. Serve and enjoy.

Nutritional Value (Amount per Serving):
Calories 426; Fat 23 g; Carbohydrates 5.8 g; Sugar 1.2 g; Protein 46.2 g

Chapter 8: Soup & Stew Recipes

Coconut Carrot Soup

Preparation Time: 10 minutes; Cooking Time: 15 minutes; Serve: 4
Ingredients:
- 8 carrots, peeled and chopped
- 1 onion, chopped
- 2 garlic cloves, peeled
- 14 oz can coconut milk
- 1 ½ cups chicken stock
- ¼ cup butter
- 1 tbsp red curry paste
- Pepper
- Salt

Directions:
1. Add all ingredients into the instant pot and stir well.
2. Seal pot with lid and cook on high for 15 minutes.
3. Release pressure using quick release method than open the lid.
4. Puree the soup using a blender until smooth and creamy.
5. Season with pepper and salt.
6. Serve and enjoy.

Nutritional Value (Amount per Serving):
Calories 253; Fat 22.7 g; Carbohydrates 12.6 g; Sugar 5 g; Protein 2.5 g

Squash Cauliflower Soup

Preparation Time: 10 minutes; Cooking Time: 15 minutes; Serve: 6
Ingredients:
- 1 onion, diced
- 2 tsp olive oil
- 2 garlic cloves, minced
- 1 lb cauliflower, chopped
- 1 lb butternut squash, cubed
- 2 cups chicken stock
- 1 tsp paprika
- ½ tsp dried thyme
- ¼ tsp red pepper flakes
- ½ cup heavy cream
- ½ tsp salt

Directions:
1. Add oil into the instant pot and set the pot on sauté mode.
2. Add onion and garlic to the pot and sauté for 5 minutes.
3. Add paprika, thyme, and red pepper flakes and sauté for a minute.
4. Add squash and stir well and cook for 2 minutes.
5. Add cauliflower and stir to mix.
6. Pour chicken stock into the pot and stir well.
7. Seal pot with lid and cook on high for 5 minutes.
8. Release pressure using quick release method than open the lid.
9. Puree the soup using a blender until smooth and creamy.
10. Serve and enjoy.

Nutritional Value (Amount per Serving):
Calories 111; Fat 5.7 g; Carbohydrates 13 g; Sugar 4.4 g; Protein 2.9 g

Creamy Squash Soup

Preparation Time: 10 minutes; Cooking Time: 10 minutes; Serve: 6
Ingredients:
- 6 cups butternut squash, peeled and cubed
- 1/8 tsp nutmeg
- 1/8 tsp cayenne pepper
- 2 tsp thyme
- 3 cups vegetable stock
- 1 onion, chopped
- 2 tbsp butter
- ¼ cup heavy cream
- Pepper
- Salt

Directions:
1. Add butter into the instant pot and set the pot on sauté mode.
2. Add onion to the pot and sauté for 3 minutes.
3. Add squash, nutmeg, cayenne, thyme, stock, and salt. Stir well.
4. Seal pot with lid and cook on high for 5 minutes.
5. Allow to release pressure naturally then open the lid.
6. Add heavy cream and stir well.
7. Puree the soup using a blender until smooth and creamy.
8. Season soup with pepper and salt.
9. Serve and enjoy.

Nutritional Value (Amount per Serving):
Calories 88; Fat 7 g; Carbohydrates 8.1 g; Sugar 1.8 g; Protein 1.9 g

Pork Soup

Preparation Time: 10 minutes; Cooking Time: 30 minutes; Serve: 2
Ingredients:
- ½ lb ground pork
- ½ tsp ground ginger
- 1 tbsp olive oil
- 1 ½ cup cabbage, chopped
- 1 tbsp soy sauce
- 2 cup chicken stock
- 1 cup carrot, peeled and shredded
- 1 small onion, chopped
- Pepper
- Salt

Directions:
1. Add oil into the instant pot and set the pot on sauté mode.
2. Add meat to the pot and sauté for 3-4 minutes.
3. Add remaining ingredients and stir well to combine.
4. Seal pot with lid and cook o high for 25 minutes.
5. Release pressure using quick release method than open the lid.
6. Season soup with pepper and salt.

7. Serve and enjoy.

Nutritional Value (Amount per Serving):
Calories 288; Fat 11.7 g; Carbohydrates 13.4 g; Sugar 6.7 g; Protein 32.4 g

Mushroom Chicken Stew

Preparation Time: 10 minutes; Cooking Time: 38 minutes; Serve: 4

Ingredients:
- 1 lb turkey breast, skinless, boneless, and cut into pieces
- 1 tbsp olive oil
- 2 tbsp butter
- 12 oz mushrooms, sliced
- 1 lb chicken breast, skinless, boneless, and cut into pieces
- 1 tbsp cayenne pepper
- ½ tsp pepper
- 1 tsp salt

Directions:
1. Add oil into the instant pot and set the pot on sauté mode.
2. Add turkey breast, cayenne pepper, pepper, and salt. Stir well.
3. Pour 2 cups of water into the pot and stir well.
4. Seal pot with lid and cook on high for 13 minutes.
5. Release pressure using quick release method than open the lid.
6. Add chicken breast, 1 cup water, and butter. Stir well.
7. Seal pot with lid and cook for 15 minutes.
8. Release pressure using quick release method than open the lid.
9. Add celery and mushrooms and cook on sauté mode for 10 minutes.
10. Serve warm and enjoy.

Nutritional Value (Amount per Serving):
Calories 351; Fat 14.5 g; Carbohydrates 8.5 g; Sugar 5.6 g; Protein 46.3 g

Chicken Veggie Stew

Preparation Time: 10 minutes; Cooking Time: 40 minutes; Serve: 5

Ingredients:
- 2 lbs whole chicken
- ½ tsp black pepper
- 1 tbsp cayenne pepper
- 4 cups chicken stock
- 3 tbsp olive oil
- 1 tomato, chopped
- 1 onion, chopped
- 7 oz cauliflower, chopped
- 10 oz broccoli, chopped
- 2 tsp salt

Directions:
1. Season chicken with salt and set aside.
2. Add oil into the instant pot and set the pot on sauté mode.
3. Add onion to the pot and sauté for 3-4 minutes.
4. Add tomato and cook for 5 minutes.
5. Add remaining ingredients and stir well.

6. Seal pot with lid and cook on high for 30 minutes.
7. Allow to release pressure naturally then open the lid.
8. Stir well and serve.

Nutritional Value (Amount per Serving):
Calories 469; Fat 22.8 g; Carbohydrates 9.7 g; Sugar 3.9 g; Protein 55.9 g

Venison Stew

Preparation Time: 10 minutes; Cooking Time: 28 minutes; Serve: 4
Ingredients:
- 1 lb venison shoulder, cut into pieces
- 2 garlic cloves
- 3 cups chicken stock
- 3 cups water
- 1 tbsp olive oil
- 2 green chilies, chopped
- 3 dried chilies
- 1 tsp pepper
- 1 tsp salt

Directions:
1. Add oil into the instant pot and set the pot on sauté mode. Season meat with pepper and salt.
2. Add meat into the pot and sauté for 3 minutes.
3. Add garlic and sauté for 1-2 minutes.
4. Add remaining ingredients and stir well.
5. Seal pot with lid and cook on high for 25 minutes.
6. Allow to release pressure naturally then open the lid.
7. Stir well and serve warm.

Nutritional Value (Amount per Serving):
Calories 168; Fat 7 g; Carbohydrates 1.6 g; Sugar 0.7 g; Protein 25.3 g

Creamy Taco Soup

Preparation Time: 10 minutes; Cooking Time: 20 minutes; Serve: 8
Ingredients:
- 2 lbs ground beef
- ½ cup heavy cream
- 8 oz cream cheese
- 4 cups chicken broth
- 20 oz can tomato, diced
- 2 tsp ground cumin
- 2 tbsp chili powder
- 3 garlic cloves, minced
- 1 tbsp olive oil
- Pepper
- Salt

Directions:
1. Add oil into the instant pot and set the pot on sauté mode.
2. Add beef in the pot and sauté for 10 minutes.
3. Add remaining ingredients except for heavy cream and cream cheese. Stir to combine.
4. Seal pot with lid and select soup mode and set timer for 10 minutes.

5. Allow to release pressure naturally then open the lid.
6. Stir in heavy cream and cream cheese.
7. Stir well and serve.

Nutritional Value (Amount per Serving):
Calories 394; Fat 22.6 g; Carbohydrates 6.7 g; Sugar 3 g; Protein 40.1 g

Asparagus Soup

Preparation Time: 10 minutes; Cooking Time: 45 minutes; Serve: 6
Ingredients:
- 2 lbs asparagus, halved
- ½ tsp thyme
- 4 cups chicken stock
- 1 cup ham, chopped
- 4 garlic cloves, crushed
- 1 onion, chopped
- 2 tbsp butter
- Pepper
- Salt

Directions:
1. Add butter into the instant pot and set the pot on sauté mode.
2. Add onion to the pot and sauté for 5 minutes.
3. Add ham, garlic, and stock. Stir well and cook for 2-3 minutes.
4. Add remaining ingredients and stir well.
5. Seal pot with lid and select soup mode and cook for 45 minutes.
6. Release pressure using quick release method than open the lid.
7. Puree the soup using a blender until smooth and creamy.
8. Serve and enjoy.

Nutritional Value (Amount per Serving):
Calories 118; Fat 6.4 g; Carbohydrates 9.7 g; Sugar 4.1 g; Protein 7.9 g

Creamy Tomato Soup

Preparation Time: 10 minutes; Cooking Time: 8 minutes; Serve: 8
Ingredients:
- 4 cups tomatoes, peeled, seeded and chopped
- ½ cup heavy cream
- 1 ½ cups unsweetened almond milk
- ½ tsp baking soda
- 1 cup chicken stock
- Pepper
- Salt

Directions:
1. Add tomatoes and stock into the instant pot and stir well. Season with pepper and salt.
2. Seal pot with lid and cook on high for 3 minutes.
3. Release pressure using quick release method than open the lid.
4. Add baking soda to the pot and stir to combine.
5. Stir in heavy cream, almond milk, pepper, and salt.
6. Puree the soup using a blender until smooth and cook on sauté mode for 5 minutes.

7. Stir well and serve.

Nutritional Value (Amount per Serving):
Calories 51; Fat 3.7 g; Carbohydrates 4.2 g; Sugar 2.5 g; Protein 1.2 g

Thyme Asparagus Ham Soup

Preparation Time: 10 minutes; Cooking Time: 45 minutes; Serve: 4

Ingredients:
- 1 ½ lbs asparagus, trimmed and chopped
- 4 cups chicken stock
- 2 tsp garlic, minced
- 3 tbsp butter
- 1 onion, diced
- ¾ cup ham, diced
- ½ tsp thyme

Directions:
1. Add butter into the instant pot and set the pot on sauté mode.
2. Add onion to the pot and sauté for 3 minutes.
3. Add garlic and ham and sauté for a minute.
4. Add stock and thyme. Stir well.
5. Seal pot with lid and select soup mode and cook for 45 minutes.
6. Release pressure using quick release method than open the lid.
7. Puree the soup using a blender until smooth.
8. Serve and enjoy.

Nutritional Value (Amount per Serving):
Calories 175; Fat 11.6 g; Carbohydrates 11.4 g; Sugar 5.1 g; Protein 9.1 g

Beef Pork Soup

Preparation Time: 10 minutes; Cooking Time: 25 minutes; Serve: 8

Ingredients:
- ½ cup Monterey Jack cheese, grated
- 2 tbsp fresh coriander, chopped
- 4 cups chicken stock
- 2 tbsp taco seasonings
- 20 oz Rotel tomatoes, diced
- 16 oz cream cheese
- 1 lb ground beef
- 1 lb ground pork

Directions:
1. Add meat into the instant pot and cook meat on sauté mode for 10 minutes.
2. Add Rotel, cream cheese, and taco seasonings. Stir to combine.
3. Seal pot with lid and cook on high for 15 minutes.
4. Release pressure using quick release method than open the lid.
5. Add coriander and stir well.
6. Top with Monterey jack cheese and serve.

Nutritional Value (Amount per Serving):
Calories 434; Fat 27.8 g; Carbohydrates 6 g; Sugar 0.9 g; Protein 38.9 g

Tomato Coconut Soup

Preparation Time: 10 minutes; Cooking Time: 5 minutes; Serve: 4

Ingredients:
- 6 tomatoes, quartered
- 1 tsp turmeric
- ½ tsp cayenne pepper
- 1 tsp ginger, minced
- 1 tsp garlic, minced
- ¼ cup coriander leaves, chopped
- 1 onion, diced
- 14 oz can coconut milk
- Pepper
- Salt

Directions:
1. Add all ingredients into the instant pot and stir to combine.
2. Seal pot with lid and cook on high for 5 minutes.
3. Allow to release pressure naturally then open the lid.
4. Puree the soup using a blender until smooth.
5. Season soup with pepper and salt.
6. Serve warm and enjoy.

Nutritional Value (Amount per Serving):
Calories 245; Fat 21.7 g; Carbohydrates 13.6 g; Sugar 6.1 g; Protein 4.1 g

Tomato Chicken Soup

Preparation Time: 10 minutes; Cooking Time: 5 minutes; Serve: 6

Ingredients:
- 2 cups Swiss chard, chopped
- 1 ½ cups celery stalks, chopped
- 1 lb chicken thighs, boneless and cut into chunks
- 1 tsp turmeric powder
- 1 tbsp chicken broth base
- 10 oz Rotel can tomatoes
- 1 cup coconut milk
- 1 oz ginger
- 5 garlic cloves
- 1 onion

Directions:
1. Add onion, half coconut milk, broth base, turmeric, tomatoes, ginger, and garlic into the food processor and process until smooth.
2. Transfer blended mixture into the instant pot. Add Swiss chard, celery, and chicken and stir well.
3. Seal pot with lid and cook on high for 5 minutes.
4. Allow to release pressure naturally then open the lid.
5. Add remaining coconut milk and stir well.
6. Serve and enjoy.

Nutritional Value (Amount per Serving):
Calories 283; Fat 15.7 g; Carbohydrates 12 g; Sugar 4.4 g; Protein 24.4 g

Italian Mushrooms Chicken Soup

Preparation Time: 10 minutes; Cooking Time: 15 minutes; Serve: 4
Ingredients:
- 1 lb chicken breast, cut into chunks
- 1 tsp Italian seasoning
- 2 ½ cups chicken stock
- 1 yellow squash, chopped
- 2 cups mushrooms, sliced
- 3 garlic cloves, minced
- 1 onion, diced
- 1 tsp salt

Directions:
1. Add all ingredients into the instant pot and stir well.
2. Seal pot with lid and cook on high for 15 minutes.
3. Allow to release pressure naturally then open the lid.
4. Remove chicken from pot and using blender puree the veggie mixture.
5. Shred the chicken using a fork. Return shredded chicken to the pot and stir well.
6. Serve and enjoy.

Nutritional Value (Amount per Serving):
Calories 169; Fat 3.8 g; Carbohydrates 6.7 g; Sugar 3.2 g; Protein 26.6 g

Garlic Kale Chicken Soup

Preparation Time: 10 minutes; Cooking Time: 5 minutes; Serve: 4
Ingredients:
- 2 cups chicken breast, cooked
- 2 tsp garlic, minced
- ½ tsp cinnamon
- 4 cups chicken stock
- 1 onion, diced
- 12 oz kale
- 1 tsp black pepper
- 1 tsp salt

Directions:
1. Add all ingredients into the instant pot and stir well.
2. Seal pot with lid and cook on high for 5 minutes.
3. Allow to release pressure naturally then open the lid.
4. Stir well and serve warm.

Nutritional Value (Amount per Serving):
Calories 175; Fat 2.8 g; Carbohydrates 13.7 g; Sugar 1.9 g; Protein 24.1 g

Artichoke Chicken Stew

Preparation Time: 10 minutes; Cooking Time: 11 minutes; Serve: 8
Ingredients:
- 1 lb chicken, cooked and shredded
- 1 tbsp parsley
- 2 garlic cloves, minced
- 13 oz can artichokes, chopped
- 1 lb mushrooms, quartered
- 2 tbsp lemon juice

- 1 tsp dry sherry
- 1 cup coconut milk
- 1 cup chicken stock
- 2 cups spinach, chopped
- 1/4 cup nutritional yeast
- 1/2 tsp thyme
- 1 tbsp olive oil
- 1/2 small onion, sliced
- 1 tsp salt

Directions:
1. Add oil into the instant pot and set the pot on sauté mode.
2. Add onion into the pot and sauté for 6 minutes.
3. Add remaining ingredients except for spinach into the pot and stir well.
4. Seal pot with lid and select manual and cook on low pressure for 5 minutes.
5. Release pressure using quick release method than open the lid.
6. Add spinach and stir until spinach is wilted.
7. Stir and serve.

Nutritional Value (Amount per Serving):
Calories 234; Fat 11.4 g; Carbohydrates 12.5 g; Sugar 2.8 g; Protein 23.5 g

Dijon Mushroom Stew

Preparation Time: 10 minutes; Cooking Time: 19 minutes; Serve: 4
Ingredients:
- 1 1/2 lbs chicken thighs, diced
- 1/3 cup sour cream
- 1/4 tsp nutmeg powder
- 1 bay leaf
- 4 garlic cloves, diced
- 7 oz mushrooms, sliced
- 2 tbsp olive oil
- 1 tsp Dijon mustard
- 1/2 cup chicken stock
- 1/2 tsp black pepper
- 1 onion, sliced
- 1 tsp salt

Directions:
1. Add olive oil into the instant pot and set the pot on sauté mode.
2. Add onion and sauté for 4 minutes.
3. Add chicken, mustard, water, stock, pepper, nutmeg, bay leaf, garlic, and mushrooms and stir well.
4. Seal pot with lid and select poultry setting and set timer for 15 minutes.
5. Allow to release pressure naturally then open the lid.
6. Turn off the instant pot. Add sour cream and stir well.
7. Serve and enjoy.

Nutritional Value (Amount per Serving):
Calories 497; Fat 25.7 g; Carbohydrates 6.4 g; Protein 58.6 g; Sugar 2.2 g

Thyme Basil Tomato Soup

Preparation Time: 10 minutes; Cooking Time: 35 minutes; Serve: 6
Ingredients:

- 28 oz can whole tomatoes
- 1 3/4 cup coconut milk
- 3 1/2 cups chicken broth
- 1 cup onion, diced
- 1/3 cup Romano cheese, grated
- 2 bay leaves
- 1/2 cup fresh basil, chopped
- 1 fresh thyme sprig
- 1 cup carrots, diced
- 1 cup celery, diced
- 1 tbsp butter
- 2 tbsp olive oil
- Pepper
- Salt

Directions:
1. Add olive oil and butter into the instant pot and set the pot on sauté mode.
2. Add celery, onion, and carrots and sauté for 5 minutes.
3. Add flour and cook for another 1 minute. Stir constantly.
4. Add remaining ingredients into the instant pot and stir well.
5. Seal pot with lid and cook on manual high pressure for 30 minutes.
6. Release pressure using quick release method than open the lid.
7. Puree the soup using a blender until smooth.
8. Stir well and serve.

Nutritional Value (Amount per Serving):
Calories 299; Fat 25.6 g; Carbohydrates 13 g; Sugar 7 g; Protein 7.8 g

Zesty Cabbage Soup

Preparation Time: 10 minutes; Cooking Time: 6 minutes; Serve: 8

Ingredients:
- 13 oz can tomato, diced
- 3 cups cabbage, chopped
- 1/2 onion, sliced
- 4 garlic cloves, diced
- 2 tbsp butter
- 6 oz tomato paste
- 13 oz can have stewed tomatoes
- 4 cups water
- 1/4 tsp pepper
- 1 1/2 tsp salt

Directions:
1. Add butter into the instant pot and set the pot on sauté mode.
2. Add onion and garlic and sauté for 2 minutes.
3. Add cabbage, water, tomato paste, and tomatoes. Stir well.
4. Seal pot with lid and cook on manual high pressure for 4 minutes.
5. Allow to release pressure naturally then open the lid.
6. Season with pepper and salt.
7. Serve and enjoy.

Nutritional Value (Amount per Serving):
Calories 77; Fat 3.1 g; Carbohydrates 12 g; Sugar 7 g; Protein 2.4 g

Tasty Asparagus Bacon Soup

Preparation Time: 10 minutes; Cooking Time: 10 minutes; Serve: 4

Ingredients:
- 1 bunch asparagus, trimmed and cut into pieces
- 3 cups chicken stock
- 3 tbsp olive oil
- 5 bacon slices, cut into 2" pieces
- 1 medium onion, chopped
- Pepper
- Salt

Directions:
1. Add all ingredients except olive oil into the instant pot and stir well.
2. Seal pot with lid and cook on high pressure for 10 minutes.
3. Allow to release pressure naturally then open the lid.
4. Puree the using blender until smooth.
5. Season with pepper and salt.
6. Serve and enjoy.

Nutritional Value (Amount per Serving):
Calories 265; Fat 21.5 g; Carbohydrates 4.9 g; Sugar 2.3 g; Protein 13.5 g

Dill Celery Coconut Soup

Preparation Time: 10 minutes; Cooking Time: 30 minutes; Serve: 4

Ingredients:
- 6 cups celery stalk, chopped
- 1/2 tsp dill
- 1 cup coconut milk
- 2 cups vegetable stock
- 1 medium onion, chopped
- 1/4 tsp salt

Directions:
1. Add all ingredients into the instant pot and stir well.
2. Seal pot with lid and select soup mode it takes 30 minutes.
3. Release pressure using quick release method than open lid carefully.
4. Puree the soup using a blender until smooth.
5. Stir well and serve.

Nutritional Value (Amount per Serving):
Calories 179; Fat 15.6 g; Carbohydrates 11 g; Sugar 6.2 g; Protein 2.8 g

Vegetable Soup

Preparation Time: 10 minutes; Cooking Time: 10 minutes; Serve: 4

Ingredients:
- 1 medium onion, diced
- 3 cups vegetable stock
- 1/4 tsp pepper
- 2 garlic cloves, chopped
- 1/2 cup fennel, diced
- 1 cup celery stalk, diced
- 2 medium carrot, diced

Directions:
1. Add oil, onion, and garlic in instant pot and set the pot on sauté mode.
2. Add remaining ingredients into the pot and stir well.

3. Seal pot with lid and cook on high pressure for 10 minutes.
4. Allow to release pressure naturally then open the lid.
5. Stir well and serve.

Nutritional Value (Amount per Serving):
Calories 41; Fat 1.6 g; Carbohydrates 9.2 g; Sugar 4.5 g; Protein 1 g

Spinach Cheese Broccoli Soup

Preparation Time: 10 minutes; Cooking Time: 6 minutes; Serve: 8
Ingredients:
- 2 cups spinach
- 4 cups chicken broth
- 1 1/2 tsp dry mustard
- 2 garlic cloves, minced
- 4 cups broccoli florets
- 1/2 cup parmesan cheese, shredded
- 1 cup cheddar cheese, shredded
- 1 onion, chopped
- 2 tbsp butter
- 1 1/2 tsp salt

Directions:
1. Add butter into the instant pot and set the pot on sauté mode.
2. Add garlic, onion, and spices and sauté for 2 minutes.
3. Add broccoli florets and stir to combine.
4. Pour broth and stir well. Seal pot with lid and cook on high pressure for 4 minutes.
5. Release pressure using quick release method than open the lid.
6. Set the instant pot on sauté mode. Add spinach and stir until spinach wilted.
7. Puree the soup using a blender until smooth.
8. Add cheese and blend again to combine.
9. Serve and enjoy.

Nutritional Value (Amount per Serving):
Calories 149; Fat 10 g; Carbohydrates 5.9 g; Sugar 1.9 g; Protein 9.7 g

Pumpkin Pepper Soup

Preparation Time: 10 minutes; Cooking Time: 6 minutes; Serve: 6
Ingredients:
- 2 cups pumpkin puree
- 1/8 tsp thyme, dried
- 1 onion, chopped
- 2 cups chicken stock
- 2 cups coconut milk
- 1/4 cup bell pepper, chopped
- 1 tsp parsley, chopped
- 1/4 tsp nutmeg
- 1/2 tsp salt

Directions:
1. Add pumpkin puree, bell pepper, onion, chicken stock, nutmeg, thyme, milk, and salt in instant pot and mix well.
2. Seal pot with lid and cook on manual high pressure for 6 minutes.
3. Allow to release pressure naturally then open the lid carefully.

4. Garnish with parsley and serve.

Nutritional Value (Amount per Serving):
Calories 82; Fat 4.5 g; Carbohydrates 10 g; Sugar 4 g; Protein 1.9 g

Cheese Soup

Preparation Time: 10 minutes; Cooking Time: 13 minutes; Serve: 6

Ingredients:
- 4 American cheese slices, chopped
- 1/2 cup parmesan cheese, grated
- 1/2 tsp paprika
- 1 tbsp dijon mustard
- 1/2 cup carrots, chopped
- 1 cup coconut milk
- 1 cup farmers cheese, shredded
- 1 cup sharp cheddar cheese, shredded
- 1/2 celery rib, chopped
- 3 cups chicken broth
- 1 tsp garlic, minced
- 1 tbsp onion, minced
- 4 tbsp butter
- Pepper
- Salt

Directions:
1. Add butter into the instant pot and select sauté.
2. Once butter is melted then add celery, onion, carrots and sauté for 5 minutes.
3. Stir in mustard, garlic, paprika, pepper, and salt.
4. Pour broth into the pot and stir well.
5. Seal pot with lid and cook on high pressure for 8 minutes.
6. Release pressure using quick release method than open the lid.
7. Stir in cheeses and mix until cheese is completely melted.
8. Add milk and stir well.
9. Serve and enjoy.

Nutritional Value (Amount per Serving):
Calories 426; Fat 34.1 g; Carbohydrates 5.5 g; Sugar 3.4 g; Protein 21.7 g

Zucchini Coconut Soup

Preparation Time: 10 minutes; Cooking Time: 10 minutes; Serve: 8

Ingredients:
- 10 cups zucchini, chopped
- 13 oz coconut milk
- 1 tbsp Thai curry paste
- 32 oz vegetable stock

Directions:
1. Add all ingredients into the instant pot and stir well.
2. Seal pot with lid and cook on high pressure for 10 minutes.
3. Release pressure using quick release method than open the lid.
4. Puree the soup using a blender until smooth.
5. Serve and enjoy.

Nutritional Value (Amount per Serving):

Calories 137; Fat 11.3 g; Carbohydrates 8.7 g; Sugar 4.9 g; Protein 3.2 g

Thai Carrot Soup

Preparation Time: 10 minutes; Cooking Time: 17 minutes; Serve: 6
Ingredients:
- 1 1/4 lbs carrot, chopped
- 1/2 tsp curry powder
- 1 tsp garlic powder
- 1 tsp sea salt
- 4 cups chicken broth
- 2 tsp ginger, grated
- 1 jalapeno pepper, chopped
- 1 medium onion, chopped
- 1/2 cup coconut milk
- 1/4 tsp cayenne pepper
- 1/4 tsp turmeric
- 1/4 tsp garam masala
- 1 tbsp olive oil

Directions:
1. Add olive oil into the instant pot and set the pot on sauté mode.
2. Add onion into the pot and sauté for 5 minutes.
3. Add carrot and pepper and sauté for minutes.
4. Add remaining ingredients except for coconut milk and stir well.
5. Seal pot with lid and select cook on high for 12 minutes.
6. Release pressure using quick release method than open the lid.
7. Puree the soup using a blender until smooth.
8. Stir in coconut milk and serve.

Nutritional Value (Amount per Serving):
Calories 143; Fat 8.1 g; Carbohydrates 13.8 g; Sugar 6.8 g; Protein 4.9 g

Curried Squash Soup

Preparation Time: 10 minutes; Cooking Time: 10 minutes; Serve: 4
Ingredients:
- 4 yellow squash, chopped
- 1/2 cup coconut milk
- 3 garlic cloves, chopped
- 1 small onion, chopped
- 1/2 tsp cumin
- 1 1/2 tsp curry powder
- 4 cups vegetable broth
- 1/4 tsp pepper
- 1/2 tsp salt

Directions:
1. Add all ingredients except coconut milk into the instant pot and stir well.
2. Seal pot with lid and cook on manual high pressure for 10 minutes.
3. Release pressure using quick release method than open the lid.
4. Puree the soup using a blender until smooth.
5. Add coconut milk and stir well.
6. Season with pepper and salt.
7. Serve and enjoy.

Nutritional Value (Amount per Serving):
 Calories 153; Fat 9 g; Carbohydrates 12 g; Sugar 5.9 g; Protein 8.4 g

Coconut Celery Chicken Soup

Preparation Time: 10 minutes; Cooking Time: 15 minutes; Serve: 6
Ingredients:
- 2 chicken breasts, skinless and boneless
- 14 oz coconut milk
- 4 cups chicken broth
- 2 celery stalks, diced
- 1/2 onion, diced
- 2 carrots, diced

Directions:
1. Add 1 cup chicken broth and chicken into the instant pot and stir well.
2. Seal pot with lid and select poultry setting and set timer for 8 minutes.
3. Release pressure using quick release method than open the lid.
4. Add remaining ingredients and stir well.
5. Again, seal pot with lid and select soup setting for 15 minutes.
6. Release pressure using quick release method than open the lid carefully.
7. Serve and enjoy.

Nutritional Value (Amount per Serving):
 Calories 283; Fat 20.3 g; Carbohydrates 7.3 g; Sugar 4.1 g; Protein 19.1 g

Mushroom Steak Soup

Preparation Time: 10 minutes; Cooking Time: 15 minutes; Serve: 6
Ingredients:
- 1 lb steak, diced
- 2 tbsp oregano
- 2 tbsp garlic powder
- 8 oz mushrooms, sliced
- 1 large bell pepper, diced
- 2 large celery stalks, diced
- 2 large carrots, diced
- 2 cups water
- 2 cups beef stock
- 1 cup tomatoes, crushed
- 1 bay leaf
- 1 tbsp thyme
- 1 large onion, diced
- 1 tbsp salt

Directions:
1. Set the instant pot on sauté mode.
2. Add meat into the pot and cook until browned.
3. Add onion, carrots, pepper, and celery and cook until softened.
4. Add mushrooms and cook until softened.
5. Add remaining ingredients into the pot and stir well.
6. Seal pot with lid and select soup setting and set timer for 15 minutes.
7. Release pressure using quick release method than open the lid.
8. Stir and serve.

Nutritional Value (Amount per Serving):
Calories 212; Fat 4.4 g; Carbohydrates 12 g; Sugar 5.5 g; Protein 31 g

Basil Parmesan Tomato Soup

Preparation Time: 10 minutes; Cooking Time: 5 minutes; Serve: 8
Ingredients:

- 3 lbs tomatoes, cored, peeled, and diced
- 1/4 cup fresh basil
- 14.5 oz can chicken broth
- 2 garlic cloves, minced
- 1 large carrot, diced
- 2 celery stalks, diced
- 1 large onion, diced
- 1 cup half and half
- 1/2 cup parmesan cheese, shredded
- 1 tbsp tomato paste
- 3 tbsp butter
- 1/2 tsp black pepper
- 1/2 tsp salt

Directions:
1. Add butter into the instant pot and set the pot on sauté mode.
2. Add carrots, celery, and onions into the pot and sauté until tender.
3. Add stock, tomato paste, basil, tomatoes, pepper, and salt. Stir well.
4. Seal pot with lid and cook on high pressure for 5 minutes.
5. Release pressure using quick release method than open the lid.
6. Using blender puree the soup until smooth.
7. Set the instant pot on sauté mode. Add half and half and parmesan cheese. Stir well.
8. Serve and enjoy.

Nutritional Value (Amount per Serving):
Calories 152; Fat 9.8 g; Carbohydrates 11 g; Sugar 6.2 g; Protein 5.9 g

Creamy Lemon Mushroom Soup

Preparation Time: 10 minutes; Cooking Time: 13 minutes; Serve: 8
Ingredients:

- 4 cups shiitake mushrooms, sliced
- 4 cups chicken broth
- 2 garlic cloves, minced
- 1 medium onion, sliced
- 2 cups half and half
- 1 lemon juice
- 3 fresh thyme sprigs
- 1/4 cup butter
- 1 tsp sea salt

Directions:
1. Add butter into the instant pot and set the pot on sauté mode.
2. Add garlic, onion, and mushrooms into the pot and sauté for 3 minutes.
3. Add lemon juice, thyme, broth, pepper, and salt. Stir well.
4. Seal pot with lid and cook on manual high pressure for 10 minutes.

5. Release pressure using quick release method than open the lid.
6. Add half and half and stir well.
7. Using blender puree the soup until smooth.
8. Serve and enjoy.

Nutritional Value (Amount per Serving):
Calories 194; Fat 13 g; Carbohydrates 13 g; Sugar 3.7 g; Protein 5.6 g

Italian Cabbage Soup

Preparation Time: 10 minutes; Cooking Time: 20 minutes; Serve: 6
Ingredients:
- 2 leeks, chopped
- 1 garlic clove, minced
- 2 carrots, diced
- 1 bell pepper, diced
- 3 celery ribs, diced
- 1/2 cabbage head, chopped
- 2 tbsp coconut oil
- 2 cups mixed salad greens
- 1 tsp Creole seasoning
- 1 tsp Italian seasoning
- 4 cups chicken broth
- Pepper
- Salt

Directions:
1. Add coconut oil into the instant pot and set the pot on sauté mode.
2. Add all ingredients except salad greens into the instant pot and stir well.
3. Seal pot with lid and select soup setting and set timer for 20 minutes.
4. Release pressure using quick release method than open the lid.
5. Add salad greens and stir until it wilts.
6. Serve and enjoy.

Nutritional Value (Amount per Serving):
Calories 124; Fat 5.9 g; Carbohydrates 13 g; Sugar 5.7 g; Protein 5.5 g

Broccoli Carrot Soup

Preparation Time: 10 minutes; Cooking Time: 30 minutes; Serve: 4
Ingredients:
- 2 cups broccoli florets, chopped
- 2 small carrots, diced
- 2 celery stalks, sliced
- 1 onion, diced
- 1 1/2 cup heavy whipping cream
- 32 oz vegetable broth
- 2 tbsp olive oil
- 1/2 tsp pepper
- 1/2 tsp salt

Directions:
1. Add olive oil into the instant pot and set the pot on sauté mode.
2. Add onion, carrots, and celery into the pot and sauté until tender.
3. Add remaining ingredients except whipping cream into the pot and stir well.

4. Seal pot with lid and select soup setting.
5. Allow to release pressure naturally then open the lid.
6. Add heavy whipping cream and stir well.
7. Serve and enjoy.

Nutritional Value (Amount per Serving):
Calories 290; Fat 25 g; Carbohydrates 10 g; Protein 7.4 g; Sugar 4 g

Coconut Cauliflower Soup

Preparation Time: 10 minutes; Cooking Time: 10 minutes; Serve: 6
Ingredients:
- 1 lb cauliflower florets
- 3 cups vegetable broth
- 1 cup coconut milk
- 1 medium fennel bulbs, chopped
- 3 garlic cloves, minced
- 1 onion, sliced
- 1 tbsp olive oil
- 2 tsp salt

Directions:
1. Add oil into the instant pot and set the pot on sauté mode.
2. Add onion into the pot and sauté until translucent.
3. Add cauliflower, fennel, and garlic and sauté for 5 minutes.
4. Pour coconut milk and broth into the instant pot and stir well.
5. Seal pot with lid and select soup setting and set timer for 5 minutes.
6. Allow to release pressure naturally then open the lid.
7. Puree the soup using a blender until smooth.
8. Serve and enjoy.

Nutritional Value (Amount per Serving):
Calories 171; Fat 12 g; Carbohydrates 11 g; Sugar 4.3 g; Protein 5.6 g

Jalapeno Chicken Soup

Preparation Time: 10 minutes; Cooking Time: 33 minutes; Serve: 10
Ingredients:
- 1 lb chicken breasts, skinless and boneless
- 1 jalapeno pepper, sliced
- 4 garlic cloves, diced
- 1 medium onion, chopped
- 2 medium celery stalks, chopped
- 2 medium carrots, peeled and chopped
- 2 tbsp apple cider vinegar
- 1 cup water
- 8 cup chicken stock
- 1 tbsp ginger root, diced
- 1 tbsp olive oil
- Black pepper
- Salt

Directions:
1. Add olive oil into the instant pot and set the pot on sauté mode.
2. Add ginger, jalapeno, garlic, onion, celery, and carrots and sauté for 3 minutes.

3. Add stock, chicken breasts, and vinegar. Stir well.
4. Seal pot with lid and select soup setting.
5. Release pressure using quick release method than open the lid.
6. Shred chicken using a fork and stir well.
7. Season with pepper and salt.
8. Serve and enjoy.

Nutritional Value (Amount per Serving):
Calories 120; Fat 5.3 g; Carbohydrates 3.7 g; Protein 14.1 g; Sugar 1.8 g

Chicken Curry Soup

Preparation Time: 10 minutes; Cooking Time: 10 minutes; Serve: 6
Ingredients:
- 1 lb chicken thighs, skinless and boneless
- 4 oz baby spinach
- 1 cup mushrooms, sliced
- 1 tsp ginger, chopped
- 3 garlic cloves, crushed
- 1/2 onion, diced
- 1 1/2 cups coconut milk
- 1/4 cup cilantro, chopped
- 1 tsp garam masala
- 1/2 tsp cayenne pepper
- 1/2 tsp turmeric
- 1 tsp salt

Directions:
1. Add all ingredients into the instant pot and stir well.
2. Seal pot with lid and cook on manual high pressure for 10 minutes.
3. Allow to release naturally then open the lid.
4. Remove chicken from instant pot and shred using a fork.
5. Return shredded chicken into the instant and stir well.
6. Serve and enjoy.

Nutritional Value (Amount per Serving):
Calories 297; Fat 20.1 g; Carbohydrates 6.2 g; Sugar 2.7 g; Protein 24.4 g

Thyme Onion Soup

Preparation Time: 10 minutes; Cooking Time: 25 minutes; Serve: 8
Ingredients:
- 8 cups onions, peel and slice
- 1 tbsp balsamic vinegar
- 2 tbsp olive oil
- 2 large fresh thyme sprigs
- 2 bay leaves
- 6 cups vegetable stock
- 1 tsp salt

Directions:
1. Add oil into the instant pot and set the pot on sauté mode.
2. Add onion into the pot and cook until translucent, about 15 minutes.

3. Add remaining ingredients into the instant pot and stir well.
4. Seal pot with lid and cook on manual high pressure for 10 minutes.
5. Allow to release pressure naturally then open the lid.
6. Discard bay leaves and thyme from soup mixture.
7. Puree the soup using a blender until smooth and creamy.
8. Serve and enjoy.

Nutritional Value (Amount per Serving):
Calories 83; Fat 5 g; Carbohydrates 12 g; Sugar 6.4 g; Protein 1.3 g

Chicken Poblano Soup

Preparation Time: 10 minutes; Cooking Time: 15 minutes; Serve: 8
Ingredients:
- 1 1/2 lbs chicken breast, boneless and cut into chunks
- 2 1/2 cups water
- 5 garlic cloves
- 3 poblano peppers, chopped
- 1 cup onion, diced
- 2 oz cream cheese, cut into chunks
- 1 tsp ground cumin
- 1 tsp ground coriander
- 1/4 cup cilantro, chopped
- 1 cup cauliflower, diced
- 1 tsp salt

Directions:
1. Add all ingredients except cream cheese into the instant pot and stir well.
2. Seal pot with lid and cook on high pressure for 15 minutes.
3. Allow to release pressure naturally then open the lid.
4. Remove chicken from instant pot and set aside.
5. Puree the soup and vegetables using a blender.
6. Set the instant pot on sauté mode. Add cream cheese and stir to well combine.
7. Shred the chicken using a fork. Return shredded chicken into the instant pot and stir well.
8. Serve and enjoy.

Nutritional Value (Amount per Serving):
Calories 141; Fat 4.7 g; Carbohydrates 4.5 g; Sugar 1.8 g; Protein 19.5 g

Ranch Chicken Soup

Preparation Time: 10 minutes; Cooking Time: 10 minutes; Serve: 3
Ingredients:
- 2 chicken breasts, skinless and boneless
- 2 tbsp butter
- 1 tbsp ranch dressing
- 1 garlic clove, chopped
- 1/4 cup onion, chopped
- 1 cup heavy cream
- 2 cups cheddar cheese, shredded
- 1/3 cup hot sauce
- 1/2 cup celery, diced
- 3 cups chicken broth

Directions:
1. Add all ingredients except cheese and cream into the instant pot and stir well.
2. Seal pot with lid and cook on high for 10 minutes.
3. Release pressure using quick release method than open the lid.
4. Remove chicken from pot and using fork shred the chicken.
5. Return shredded chicken into the pot and stir well.
6. Add cheese and cream and stir to well combine.
7. Serve and enjoy.

Nutritional Value (Amount per Serving):
Calories 745; Fat 56 g; Carbohydrates 5.4 g; Sugar 2.2 g; Protein 53 g

Tasty Tomato Cream Soup

Preparation Time: 10 minutes; Cooking Time: 5 minutes; Serve: 8
Ingredients:
- 1 cup heavy cream
- 2 cups chicken stock
- 1 tsp onion powder
- 1 tsp garlic powder
- 2 tsp basil
- 2 tsp thyme
- 3 garlic cloves, minced
- 1/2 onion, diced
- 14 oz can tomato, diced
- Pepper
- Salt

Directions:
1. Add all ingredients except heavy cream into the instant pot and stir well.
2. Seal pot with lid and cook on high for 5 minutes.
3. Release pressure using quick release method than open the lid.
4. Add heavy cream and stir well. Season soup with pepper and salt.
5. Serve and enjoy.

Nutritional Value (Amount per Serving):
Calories 72; Fat 5.7 g; Carbohydrates 4.8 g; Sugar 2.4 g; Protein 1.2 g

Broccoli Soup

Preparation Time: 10 minutes; Cooking Time: 10 minutes; Serve: 4
Ingredients:
- 1 cup heavy cream
- 4 cups chicken stock
- 2 cups cheddar cheese, grated
- 1 cup onion, diced
- 9 oz broccoli florets
- 1/2 tsp pepper
- 1 tsp sea salt

Directions:
1. Add broccoli, cheese, onion, pepper, and salt into the instant pot and stir well.
2. Add stock and stir well. Seal pot with lid and cook on high for 7 minutes.
3. Release pressure using quick release method than open the lid.

4. Transfer one cup of instant pot soup to the blender with heavy cream and blend until smooth.
5. Return blended mixture to the instant pot and stir well and cook on sauté mode for 5 minutes.
6. Season soup with pepper and salt.
7. Serve and enjoy.

Nutritional Value (Amount per Serving):
Calories 375; Fat 30.6 g; Carbohydrates 9.4 g; Sugar 3.3 g; Protein 17.5 g

Rosemary Lamb Stew

Preparation Time: 10 minutes; Cooking Time: 85 minutes; Serve: 8
Ingredients:
- 1/2 cup parmesan cheese
- 1 cup sour cream
- ½ lbs mushrooms, sliced
- 4 lbs lamb shoulder, cut into chunks
- 4 cups chicken stock
- 1 cup tomato puree
- ½ cup red wine vinegar
- 3 celery stalks, diced
- ¼ cup rosemary, chopped
- 1 onion, diced
- 3 garlic cloves, minced
- ¼ cup olive oil
- 1 tsp salt

Directions:
1. Add oil, celery, rosemary, onion, and garlic to the pot and cook on sauté mode for 5 minutes.
2. Add tomato puree, vinegar, pepper, and salt and cook for 5 minutes.
3. Add stock and meat and stir well.
4. Seal pot with lid and cook on meat/stew mode for 60 minutes.
5. Allow to release pressure naturally then open the lid.
6. Set pot on sauté mode. Add mushrooms and cook for 15 minutes.
7. Serve and enjoy.

Nutritional Value (Amount per Serving):
Calories 598; Fat 31.1 g; Carbohydrates 8.6 g; Sugar 3.1 g; Protein 68.6 g

Cauliflower Broccoli Chicken Stew

Preparation Time: 10 minutes; Cooking Time: 50 minutes; Serve: 5
Ingredients:
- 3 lbs whole chicken
- 1 tbsp cayenne pepper
- 4 cups chicken stock
- 3 tbsp olive oil
- 1 tomato, chopped
- 1 onion, chopped
- 7 oz cauliflower, chopped
- 10 oz broccoli, chopped
- ½ tsp pepper
- 2 tsp salt

Directions:

1. Season chicken with pepper and salt. Set aside.
2. Add oil into the instant pot and set the pot on sauté mode.
3. Add onion to the pot and sauté for 3-4 minutes. Add tomato and sauté for 5 minutes.
4. Add remaining ingredients and stir well.
5. Seal pot with lid and cook on high pressure for 30 minutes.
6. Allow to release pressure naturally then open the lid.
7. Serve and enjoy.

Nutritional Value (Amount per Serving):
Calories 641; Fat 29.5 g; Carbohydrates 9.7 g; Sugar 3.9 g; Protein 82.2 g

Chapter 9: Beef Recipes

Flavorful Corned Beef

Preparation Time: 10 minutes; Cooking Time: 90 minutes; Serve: 8
Ingredients:
- 4 lbs corned beef
- 1 bay leaf
- 1 onion, quartered
- 2 cups chicken stock
- 12 oz beer
- Pepper

Directions:
1. Place meat into the instant pot and cover with stock and beer.
2. Add bay leaf and onion on top. Season with pepper.
3. Seal pot with lid and cook on high for 90 minutes.
4. Allow to release pressure naturally then open the lid.
5. Remove meat from pot. Cut meat into the slices and serve.

Nutritional Value (Amount per Serving):
Calories 411; Fat 28.5 g; Carbohydrates 3 g; Sugar 0.8 g; Protein 30.9 g

Herb Meatloaf

Preparation Time: 10 minutes; Cooking Time: 30 minutes; Serve: 6
Ingredients:
- 2 lbs ground beef
- 1 ½ cups water
- 2 eggs
- 3 tbsp olive oil
- 1 tsp garlic salt
- ½ tsp sage
- 1 tsp parsley
- 1 tsp oregano
- 1 tsp thyme
- 1 tsp rosemary

Directions:
1. Pour water into the instant pot and place trivet in the pot.
2. Spray loaf pan with cooking spray.
3. Add all ingredients into the large mixing bowl and mix until well combined.
4. Pour bowl mixture into the prepared pan and press down gently.
5. Place loaf pan on top of the trivet.
6. Seal pot with lid and cook on high for 30 minutes.
7. Allow to release pressure naturally then open the lid.
8. Serve and enjoy.

Nutritional Value (Amount per Serving):
Calories 366; Fat 18 g; Carbohydrates 0.9 g; Sugar 0.2 g; Protein 47.9 g

Italian Beef Roast

Preparation Time: 10 minutes; Cooking Time: 50 minutes; Serve: 6
Ingredients:
- 2 ½ lbs beef roast
- 1 cup beef stock
- 1 cup red wine
- 2 tbsp Italian seasoning
- 2 tbsp olive oil
- 1 bell pepper, chopped
- 2 celery stalks, chopped
- 2 garlic cloves, sliced
- 1 onion, sliced

Directions:
1. Add 1 tablespoon of olive oil into the instant pot and set the pot on sauté mode.
2. Add meat into the pot and sear from all the sides. Transfer seared meat to a plate.
3. Add remaining oil, peppers, celery, and onions to the pot and sauté for 3 minutes.
4. Add seasoning and garlic and sauté for a minute.
5. Return meat to the pot.
6. Pour stock and red wine over the meat.
7. Seal pot with lid and cook on high for 40 minutes.
8. Allow to release pressure naturally then open the lid.
9. Serve and enjoy.

Nutritional Value (Amount per Serving):
Calories 457; Fat 18 g; Carbohydrates 5.3 g; Sugar 2.6 g; Protein 58.4 g

Ginger Garlic Beef

Preparation Time: 10 minutes; Cooking Time: 45 minutes; Serve: 4
Ingredients:
- 2 lbs beef roast
- 1 cup water
- 1 tsp garlic powder
- 1 tsp thyme
- 4 garlic cloves
- 1 tsp ginger, grated
- ½ tsp salt

Directions:
1. Mix together all spices and rub over the meat.
2. Place meat into the instant pot. Add garlic cloves on top.
3. Pour water around the meat.
4. Seal pot with lid and cook on high for 45 minutes.
5. Release pressure using quick release method than open the lid.
6. Remove meat from pot and shred using a fork.
7. Serve and enjoy.

Nutritional Value (Amount per Serving):
Calories 430; Fat 14.2 g; Carbohydrates 2 g; Sugar 0.2 g; Protein 69.2 g

Delicious Cajun Cheese Beef

Preparation Time: 10 minutes; Cooking Time: 12 minutes; Serve: 4
Ingredients:
- 1 lb ground beef
- 1 tbsp olive oil
- 2 tbsp tomato paste
- 1 cup beef broth
- 12 oz Mexican cheese
- 1 tbsp Cajun seasoning

Directions:
1. Add oil into the instant pot and set the pot on sauté mode.
2. Add meat to the pot and sauté until browned.
3. Add Cajun seasoning and tomato paste. Stir well.
4. Pour broth over meat.
5. Seal pot with lid and cook on high for 7 minutes.
6. Release pressure using quick release method than open the lid.
7. Add cheese and stir well.
8. Seal pot again and cook on high for 5 minutes.
9. Release pressure using quick release method than open the lid.
10. Stir well and serve.

Nutritional Value (Amount per Serving):
Calories 561; Fat 38.3 g; Carbohydrates 4.8 g; Sugar 1.1 g; Protein 54.2 g

Lemon Chili Chuck Roast

Preparation Time: 10 minutes; Cooking Time: 65 minutes; Serve: 4
Ingredients:
- 2 lbs chuck roast
- 1 tbsp oregano
- 1 tbsp cumin
- 3 garlic cloves, minced
- 8 oz can green chilies, chopped
- 2 lemon juice
- 1 onion, sliced
- ½ cup water
- ½ tsp pepper

Directions:
1. Add all ingredients into the instant pot and stir well.
2. Seal pot with lid and cook on high for 60 minutes.
3. Release pressure using quick release method than open the lid.
4. Remove meat from pot and shred the meat using a fork.
5. Return shredded meat to the pot and cook on sauté mode for 5 minutes.
6. Serve and enjoy.

Nutritional Value (Amount per Serving):
Calories 532; Fat 19.7 g; Carbohydrates 8 g; Sugar 1.8 g; Protein 76.4 g

Easy Short Beef Ribs

Preparation Time: 10 minutes; Cooking Time: 35 minutes; Serve: 4
Ingredients:
- 2 lbs beef short ribs
- 1 tbsp ginger, grated
- 1 tsp five spice powder
- 2 tsp garlic, minced
- ¼ cup Swerve
- 1/3 cup coconut aminos
- ½ cup chicken stock

Directions:
1. In a bowl, whisk together stock, ginger, spice powder, garlic, swerve, and coconut aminos.
2. Place ribs into the instant pot.
3. Pour stock mixture over the ribs.
4. Seal pot with lid and select meat/stew mode and cook for 35 minutes.
5. Allow to release pressure naturally then open the lid.
6. Serve and enjoy.

Nutritional Value (Amount per Serving):
Calories 493; Fat 20.6 g; Carbohydrates 5.6 g; Sugar 0.2 g; Protein 65.8 g

Easy Bolognese Sauce

Preparation Time: 10 minutes; Cooking Time: 15 minutes; Serve: 4
Ingredients:
- 14 oz marinara sauce, sugar-free
- ¼ cup parsley, chopped
- 2 tsp garlic, minced
- 1 lb ground beef

Directions:
1. Add all ingredients into the instant pot and stir well.
2. Seal pot with lid and cook on high for 8 minutes.
3. Release pressure using quick release method than open the lid.
4. Stir well and serve.

Nutritional Value (Amount per Serving):
Calories 262; Fat 7.9 g; Carbohydrates 8.6 g; Sugar 4.8 g; Protein 36.2 g

Tender & Juicy Chuck Roast

Preparation Time: 10 minutes; Cooking Time: 80 minutes; Serve: 4
Ingredients:
- 2 lbs chuck roast
- 2 cups chicken broth
- 2 tbsp olive oil
- 1 onion, sliced
- Pepper
- Salt

Directions:
1. Add oil into the instant pot and set the pot on sauté mode.

2. Season meat with pepper and salt.
3. Place meat into the pot and sear from all the sides until browned.
4. Pour chicken broth over the meat.
5. Seal pot with lid and cook on high for 70 minutes.
6. Release pressure using quick release method than open the lid.
7. Serve and enjoy.

Nutritional Value (Amount per Serving):
Calories 580; Fat 26.5 g; Carbohydrates 3.1 g; Sugar 1.5 g; Protein 77.6 g

Basil Cheese Beef

Preparation Time: 10 minutes; Cooking Time: 35 minutes; Serve: 4
Ingredients:
- 1 lb ground beef
- 1 tbsp olive oil
- ½ cup mozzarella cheese, shredded
- ½ cup tomato puree
- 1 tsp basil
- 1 tsp oregano
- ½ onion, diced
- 1 carrot, sliced
- 14 oz can tomato, diced

Directions:
1. Add oil into the instant pot and set the pot on sauté mode.
2. Add onion to the pot and sauté for 2 minutes.
3. Add meat and cook until browned.
4. Add can tomatoes, oregano, basil, and tomato puree. Stir well.
5. Seal pot with lid and cook on high for 15 minutes.
6. Release pressure using quick release method than open the lid.
7. Add mozzarella cheese and cook on sauté mode for 5 minutes.
8. Serve and enjoy.

Nutritional Value (Amount per Serving):
Calories 297; Fat 11.3 g; Carbohydrates 11 g; Sugar 6.2 g; Protein 37.1 g

Beef with Carrot & Cabbage

Preparation Time: 10 minutes; Cooking Time: 35 minutes; Serve: 8
Ingredients:
- 3 lbs corned beef, chopped
- ½ tsp cumin
- 1 tsp garlic powder
- 3 cups chicken broth
- 1 tbsp butter
- 2 bacon slices, diced
- 3 lbs cabbage, chopped
- 1 onion, chopped
- 1 celery stalk, chopped
- 1 carrot, sliced
- ½ tsp salt

Directions:
1. Add butter into the instant pot and set the pot on sauté mode.

2. Add bacon to the pot and cook until crisp.
3. Add meat and cook until browned.
4. Add remaining ingredients and stir well.
5. Seal pot with lid and cook on high for 35 minutes.
6. Release pressure using quick release method than open the lid.
7. Serve and enjoy.

Nutritional Value (Amount per Serving):
Calories 395; Fat 25.4 g; Carbohydrates 12.7 g; Sugar 6.8 g; Protein 28.9 g

Paprika Corned Beef

Preparation Time: 10 minutes; Cooking Time: 45 minutes; Serve: 4
Ingredients:
- 2 lbs corned beef
- 2 cups water
- ½ tbsp garlic powder
- 2 tbsp olive oil
- ½ tsp ground cloves
- 1 ½ tbsp pepper
- ½ tbsp swerve
- ½ tbsp onion powder
- 1 tsp paprika
- ½ tbsp salt

Directions:
1. Place meat into the instant pot.
2. Pour water over the meat.
3. Seal pot with lid and cook on high for 45 minutes.
4. Release pressure using quick release method than open the lid.
5. In a bowl, mix together spices and oil and rub the spice mixture into the meat.
6. Cook on sauté mode until meat is browned.
7. Serve and enjoy.

Nutritional Value (Amount per Serving):
Calories 460; Fat 35.6 g; Carbohydrates 3.7 g; Sugar 0.7 g; Protein 31 g

Flavorful Pepperoncini Roast

Preparation Time: 10 minutes; Cooking Time: 90 minutes; Serve: 8
Ingredients:
- 5 lbs beef roast
- ¼ cup butter
- 6 pepperoncini
- 1 cup chicken stock

Directions:
1. Add all ingredients into the instant pot and stir well.
2. Seal pot with lid and cook on high for 90 minutes.
3. Allow to release pressure naturally then open the lid.
4. Slices the meat and serve.

Nutritional Value (Amount per Serving):
Calories 586; Fat 23.5 g; Carbohydrates 2.3 g; Sugar 0.8 g; Protein 86.4 g

Ginger Garlic Broccoli Beef

Preparation Time: 10 minutes; Cooking Time: 50 minutes; Serve: 4
Ingredients:
- 1 lb beef, chopped
- 1 tsp ground ginger
- 1 tsp garlic, minced
- ¼ cup coconut aminos
- 1 tbsp fish sauce
- 12 oz broccoli, chopped
- 1 onion, chopped
- Pepper
- Salt

Directions:
1. Add all ingredients except broccoli into the instant pot and stir well.
2. Seal pot with lid and cook on meat/stew mode.
3. Release pressure using quick release method than open the lid.
4. Set pot on sauté mode.
5. Add broccoli to the pot and sauté for 5 minutes.
6. Stir well and serve.

Nutritional Value (Amount per Serving):
Calories 255; Fat 7.4 g; Carbohydrates 9 g; Sugar 2.8 g; Protein 37.4 g

Herb Vinegar Beef

Preparation Time: 10 minutes; Cooking Time: 90 minutes; Serve: 6
Ingredients:
- 3 lbs chuck roast
- ½ tsp ground ginger
- 1 tsp marjoram
- 1 tsp onion powder
- 1 tsp oregano
- 5 garlic cloves
- ¼ cup apple cider vinegar
- 1 tsp basil
- 1 cup chicken broth
- 1 tsp salt

Directions:
1. Using sharp knife make slit cut on meat then press garlic inside the slit.
2. Mix together spices and herbs and rub over the meat.
3. Place meat into the instant pot.
4. Pour broth and vinegar over the meat.
5. Seal pot with lid and cook on high for 90 minutes.
6. Allow to release pressure naturally then open the lid.
7. Serve and enjoy.

Nutritional Value (Amount per Serving):
Calories 505; Fat 19.1 g; Carbohydrates 1.7 g; Sugar 0.4 g; Protein 76 g

Spicy Beef Chili

Preparation Time: 10 minutes; Cooking Time: 13 minutes; Serve: 6
Ingredients:
- 2 lbs ground beef
- 2 cups celery, sliced
- 3 cups onions, chopped
- 2 tbsp olive oil
- 1 1/2 cups beef stock
- 2 tbsp chili powder
- 25 oz tomatoes, chopped
- Pepper
- Salt

Directions:
1. Add oil into the instant pot and set the pot on sauté mode.
2. Add onions and celery and cook for 5 minutes.
3. Add ground beef and cook until meat is no longer pink.
4. Add stock, chili powder, tomatoes, pepper, and salt. Stir well.
5. Seal pot with lid and cook on soup setting for 8 minutes.
6. Allow to release pressure naturally then open the lid.
7. Serve and enjoy.

Nutritional Value (Amount per Serving):
Calories 382; Fat 14 g; Carbohydrates 12 g; Sugar 6.2 g; Protein 48 g

Cajun Pepper Beef

Preparation Time: 10 minutes; Cooking Time: 15 minutes; Serve: 4
Ingredients:
- 1 lb lean minced beef
- 1 roasted red pepper, chopped
- 2 tsp coconut oil
- 1 tbsp pickled jalapeno, chopped
- 1 can tomato, chopped
- 2 tsp Cajun seasoning
- 3 garlic cloves, minced
- 1 onion, chopped
- 1/2 tsp black pepper
- 1/2 tsp sea salt

Directions:
1. Add olive oil into the instant pot and set the instant pot on sauté mode.
2. Add onion into the pot and sauté until translucent.
3. Add Cajun seasoning and garlic and sauté for 1 minute.
4. Add beef and peppers and cook until meat is no longer pink.
5. Add water and tomatoes and mix well.
6. Seal pot with lid and cook on manual high pressure for 15 minutes.
7. Release pressure using quick release method the open the lid.
8. Serve and enjoy.

Nutritional Value (Amount per Serving):
Calories 188; Fat 8 g; Carbohydrates 4.6 g; Sugar 2 g; Protein 24.5 g

Spicy Taco Meat

Preparation Time: 10 minutes; Cooking Time: 18 minutes; Serve: 6
Ingredients:
- 1 1/2 lbs beef minced
- 2 large tomatoes, chopped
- 3 garlic cloves, minced
- 1 bell pepper, chopped
- 1 onion, chopped
- 1/4 tsp smoked paprika
- 1/2 tsp garlic powder
- 1/2 tsp onion powder
- 1/2 tsp dried basil
- 1 tsp paprika
- 1 tsp oregano
- 1/2 tbsp olive oil
- 1/2 tsp ground cumin
- 1/4 tsp black pepper
- 1 tsp salt

Directions:
1. Add oil into the instant pot and set the pot on sauté mode.
2. Add meat into the pot and sauté for 3 minutes.
3. Add remaining ingredients into the pot and stir well.
4. Seal pot with lid and cook on high for 15 minutes.
5. Release pressure using quick release method than open the lid.
6. Serve and enjoy.

Nutritional Value (Amount per Serving):
Calories 252; Fat 8.5 g; Carbohydrates 7 g; Sugar 3.6 g; Protein 35 g

Spicy Beef Chili

Preparation Time: 10 minutes; Cooking Time: 35 minutes; Serve: 4
Ingredients:
- 1 lb beef
- 1 onion, diced
- 1 bell pepper, diced
- 1 tbsp Worcestershire sauce
- 1 tbsp parsley, chopped
- 1 tsp onion powder
- 26 oz tomatoes, chopped
- 1 tsp garlic powder
- 1 tsp paprika
- 4 tsp chili powder
- 2 carrots, chopped
- 1/2 tsp black pepper
- 1 tsp sea salt

Directions:
1. Set the instant pot on sauté mode.
2. Add ground beef into the pot and cook until brown.
3. Add remaining ingredients into the pot and stir well.
4. Seal pot with lid and select meat/stew setting and cook for 35 minutes.
5. Release pressure using quick release method than open the lid.
6. Serve and enjoy.

Nutritional Value (Amount per Serving):

Calories 197; Fat 5.4 g; Carbohydrates 12 g; Protein 25 g; Sugar 6.9 g

Delicious Beef Curry

Preparation Time: 10 minutes; Cooking Time: 30 minutes; Serve: 4
Ingredients:
- 2 lbs stewing beef, cut into cubes
- 1 tsp ground black pepper
- 1/4 cup cilantro, chopped
- 1/2 cup tomatoes, crushed
- 3 garlic cloves, minced
- 1 onion, chopped
- 1/2 cup chicken stock
- 1/2 tsp coriander
- 1/2 tsp cumin
- 1 tbsp garam masala
- 1 tsp turmeric
- 1 tbsp olive oil
- 1/2 tsp lemon zest
- 1/2 tsp smoked paprika
- 1/2 tsp cayenne pepper
- 1 tsp salt

Directions:
1. Set the instant pot on sauté mode.
2. Add oil, spices, garlic, onion, pepper, and salt into the pot and stir well and cook until onion becomes translucent.
3. Stir in crushed tomatoes and bring to boil.
4. Pour pot mixture into the blender and blend until smooth.
5. Brown the meat on all sides then pour the blended mixture, lemon zest, and stock over meat.
6. Seal pot with lid and cook on high pressure for 30 minutes.
7. Allow to release pressure naturally then open the lid.
8. Serve and enjoy.

Nutritional Value (Amount per Serving):
Calories 476; Fat 17 g; Carbohydrates 5.5 g; Protein 69 g; Sugar 2 g

Easy Taco Meat

Preparation Time: 10 minutes; Cooking Time: 30 minutes; Serve: 8
Ingredients:
- 2 lbs lean ground beef
- 1/4 cup taco seasoning
- 1 cup chicken stock

Directions:
1. Add all ingredients into the pot and stir well.
2. Seal pot with lid and cook on manual high pressure for 25 minutes.
3. Allow to release pressure naturally then open the lid.
4. Set pot on sauté mode for 5 minutes or until liquid absorbed.
5. Serve and enjoy.

Nutritional Value (Amount per Serving):

Calories 272; Fat 7.1 g; Carbohydrates 12 g; Sugar 3.1 g; Protein 34 g

Beef Brisket

Preparation Time: 10 minutes; Cooking Time: 1 hour 40 minutes; Serve: 4
Ingredients:
- 3 1/2 lbs beef brisket, cut into pieces
- 1 tbsp butter
- 1/4 cup cilantro, chopped
- 1 cup chicken stock
- 2 tbsp chipotle powder
- 1 tsp sea salt

Directions:
1. Add butter into the instant pot and select sauté.
2. Add brisket into the pot and sauté until lightly brown.
3. Add remaining ingredients into the pot and mix well.
4. Seal pot with lid and select meat/stew setting and set the timer for 1 hour 40 minutes.
5. Release pressure using quick release method than open the lid.
6. Slice and serve.

Nutritional Value (Amount per Serving):
Calories 765; Fat 27 g; Carbohydrates 0.2 g; Sugar 0.2 g; Protein 120 g

Apple Cider Beef

Preparation Time: 10 minutes; Cooking Time: 90 minutes; Serve: 8
Ingredients:
- 3 lbs corned beef brisket
- 12 oz apple cider
- 1 cup chicken broth

Directions:
1. Place beef brisket into the instant pot.
2. Pour chicken broth and apple juice over brisket.
3. Seal pot with lid and select manual and set timer for 90 minutes.
4. Allow to release pressure naturally then open the lid.
5. Slice and serve.

Nutritional Value (Amount per Serving):
Calories 313; Fat 21 g; Carbohydrates 5.1 g; Sugar 4.7 g; Protein 23 g

Lime Beef Tacos

Preparation Time: 10 minutes; Cooking Time: 60 minutes; Serve: 4
Ingredients:
- 1 1/2 lbs beef roast
- 1 cup water
- 1 tsp ground cumin
- 2 fresh lime juices
- Pepper
- Salt

Directions:
1. Place beef roast into the instant pot.
2. Add remaining ingredients into the pot.
3. Seal pot with lid and select manual and set timer for 60 minutes.
4. Release pressure using quick release method than open the lid.
5. Shred the meat using a fork and serve.

Nutritional Value (Amount per Serving):
Calories 318; Fat 10 g; Carbohydrates 0.3 g; Sugar 0 g; Protein 51 g

Flavors Balsamic Beef Roast

Preparation Time: 10 minutes; Cooking Time: 30 minutes; Serve: 6
Ingredients:
- 3 lbs beef roast, boneless and cut into pieces
- 1/2 cup balsamic vinegar
- 1 cup chicken stock
- 4 garlic cloves, chopped
- 1/2 tsp red pepper flakes
- 1 tbsp soy sauce
- 1 tbsp Worcestershire sauce

Directions:
1. Place beef roast into the instant pot.
2. In a bowl, mix together all remaining ingredients and pour over beef roast.
3. Seal pot with lid and cook on high pressure for 30 minutes.
4. Allow to release pressure naturally then open the lid.
5. Stir and serve.

Nutritional Value (Amount per Serving):
Calories 435; Fat 14.3 g; Carbohydrates 1.8 g; Sugar 0.8 g; Protein 69.2 g

Spicy Texas Chili

Preparation Time: 10 minutes; Cooking Time: 30 minutes; Serve: 6
Ingredients:
- 2 lbs beef, cut into pieces
- 1 bottle shiner
- 1 tsp cumin
- 1 tsp red pepper flakes
- 2 tsp garlic, minced
- 8 tbsp chili powder
- 28 oz tomatoes, diced
- 1 onion, diced
- 1 1/2 tsp salt

Directions:
1. Brown onion and meat in instant pot.
2. Add remaining ingredients into the instant pot and stir well.
3. Seal pot with lid and cook on high pressure for 30 minutes.
4. Release pressure using quick release method than open the lid.
5. Stir and serve.

Nutritional Value (Amount per Serving):

Calories 347; Fat 11.5 g; Carbohydrates 13 g; Sugar 5 g; Protein 48.6 g

Indian Beef Curry

Preparation Time: 10 minutes; Cooking Time: 30 minutes; Serve: 4
Ingredients:
- 2 lbs stewing beef, cut into cubes
- 1/2 tsp coriander
- 1/2 tsp cumin
- 1 tbsp garam masala
- 1 tsp turmeric
- 1 tsp ground black pepper
- 1/4 cup cilantro, chopped
- 1/2 cup tomatoes, crushed
- 3 garlic cloves, minced
- 1/2 cup beef stock
- 1 tbsp olive oil
- 1/2 tsp lemon zest
- 1/2 tsp smoked paprika
- 1/2 tsp cayenne pepper
- 1 onion, chopped
- 1 tsp salt

Directions:
1. Set instant pot on sauté mode.
2. Add oil, spices, garlic, onion, pepper, and salt into the pot and stir well and cook until onion becomes softens.
3. Stir in crushed tomatoes. Bring to boil.
4. Pour pot mixture into the blender and blend until smooth.
5. Brown the meat on all sides then pour the blended mixture, lemon zest, and stock over meat.
6. Seal pot with lid and cook on high pressure for 30 minutes.
7. Allow to release pressure naturally then open the lid.
8. Serve and enjoy.

Nutritional Value (Amount per Serving):
Calories 478; Fat 18 g; Carbohydrates 5.4 g; Sugar 1.9 g; Protein 70.1 g

Delicious Italian Beef

Preparation Time: 10 minutes; Cooking Time: 60 minutes; Serve: 8
Ingredients:
- 5 lbs chuck roast
- 16 oz pepperoncini peppers, sliced
- 1/2 onion, sliced
- 1 tbsp olive oil
- 1 packet Italian seasoning mix
- 1 cup water

Directions:
1. Add olive oil into the instant pot and set the instant pot on sauté mode.
2. Add meat into the pot and cook until brown for 5-6 minutes on each side.
3. Add remaining ingredients into the pot and stir well.
4. Seal pot with lid and select manual and set timer for 55 minutes.
5. Release pressure using quick release method than open the lid.
6. Shred the meat using a fork and serve.

Nutritional Value (Amount per Serving):
Calories 630; Fat 25.3 g; Carbohydrates 4.6 g; Sugar 0.3 g; Protein 93.7 g

Creamy Spicy Beef Curry

Preparation Time: 10 minutes; Cooking Time: 20 minutes; Serve: 4
Ingredients:
- 1 lb beef chuck roast, cut into pieces
- 1/2 tsp ground coriander
- 1/2 tsp cayenne pepper
- 1/2 cup fresh cilantro, chopped
- 4 garlic cloves, chopped
- 1 tsp ground cumin
- 1 small onion, quarters
- 2 tomatoes, quarters
- 1 tsp garam masala
- 1 tsp salt

Directions:
1. Add tomatoes, cilantro, garlic, and onion into the blender and blend until smooth.
2. Add cumin, cayenne, garam masala, coriander, and salt and blend until combined.
3. Place beef into the instant pot then pour vegetable puree over the beef.
4. Seal pot with lid and cook on high pressure for 20 minutes.
5. Allow to release pressure naturally then open the lid.
6. Stir and serve.

Nutritional Value (Amount per Serving):
Calories 437; Fat 31.9 g; Carbohydrates 5.4 g; Sugar 2.4 g; Protein 30.8 g

Tomatillo Beef Chili

Preparation Time: 10 minutes; Cooking Time: 35 minutes; Serve: 8
Ingredients:
- 1 lb ground beef
- 1 tbsp chili powder
- 1 tbsp ground cumin
- 1 jalapeno pepper, chopped
- 1 tsp garlic powder
- 6 oz tomato paste
- 1/2 onion, chopped
- 3 tomatillos, chopped
- 1 lb ground pork
- Salt

Directions:
1. Set instant pot on sauté mode.
2. Add beef and pork into the pot and cook until brown.
3. Add remaining ingredients into the pot and stir well to combine.
4. Seal pot with lid and cook on high pressure for 35 minutes.
5. Allow to release pressure naturally then open the lid.
6. Stir and serve.

Nutritional Value (Amount per Serving):
Calories 218; Fat 6.1 g; Carbohydrates 6.6 g; Sugar 3.1 g; Protein 33.5 g

Tasty Korean Beef

Preparation Time: 10 minutes; Cooking Time: 10 minutes; Serve: 4
Ingredients:
- 1 lb ground beef
- 1 garlic clove, minced
- 3 green onion, sliced
- 1/4 tsp pepper
- 1/4 tsp red pepper flakes
- 1/4 tsp ground ginger
- 2 tsp sesame oil
- 1/4 cup soy sauce

Directions:
1. Add oil into the instant pot and set the pot on sauté mode.
2. Add meat into the pot and cook until brown, about 5 minutes.
3. Add remaining ingredients into the pot and stir well.
4. Seal pot with lid and cook for 5 minutes.
5. Release pressure using quick release method than open the lid.
6. Serve and enjoy.

Nutritional Value (Amount per Serving):
Calories 245; Fat 9.4 g; Carbohydrates 2.5 g; Sugar 0.6 g; Protein 35.7 g

Jalapeno Cajun Beef

Preparation Time: 10 minutes; Cooking Time: 15 minutes; Serve: 4
Ingredients:
- 1 lb lean minced beef
- 2 tsp Cajun seasoning
- 1 tbsp pickled jalapeno, chopped
- 1 can tomato, chopped
- 1 roasted red pepper, chopped
- 3 garlic cloves, minced
- 1 onion, chopped
- 2 tsp olive oil
- 1/2 tsp black pepper
- 1/2 tsp sea salt

Directions:
1. Add olive oil into the instant pot and set the instant pot on sauté mode.
2. Add onion into the pot and sauté until softened.
3. Add Cajun seasoning and garlic and sauté for a minute.
4. Add beef and peppers and cook until meat is browned.
5. Add water and tomatoes and stir well.
6. Seal pot with lid and cook on manual high pressure for 15 minutes.
7. Release pressure using quick release method the open the lid.
8. Stir and serve.

Nutritional Value (Amount per Serving):
Calories 196; Fat 8.1 g; Carbohydrates 5.8 g; Sugar 2 g; Protein 24.8 g

Chili Lime Shredded Beef

Preparation Time: 10 minutes; Cooking Time: 60 minutes; Serve: 4
Ingredients:
- 2 lbs beef chuck roast, boneless
- 1/2 cup beef broth
- 1 tbsp fresh lime juice
- 1 tsp oregano
- 1 tbsp chili powder
- 1 large onion, sliced
- 1 tsp garlic powder
- 1 tsp salt

Directions:
1. In a small bowl, mix together, chili powder, oregano, garlic powder, and salt.
2. Rub bowl mixture all over chuck roast.
3. Add sliced onion in instant pot then place chuck roast over the onion.
4. Pour broth and lime juice over roast.
5. Seal pot with lid and select manual and set timer for 60 minutes.
6. Allow to release pressure naturally then open the lid.
7. Shred the meat using a fork and serve.

Nutritional Value (Amount per Serving):
Calories 853; Fat 63.7 g; Carbohydrates 5.4 g; Sugar 2 g; Protein 60.7 g

Herb Almond Meatloaf

Preparation Time: 10 minutes; Cooking Time: 35 minutes; Serve: 6
Ingredients:
- 1 lb ground beef
- 1 tbsp Dijon mustard
- 1 cup almond flour
- 1/2 tsp garlic powder
- 1/2 tsp thyme, dried
- 1 large egg
- 1/2 cup ketchup
- 1 medium onion, chopped
- 1 apple, chopped
- 2 tsp parsley, dried
- 1/4 tsp pepper
- 1/4 tsp salt

Directions:
1. Spray a loaf pan with cooking spray and set aside.
2. In a bowl, combine together all ingredients and pour into the prepared loaf pan.
3. Pour 1 cup water into the instant pot then place a trivet in the pot.
4. Place loaf pan on top of the trivet.
5. Seal pot with lid and select manual and set timer for 35 minutes.
6. Release pressure using quick release method than open the lid carefully.
7. Cut into slices and serve.

Nutritional Value (Amount per Serving):
Calories 222; Fat 8.1 g; Carbohydrates 12.4 g; Sugar 5 g; Protein 25.5 g

Coconut Beef Brisket

Preparation Time: 10 minutes; Cooking Time: 52 minutes; Serve: 4
Ingredients:
- 1 1/2 lbs beef brisket
- 2 tbsp coconut sugar
- 1 tsp thyme, dried
- 2 cups beef stock
- 1 tsp onion powder
- 1 tsp mustard powder
- 1 tsp ground black pepper
- 1/2 tsp paprika
- 1 tsp salt

Directions:
1. In a small bowl, mix together thyme, paprika, onion powder, mustard, black pepper, coconut sugar, and salt.
2. Rub bowl mixture all over beef brisket.
3. Place beef brisket in instant pot and select sauté and cook brisket for 2 minutes.
4. Pour beef stock over brisket.
5. Seal pot with lid and cook on high for 50 minutes.
6. Allow to release pressure naturally then open the lid.
7. Slice beef brisket and serve.

Nutritional Value (Amount per Serving):
Calories 333; Fat 11.2 g; Carbohydrates 1.5 g; Sugar 0.3 g; Protein 53.4 g

Creamy Flank Steak

Preparation Time: 10 minutes; Cooking Time: 25 minutes; Serve: 2
Ingredients:
- 1 lb flank steak
- 2 tbsp onion soup mix
- 1/4 cup olive oil
- 1/2 tbsp Worcestershire sauce
- 2 tbsp apple cider vinegar

Directions:
1. Place flank steak in instant pot and sauté meat until brown.
2. Add olive oil, onion soup mix, vinegar, and Worcestershire sauce over the steak.
3. Seal pot with lid and cook on high for 25 minutes.
4. Allow to release pressure naturally then open the lid.
5. Serve and enjoy.

Nutritional Value (Amount per Serving):
Calories 678; Fat 44.1 g; Carbohydrates 4.9 g; Sugar 2.8 g; Protein 63.1 g

Tasty Beef Bourguignon

Preparation Time: 10 minutes; Cooking Time: 20 minutes; Serve: 6
Ingredients:

- 2 lbs round steak, cut into pieces
- 1 cup mushrooms, quartered
- 3 bacon slices, cooked
- 2 carrots, sliced
- 1/2 cup beef stock
- 1 cup dry red wine
- 2 garlic cloves, minced
- 1/4 tsp basil
- 1 onion, chopped

Directions:
1. Add all ingredients into the instant pot and stir well.
2. Seal pot with lid and cook on high for 20 minutes.
3. Allow to release pressure naturally then open the lid.
4. Stir and serve.

Nutritional Value (Amount per Serving):
Calories 432; Fat 18.6 g; Carbohydrates 5.6 g; Sugar 2.3 g; Protein 50.2 g

Ranch Roast

Preparation Time: 10 minutes; Cooking Time: 45 minutes; Serve: 8
Ingredients:
- 4 lbs pot roast
- 4 celery stalks, sliced
- 3 large carrots, peeled and sliced
- 2 tbsp olive oil
- 1 packet ranch seasoning
- 2 cups chicken stock
- 1 tsp black pepper
- 1 tsp sea salt

Directions:
1. Add oil into the instant pot and set the pot on sauté mode.
2. Add meat into the pot and sauté until brown.
3. Remove meat from pot and set aside.
4. Add carrots and celery and sauté for 5 minutes.
5. Add stock and stir well.
6. Return meat into the pot and season with ranch seasoning.
7. Seal pot with lid and cook on high for 40 minutes.
8. Allow to release pressure naturally then open the lid.
9. Stir and serve.

Nutritional Value (Amount per Serving):
Calories 799; Fat 57.7 g; Carbohydrates 3.3 g; Sugar 1.6 g; Protein 62.7 g

Thai Beef Roast

Preparation Time: 10 minutes; Cooking Time: 48 minutes; Serve: 8
Ingredients:
- 3 lbs chuck roast
- 1/2 cup sweet chili sauce
- 1/2 cup orange juice
- 1 tsp curry powder
- 2 tbsp olive oil
- 1 tsp garlic powder
- Pepper
- Salt

Directions:
1. Add olive oil into the instant pot and set the pot on sauté mode.
2. Add roast into the pot and brown the roast for 2-3 minutes per side.
3. Add remaining ingredients into the pot and stir well.
4. Seal pot with lid and cook on manual high pressure for 45 minutes.
5. Release pressure using quick release method than open the lid.
6. Shred the meat using a fork.
7. Stir and serve.

Nutritional Value (Amount per Serving):
Calories 436; Fat 17.7 g; Carbohydrates 8 g; Sugar 7.4 g; Protein 56.4 g

Ancho Chili Taco Meat

Preparation Time: 10 minutes; Cooking Time: 25 minutes; Serve: 6
Ingredients:
- 2 lbs ground beef
- 2 cups chicken stock
- 1/2 tsp chipotle powder
- 1 tsp Ancho chili powder
- 2 tsp onion powder
- 2 tsp cumin
- 2 tsp paprika
- 2 tsp garlic powder
- 1 tsp salt

Directions:
1. Add all ingredients into the instant pot and stir well.
2. Seal pot with lid and cook on high for 25 minutes.
3. Release pressure using quick release method than open the lid.
4. Stir and serve.

Nutritional Value (Amount per Serving):
Calories 295; Fat 9.9 g; Carbohydrates 2.3 g; Sugar 0.8 g; Protein 46.6 g

Pepper Rings Shredded Beef

Preparation Time: 10 minutes; Cooking Time: 70 minutes; Serve: 6
Ingredients:
- 3 lbs beef
- 1 tbsp garlic powder
- ½ cup beef broth
- 16 oz pepper rings
- Pepper
- Salt

Directions:
1. Season meat with garlic powder, pepper, and salt.
2. Place meat into the instant pot.
3. Add broth and pepper rings over the meat.
4. Seal pot with lid and cook on high for 70 minutes.
5. Allow to release pressure naturally then open the lid.
6. Shred the meat using a fork.

7. Stir well and serve.

Nutritional Value (Amount per Serving):
Calories 443; Fat 14.3 g; Carbohydrates 6.5 g; Sugar 3.1 g; Protein 70 g

Spicy Meatballs

Preparation Time: 10 minutes; Cooking Time: 30 minutes; Serve: 4

Ingredients:
- 1 lb ground beef
- ¼ tsp garlic powder
- ½ cup tomato sauce
- ½ tsp chili powder
- 2/3 cup salsa
- 1 egg
- ¼ cup arrowroot
- Pepper
- Salt

Directions:
1. Add all ingredients into the large bowl and mix until well combined.
2. Make small meatballs from mixture and place into the instant pot.
3. Seal pot with lid and cook on low for 30 minutes.
4. Release pressure using quick release method than open the lid.
5. Serve and enjoy.

Nutritional Value (Amount per Serving):
Calories 252; Fat 8.4 g; Carbohydrates 5.8 g; Sugar 2.8 g; Protein 37.2 g

Flavorful Beef Shawarma

Preparation Time: 10 minutes; Cooking Time: 5 minutes; Serve: 4

Ingredients:
- 1 lb ground beef
- ½ tsp ground coriander
- ½ tsp cumin
- ¼ tsp cayenne pepper
- ¼ tsp allspice
- ½ tsp cinnamon
- 1 tsp oregano
- 2 cups cabbage, sliced
- 1 cup bell pepper, sliced
- 1 cup onion, chopped
- 1 tsp salt

Directions:
1. Add meat into the instant pot and set the pot on sauté mode and cook for 2 minutes.
2. Add remaining ingredients and stir well.
3. Seal pot with lid and cook on high for 2 minutes.
4. Allow to release pressure naturally then open the lid.
5. Stir well and serve.

Nutritional Value (Amount per Serving):
Calories 244; Fat 7.4 g; Carbohydrates 7.7 g; Sugar 3.9 g; Protein 35.6 g

Beef Stroganoff

Preparation Time: 10 minutes; Cooking Time: 20 minutes; Serve: 4
Ingredients:
- 1 lb beef sirloin steak, cut into strips
- ½ cup sour cream
- ½ lb mushrooms, quartered
- 1 cup chicken stock
- 2 tbsp tomato paste
- 1 tsp paprika
- 2 bacon slices, diced
- 3 garlic cloves, crushed
- ½ onion, diced

Directions:
1. Add all ingredients except cream into the instant pot and stir well.
2. Seal pot with lid and cook on high for 20 minutes.
3. Allow to release pressure naturally then open the lid.
4. Serve and enjoy.

Nutritional Value (Amount per Serving):
Calories 355; Fat 17.5 g; Carbohydrates 7.2 g; Sugar 2.8 g; Protein 41.5 g

Pepper Beef Chili

Preparation Time: 10 minutes; Cooking Time: 10 minutes; Serve: 4
Ingredients:
- 1 lb ground beef
- ½ tsp ground rosemary
- ½ tsp paprika
- 1 tsp garlic powder
- ½ tsp chili powder
- ½ cup chicken stock
- 1 cup heavy cream
- 1 tbsp olive oil
- 2 garlic cloves, minced
- 1 onion, chopped
- 1 bell pepper, chopped
- 2 cups tomatoes, diced
- 1 tsp kosher salt

Directions:
1. Add oil into the instant pot and set the pot on sauté mode.
2. Add meat, bell pepper, and onion to the pot and sauté for 5 minutes. Season with garlic powder and salt.
3. Add stock and tomatoes. Stir well.
4. Seal pot with lid and cook on high for 5 minutes.
5. Release pressure using quick release method than open the lid.
6. Add rosemary, paprika, chili powder, heavy cream, and salt. Stir well.
7. Cook on sauté mode for 10 minutes.
8. Serve and enjoy.

Nutritional Value (Amount per Serving):
Calories 389; Fat 22.2 g; Carbohydrates 10.7 g; Sugar 5.4 g; Protein 36.8 g

Chapter 10: Pork Recipes

Hawaiian Pork

Preparation Time: 10 minutes; Cooking Time: 90 minutes; Serve: 8

Ingredients:
- 5 lbs pork roast, bone-in and cut into three equal pieces
- 1 cup water
- 1 tbsp Hawaiian salt
- 5 garlic cloves, minced
- 1 onion, quartered
- Pepper

Directions:
1. Place meat into the instant pot.
2. Add garlic, onion, pepper, and salt on top of meat.
3. Pour water over the meat.
4. Seal pot with lid and cook on high for 90 minutes.
5. Allow to release pressure naturally then open the lid.
6. Shred the meat using a fork.
7. Stir and serve.

Nutritional Value (Amount per Serving):
Calories 595; Fat 26.8 g; Carbohydrates 1.9 g; Sugar 0.6 g; Protein 81.1 g

Classic Pork & Cabbage

Preparation Time: 10 minutes; Cooking Time: 8 minutes; Serve: 4

Ingredients:
- 1 lb pork loin, boneless and cut into cubes
- 1 tbsp white wine vinegar
- 1 cup chicken stock
- ½ tsp pepper
- ½ tsp fennel seeds
- 1 tsp dried dill weed
- ½ small cabbage, cored and cut into wedges
- 1 onion, cut into wedges
- 2 tsp olive oil

Directions:
1. Add oil into the instant pot and set the pot on sauté mode.
2. Add onion to the pot and sauté for 2 minutes.
3. Add meat and cook for 3 minutes.
4. Add cabbage and stir well.
5. In a small bowl, mix together dill weed, pepper, and fennel seeds. Sprinkle on top of the cabbage.
6. Pour vinegar and stock on top of meat mixture.
7. Seal pot with lid and cook on high for 5 minutes.
8. Allow to release pressure naturally then open the lid.
9. Serve and enjoy.

Nutritional Value (Amount per Serving):
Calories 333; Fat 18.4 g; Carbohydrates 8.4 g; Sugar 4.2 g; Protein 32.7 g

Creamy Garlic Thyme Pork

Preparation Time: 10 minutes; Cooking Time: 10 minutes; Serve: 4

Ingredients:
- 1 lb pork sausage
- ½ tbsp olive oil
- ¼ tsp pepper
- 1 tsp thyme
- 2 cups coconut milk
- 3 garlic cloves, minced
- ¼ cup arrowroot
- ½ tsp salt

Directions:
1. Add oil into the instant pot and set the pot on sauté mode.
2. Add thyme and garlic and sauté for a minute.
3. Add meat and cook until browned.
4. Pour coconut milk and 1 ½ cups of water over meat.
5. Seal pot with lid and cook on high for 5 minutes.
6. Meanwhile, in a bowl, whisk together little coconut milk, arrowroot, pepper, and salt.
7. Release pressure using quick release method than open the lid.
8. Add arrowroot slurry to the pot and stir well and cook on sauté mode for 5 minutes.
9. Serve and enjoy.

Nutritional Value (Amount per Serving):
Calories 685; Fat 62.6 g; Carbohydrates 8.6 g; Sugar 4 g; Protein 25.3 g

Spicy Pork

Preparation Time: 10 minutes; Cooking Time: 45 minutes; Serve: 4

Ingredients:
- 2 lbs pork roast
- 1 ½ cups chicken broth
- ½ tsp pepper
- 1 tsp garlic powder
- 1 tsp ground ginger
- 1 tbsp olive oil
- 1 tsp swerve
- 1 paprika
- 1 tsp oregano
- 1 tsp thyme
- 1 tsp cumin
- ½ tsp chili powder

Directions:
1. Add oil into the instant pot and set the pot on sauté mode.
2. Mix together spices and herbs and rub over meat.
3. Cook meat on sauté mode until meat is browned.
4. Add all ingredients into the instant pot and stir well.
5. Seal pot with lid and cook on high for 45 minutes.
6. Allow to release pressure naturally then open the lid.
7. Stir well and serve.

Nutritional Value (Amount per Serving):
Calories 525; Fat 25.7 g; Carbohydrates 2.7 g; Sugar 0.5 g; Protein 60.8 g

Yummy Pork Carnitas

Preparation Time: 10 minutes; Cooking Time: 50 minutes; Serve: 4
Ingredients:
- 2 lbs pork shoulder
- 1 jalapeno, diced
- 1 tbsp olive oil
- 2 tsp garlic, minced
- 1 tsp cumin
- 1 tsp oregano
- 2 lime juice
- ½ cup water
- 2 cups chicken broth
- 1 onion, chopped

Directions:
1. Add oil into the instant pot and set the pot on sauté mode.
2. Add meat to the pot and sauté until browned.
3. Add remaining ingredients into the pot and stir well to combine.
4. Seal pot with lid and cook on high for 30 minutes.
5. Allow to release pressure naturally then open the lid.
6. Shred the meat using a fork.
7. Stir well and serve.

Nutritional Value (Amount per Serving):
Calories 734; Fat 52.9 g; Carbohydrates 6 g; Sugar 2.1 g; Protein 55.9 g

Easy Jamaican Pork

Preparation Time: 10 minutes; Cooking Time: 45 minutes; Serve: 4
Ingredients:
- 2 lbs pork shoulder
- 2 tbsp Jamaican spice rub
- 1 cup chicken broth
- 1 tbsp olive oil

Directions:
1. Add oil into the pot and set the pot on sauté mode.
2. Add meat to the pot and cook until browned.
3. Add remaining ingredients over the meat.
4. Seal pot with lid and cook on high for 45 minutes.
5. Release pressure using quick release method than open the lid.
6. Shred the meat using a fork.
7. Serve and enjoy.

Nutritional Value (Amount per Serving):
Calories 702; Fat 52.4 g; Carbohydrates 0.2 g; Sugar 0.2 g; Protein 54 g

Parmesan Pork Chops

Preparation Time: 10 minutes; Cooking Time: 50 minutes; Serve: 3
Ingredients:
- 3 pork chops, boneless
- ½ cup water
- 1 small onion, sliced
- 3 bacon slices, diced
- 1 tbsp Dijon mustard
- ¼ cup parmesan cheese, grated
- ½ cup heavy cream
- Pepper
- Salt

Directions:
1. Season pork chops with pepper and salt.
2. Add bacon slices into the instant pot and cook on sauté mode until crisp.
3. Remove bacon from pot and set aside.
4. Add pork chops into the instant pot and cook for few minutes from both the sides. Remove from pot.
5. Add onion to the pot and sauté until softened.
6. Add water and stir well. Return pork chops to the pot.
7. Seal pot with lid and cook on high for 30 minutes.
8. Allow to release pressure naturally then open the lid.
9. Remove pork chops from pot and place onto a plate.
10. Set pot on sauté mode.
11. Add Dijon mustard and cream to the pot and stir well. Bring to boil for 5-10 minutes.
12. Turn off the instant pot sauté mode.
13. Add parmesan cheese and stir until cheese is melted.
14. Pour sauce over pork chops and top with bacon.
15. Serve and enjoy.

Nutritional Value (Amount per Serving):
Calories 491; Fat 38.5 g; Carbohydrates 3.3 g; Sugar 1.1 g; Protein 29.9 g

Chili Garlic Pork

Preparation Time: 10 minutes; Cooking Time: 60 minutes; Serve: 4
Ingredients:
- 2 lbs pork shoulder
- 1 ½ cups chicken broth
- 2 tbsp olive oil
- 1 fresh lime juice
- 1 chili, chopped
- ½ onion, chopped
- 2 garlic cloves
- 1 tsp pepper

Directions:
1. Add garlic, 1 tablespoon of olive oil, pepper, lime juice, and chili into the blender and blend until smooth.
2. Rub blended mixture all over the meat.

3. Add remaining oil into the instant pot and set the pot on sauté mode.
4. Place meat into the pot and sauté until browned.
5. Seal pot with lid and cook on high for 60 minutes.
6. Allow to release pressure naturally then open the lid.
7. Cut meat into the slices and serve.

Nutritional Value (Amount per Serving):
Calories 749; Fat 56.1 g; Carbohydrates 3.4 g; Sugar 1.1 g; Protein 55 g

Garlicky Pork Shoulder

Preparation Time: 10 minutes; Cooking Time: 90 minutes; Serve: 12
Ingredients:
- 4 lbs pork shoulder, trimmed, boneless, and cut into pieces
- 9 garlic cloves, chopped
- 2 tbsp soy sauce
- 2 tbsp coconut sugar
- 1 cup chicken stock
- 2 tbsp butter
- 1 tsp salt

Directions:
1. Add butter into the instant pot and set the pot on sauté mode.
2. Add meat to the pot and sauté until browned.
3. Add remaining ingredients over the meat.
4. Seal pot with lid and cook on high for 90 minutes.
5. Allow to release pressure naturally then open the lid.
6. Shred the meat using a fork.
7. Stir well and serve.

Nutritional Value (Amount per Serving):
Calories 464; Fat 34.3 g; Carbohydrates 1 g; Sugar 0.1 g; Protein 35.6g

Mushroom Pork Chops

Preparation Time: 10 minutes; Cooking Time: 30 minutes; Serve: 4
Ingredients:
- 4 pork chops, boneless
- 1 cup mushrooms, sliced
- 10 oz water
- 10 oz can cream of mushroom soup
- 2 tbsp olive oil
- 2 garlic cloves, sliced
- Pepper
- Salt

Directions:
1. Add oil into the instant pot and set the pot on sauté mode.
2. Season pork chops with pepper and salt.
3. Add pork chops into the instant pot and sauté until browned.
4. Add remaining ingredients over the pork chops.
5. Seal pot with lid and cook on high for 30 minutes.
6. Allow to release pressure naturally then open the lid.

7. Serve and enjoy.

Nutritional Value (Amount per Serving):
Calories 361; Fat 28.2 g; Carbohydrates 7.1 g; Sugar 1.9 g; Protein 19.5 g

Cinnamon Ginger Pork Chops

Preparation Time: 10 minutes; Cooking Time: 15 minutes; Serve: 4

Ingredients:
- 2 lbs pork chops
- 1 tbsp olive oil
- 1 cup beef broth
- ½ tsp cinnamon
- 2 tbsp Dijon mustard
- ½ tsp ginger, grated
- 2 tbsp swerve
- ¼ tsp pepper
- ½ tsp salt

Directions:
1. Season pork chops with pepper and salt.
2. Add oil into the instant pot and set the pot on sauté mode.
3. Add pork chops to the pot and sauté until browned.
4. Whisk together remaining ingredients and pour over pork chops.
5. Seal pot with lid and cook on high for 15 minutes.
6. Release pressure using quick release method than open the lid.
7. Serve and enjoy.

Nutritional Value (Amount per Serving):
Calories 775; Fat 60.5 g; Carbohydrates 2.1 g; Sugar 0.3 g; Protein 52.6 g

Creamy Spinach Pork

Preparation Time: 10 minutes; Cooking Time: 20 minutes; Serve: 6

Ingredients:
- 1 lb pork shoulder, cut into cubes
- 1 tsp ginger, minced
- 1 tsp garlic, minced
- 1/3 cup half and half
- 2 tsp garam masala
- 1/2 tsp cayenne pepper
- 1/2 tsp turmeric
- 5 oz baby spinach, chopped
- 1 tbsp olive oil
- 3/4 cup water
- 1 tbsp tomato paste

Directions:
1. Add meat into the large mixing bowl and marinate with turmeric, cayenne pepper, garam masala, half and half, garlic, and ginger.
2. Add oil into the instant pot and set the pot on sauté mode.
3. Add pork into the instant pot along with marinade and tomato paste and cook on sauté mode for 5-10 minutes.
4. Pour water into the instant pot and stir well.
5. Seal pot with lid and cook on high for 10 minutes.

6. Release pressure using quick release method than open the lid.
7. Add spinach and stir until spinach is wilted.
8. Serve and enjoy.

Nutritional Value (Amount per Serving):
Calories 268; Fat 20.2 g; Carbohydrates 2.5 g; Sugar 0.5 g; Protein 18.9 g

Spiced Pork Ribs

Preparation Time: 10 minutes; Cooking Time: 45 minutes; Serve: 6
Ingredients:
- 3 lbs pork ribs
- 3/4 cup chicken broth
- For rub:
- 1 tsp garlic powder
- 1 tsp paprika
- 1/4 tsp cayenne pepper
- 1 tsp pepper
- 1 tsp onion powder
- 1 tsp cumin
- 1 tsp salt

Directions:
- In a small bowl, mix together all rub ingredients and rub over the meat.
- Pour broth into the instant pot then place ribs into the pot.
- Seal pot with lid and cook on high for 45 minutes.
- Allow to release pressure naturally then open the lid.
- Serve and enjoy.

Nutritional Value (Amount per Serving):
Calories 630; Fat 40 g; Carbohydrates 1.4 g; Sugar 0.4 g; Protein 61 g

Easy Smoked Ribs

Preparation Time: 10 minutes; Cooking Time: 35 minutes; Serve: 6
Ingredients:
- 2 1/2 lbs spareribs, boneless
- 1 tbsp liquid smoke
- 14 oz chicken broth
- 1 tbsp sea salt

Directions:
1. Season spareribs with salt and set aside.
2. Add liquid smoke and broth into the instant pot.
3. Place spareribs into the pot.
4. Seal pot with lid and cook on high for 35 minutes.
5. Release pressure using quick release method than open the lid.
6. Serve and enjoy.

Nutritional Value (Amount per Serving):
Calories 761; Fat 57 g; Carbohydrates 0.3 g; Sugar 0.2 g; Protein 56 g

Chili Garlic Pork Roast

Preparation Time: 10 minutes; Cooking Time: 25 minutes; Serve: 6
Ingredients:
- 3 lbs pork roast
- 1/2 cup apple juice
- 1 cup water
- 1 tbsp olive oil
- 1/4 tsp chili powder
- 1/2 tsp garlic powder
- 1/2 tsp onion powder
- 1/2 tsp black pepper
- 1/2 tsp salt

Directions:
1. In a small bowl, mix together all spices.
2. Rub spice mixture all over the meat.
3. Add oil into the instant pot and set the pot on sauté mode.
4. Add pork into the pot and sauté until brown.
5. Add remaining ingredients into the pot.
6. Seal pot with lid and cook on high for 25 minutes.
7. Release pressure using quick release method than open the lid.
8. Serve and enjoy.

Nutritional Value (Amount per Serving):
Calories 501; Fat 23 g; Carbohydrates 2.8 g; Sugar 2.1 g; Protein 64 g

Yummy Pork Fajitas

Preparation Time: 10 minutes; Cooking Time: 1 minute; Serve: 6
Ingredients:
- 1 1/2 lbs pork chops, cut into strips
- 2 bell peppers, cut into strips
- 14.5 oz can salsa
- 1/2 cup chicken broth
- 1 tbsp lime juice
- 1 onion, sliced
- 1 tbsp taco seasoning

Directions:
1. Add all ingredients into the instant pot. Stir well.
2. Seal pot with lid and cook on high for 1 minute.
3. Allow to release pressure naturally then open the lid.
4. Serve and enjoy.

Nutritional Value (Amount per Serving):
Calories 410; Fat 28 g; Carbohydrates 10 g; Sugar 5.2 g; Protein 27 g

Tasty Ranch Pork Chops

Preparation Time: 10 minutes; Cooking Time: 5 minutes; Serve: 6

Ingredients:
- 6 pork chops, boneless
- 1 cup water
- 1 packet ranch mix
- 1/2 cup butter
- 1 tbsp olive oil

Directions:
1. Add olive oil into the instant pot and set the pot on sauté mode.
2. Add pork chops into the pot and sauté until brown.
3. Add remaining ingredients over the pork chops.
4. Seal pot with lid and cook on high pressure for 5 minutes.
5. Allow to release pressure naturally then open the lid.
6. Serve and enjoy.

Nutritional Value (Amount per Serving):
Calories 412; Fat 37 g; Carbohydrates 0 g; Sugar 0 g; Protein 18.1 g

Lemon Apple Pork Chops

Preparation Time: 10 minutes; Cooking Time: 10 minutes; Serve: 2

Ingredients:
- 2 pork chops, boneless
- 1/4 cup apple juice
- 2 tbsp lemon pepper

Directions:
1. Set instant pot on sauté mode.
2. Season pork chops with lemon pepper and place into the instant pot.
3. Sauté pork chops until browned.
4. Pour apple juice over the pork chops.
5. Seal pot with lid and cook on high for 10 minutes.
6. Allow to release pressure naturally then open the lid.
7. Serve and enjoy.

Nutritional Value (Amount per Serving):
Calories 286; Fat 20.1 g; Carbohydrates 7.7 g; Sugar 3 g; Protein 18.7 g

Thyme Pepper Shredded Pork

Preparation Time: 10 minutes; Cooking Time: 45 minutes; Serve: 10

Ingredients:
- 18 oz pork tenderloin
- 1 tbsp fresh parsley, chopped
- 2 bay leaves
- 2 fresh thyme sprigs
- 7 oz jar roasted red peppers, drained
- 28 oz can tomatoes, crushed
- 5 garlic cloves, smashed
- 1 tsp olive oil
- 1/4 tsp pepper
- 1 tsp kosher salt

Directions:
1. Season pork with pepper and salt.

2. Add olive oil into the instant pot and set the pot on sauté mode.
3. Add garlic into the pot and sauté for a minute.
4. Add pork into the pot and sauté until lightly brown.
5. Add remaining ingredients and stir well.
6. Seal pot with lid and cook on high for 45 minutes.
7. Allow to release pressure naturally then open the lid.
8. Shred the pork using a fork.
9. Serve and enjoy.

Nutritional Value (Amount per Serving):
Calories 121; Fat 2.3 g; Carbohydrates 8.1 g; Sugar 2.7 g; Protein 14.9 g

Cheesy Pork Chops

Preparation Time: 10 minutes; Cooking Time: 8 minutes; Serve: 2
Ingredients:
- 2 pork chops, boneless
- 2 tbsp olive oil
- 1 cup water
- 2 tbsp hot sauce
- 2 tbsp butter
- 1/2 cup cheese, shredded

Directions:
1. Add oil into the instant pot and set the pot on sauté mode.
2. Add pork chops into the pot and sauté until brown.
3. Transfer pork chops into the baking dish.
4. Pour hot sauce and butter over pork chops and cover dish with foil.
5. Pour 1 cup water into the instant pot then place trivet into the pot.
6. Place baking dish on top of the trivet.
7. Seal pot with lid and cook on high pressure for 8 minutes.
8. Allow to release pressure naturally then open the lid.
9. Sprinkle cheese on top of pork chops and broil until cheese melted.
10. Serve and enjoy.

Nutritional Value (Amount per Serving):
Calories 590; Fat 54 g; Carbohydrates 0.6 g; Sugar 0.3 g; Protein 25 g

Country Style Pork Ribs

Preparation Time: 10 minutes; Cooking Time: 45 minutes; Serve: 4
Ingredients:
- 3 lbs country style pork ribs
- 3/4 cup chicken stock
- For rub:
- 1 tsp onion powder
- 1 tsp garlic powder
- 1/4 tsp cayenne pepper
- 1 tsp cumin
- 1 tsp pepper
- 1 tsp paprika
- 1 tsp salt

Directions:
1. In a small bowl, mix together all rub ingredients and rub over meat.
2. Pour stock into the instant pot then place meat into the pot.
3. Seal pot with lid and cook on high for 45 minutes.
4. Allow to release pressure naturally then open the lid.
5. Serve and enjoy.

Nutritional Value (Amount per Serving):
Calories 644; Fat 39.5 g; Carbohydrates 2.1 g; Sugar 0.6 g; Protein 66.8 g

Onion Garlic Pork Loin

Preparation Time: 10 minutes; Cooking Time: 45 minutes; Serve: 4
Ingredients:
- 2 lb pork loin
- 1 cup chicken stock
- 2 garlic cloves, crushed
- 1 tsp onion powder
- 1 tsp ground ginger
- 1/2 cup water
- 1/4 cup soy sauce

Directions:
1. In a small bowl, mix together all ingredients except meat and stock.
2. Pour stock into the instant pot.
3. Place meat into the pot then pour bowl mixture over the pork.
4. Seal pot with lid and cook high for 45 minutes.
5. Allow to release pressure naturally then open the lid.
6. Serve and enjoy.

Nutritional Value (Amount per Serving):
Calories 566; Fat 31.8 g; Carbohydrates 2.7 g; Sugar 0.7 g; Protein 63.3 g

Delicious Butter Ranch Pork Chops

Preparation Time: 10 minutes; Cooking Time: 10 minutes; Serve: 6
Ingredients:
- 6 pork chops, boneless
- 8 tbsp butter
- 1 tbsp olive oil
- 1 cup chicken stock
- 1 packet ranch seasoning
- Pepper
- Salt

Directions:
1. Season pork chops with pepper and salt.
2. Heat oil in a pan over medium heat.
3. Add pork chops and cook until brown from both the sides.
4. Remove pan from heat and set aside.
5. Place pork chops in instant pot.
6. Sprinkle ranch seasoning over the pork chops.

7. Add butter and stock over the pork.
8. Seal pot with lid and cook on high for 5 minutes.
9. Allow to release pressure naturally then open the lid.
10. Serve and enjoy.

Nutritional Value (Amount per Serving):
Calories 414; Fat 37.7 g; Carbohydrates 0.1 g; Sugar 0.1 g; Protein 18.3 g

Shredded Garlic BBQ Pork

Preparation Time: 10 minutes; Cooking Time: 60 minutes; Serve: 4

Ingredients:
- 1 lb pork shoulder
- 1/4 cup BBQ sauce, sugar-free
- 1/2 tbsp mustard powder
- 1/2 tsp garlic powder
- 1/2 tbsp onion powder
- 1/4 cup beef stock
- 1/4 tsp pepper
- 1 tsp salt

Directions:
1. Mix together all dry ingredients and rub all over the meat.
2. Place meat in instant pot and pour stock and BBQ sauce over pork.
3. Seal pot with lid and cook on high pressure for 60 minutes.
4. Allow releasing pressure naturally then open the lid.
5. Shred the meat using a fork and serve.

Nutritional Value (Amount per Serving):
Calories 346; Fat 24.7 g; Carbohydrates 2 g; Sugar 0.5 g; Protein 27.1 g

Chipotle BBQ Pork Ribs

Preparation Time: 10 minutes; Cooking Time: 25 minutes; Serve: 6

Ingredients:
- 3 lbs pork ribs rack
- 1 tsp onion powder
- 1/2 tsp chipotle powder
- 1 cup water
- 1/2 cup BBQ sauce, sugar-free
- 1 tsp garlic powder

Directions:
1. Pour water into the instant pot then place a trivet in the pot.
2. Season pork ribs with onion, garlic, and chipotle powder and place on top of the trivet.
3. Seal pot with lid and cook on high for 25 minutes.
4. Allow to release pressure naturally then the open lid.
5. Remove ribs from pot and place on baking tray and coat with BBQ sauce.
6. Broil pork ribs into the broiler for few minutes until sauce caramelized.
7. Serve and enjoy.

Nutritional Value (Amount per Serving):
Calories 531; Fat 38.1 g; Carbohydrates 2 g; Sugar 0.3 g; Protein 40.3 g

Flavors Pork Carnitas

Preparation Time: 10 minutes; Cooking Time: 55 minutes; Serve: 8
Ingredients:
- 2 lb pork shoulder blade roast, trimmed and boneless
- 1 tsp cumin
- 5 garlic cloves, cut into slivers
- 2 chipotle peppers
- 3/4 cup chicken stock
- 1/4 tsp dry oregano
- 1/2 tsp garlic powder
- 1/4 tsp dry adobo seasoning
- 2 bay leaves
- 1/2 tsp sazon
- Pepper
- Salt

Directions:
1. Season pork with pepper and salt.
2. In a large pan, brown the meat from all the sides over high heat for 5 minutes.
3. Remove meat from pan and set aside.
4. Using knife insert blade into pork about 1" deep then insert garlic slivers, do this all over.
5. Season pork with garlic powder, adobo, oregano, sazon and cumin.
6. Pour chicken stock in an instant pot. Add chipotle peppers and stir well.
7. Add bay leaves and place pork in instant pot.
8. Seal pot with lid and cook on high for 50 minutes.
9. Allow to release pressure naturally then open the lid.
10. Shred the pork using a fork and stir in juices.
11. Remove bay leaves and stir well.
12. Serve and enjoy.

Nutritional Value (Amount per Serving):
Calories 251; Fat 18.2 g; Carbohydrates 2 g; Sugar 0.7 g; Protein 20.6 g

Salsa Pork Chili Verde

Preparation Time: 10 minutes; Cooking Time: 55 minutes; Serve: 4
Ingredients:
- 2 lbs pork shoulder
- 1/2 cup water
- 1/4 tsp garlic powder
- 1/2 tsp black pepper
- 1 1/2 cups salsa verde
- 1/2 tsp oregano
- 1/4 tsp smoked paprika
- 1 tbsp olive oil
- 1/2 tsp kosher salt

Directions:
1. Mix together all spices and rub over meat.
2. Add olive oil into the instant pot and set the pot on sauté mode.
3. Add pork into the pot and sauté until brown from all the sides.
4. Add remaining ingredients into the instant pot and stir well.

5. Seal pot with lid and select meat/stew mode and set timer for 55 minutes.
6. Allow to release pressure naturally then open the lid.
7. Shred the meat using a fork and stir well.
8. Serve and enjoy.

Nutritional Value (Amount per Serving):
Calories 717; Fat 52.3 g; Carbohydrates 4.4 g; Sugar 1.4 g; Protein 54.1 g

Cinnamon Spice Ham

Preparation Time: 10 minutes; Cooking Time: 10 minutes; Serve: 8
Ingredients:
- 7 lbs ham, cut into chunks
- 2 cinnamon sticks
- 1 bay leaves
- 1/4 cup Worcestershire sauce
- 2 cups apple juice
- 4 cups chicken stock
- 1 tbsp allspice berries
- 1 tbsp black peppercorns

Directions:
1. Add all ingredients into the instant pot and stir well.
2. Seal pot with lid and cook on high for 10 minutes.
3. Allow to release pressure naturally then open the lid.
4. Stir well and serve.

Nutritional Value (Amount per Serving):
Calories 463; Fat 14.6 g; Carbohydrates 10.2 g; Sugar 7 g; Protein 73.6 g

Pork Chops with Apple Butter

Preparation Time: 10 minutes; Cooking Time: 20 minutes; Serve: 4
Ingredients:
- 2 lbs pork chops, boneless
- 3 garlic cloves, minced
- 1 onion, chopped
- 2 tbsp olive oil
- 1 cup applesauce
- 28 oz apple butter
- Pepper
- Salt

Directions:
1. Season pork chops with pepper and salt,
2. Add olive oil into the pot and set the pot on sauté mode.
3. Add pork chops into the pot and sauté until brown.
4. Add garlic and onion and sauté for 2 minutes.
5. Add remaining ingredients into the pot and stir well.
6. Seal pot with lid and cook on high for 20 minutes.
7. Allow to release pressure naturally then open the lid.
8. Serve and enjoy.

Nutritional Value (Amount per Serving):
Calories 560; Fat 42.3 g; Carbohydrates 9.3 g; Sugar 6.5 g; Protein 34.3 g

Pork Chops in Garlic Sauce

Preparation Time: 10 minutes; Cooking Time: 10 minutes; Serve: 6
Ingredients:
- 6 pork chops
- 1 cup chicken broth
- 2 tbsp butter
- 1/2 cup almond milk, unsweetened
- 2 tbsp arrowroot
- 1/4 cup garlic cloves, minced
- 1/4 tsp black pepper
- 1/2 tsp salt

Directions:
1. Add butter into the instant pot and set the pot on sauté mode.
2. Season pork chops with pepper and salt.
3. Place pork chops into the pot and cook until brown.
4. Remove chops from the pot and set aside.
5. Pour broth into the instant pot then return chops into the pot.
6. Seal pot with lid and cook on high for 8 minutes.
7. Allow to release pressure naturally then open the lid.
8. Stir in arrowroot and almond milk and cook on sauté mode until thicken about 2-3 minutes.
9. Serve and enjoy.

Nutritional Value (Amount per Serving):
Calories 353; Fat 28.8 g; Carbohydrates 3.5 g; Sugar 0.9 g; Protein 19.8 g

Cheese Butter Pork Chops

Preparation Time: 10 minutes; Cooking Time: 8 minutes; Serve: 2
Ingredients:
- 2 pork chops, boneless
- 2 tbsp butter
- 2 tbsp olive oil
- 1 cup water
- 1/2 cup cheese, shredded
- 2 tbsp hot sauce

Directions:
1. Add oil into the instant pot and set the pot on sauté mode.
2. Add pork chops into the pot and sauté until brown.
3. Remove pork chops from pot and place into the baking dish.
4. Pour hot sauce and butter over pork chops and cover dish with foil.
5. Pour 1 cup water into the pot then place trivet into the pot.
6. Place baking dish on top of the trivet.
7. Seal pot with lid and cook on high for 8 minutes.
8. Allow to release pressure naturally then open the lid.
9. Sprinkle cheese on top of pork chops and broil until cheese melted.
10. Serve and enjoy.

Nutritional Value (Amount per Serving):

Calories 593; Fat 54.8 g; Carbohydrates 0.6 g; Sugar 0.3 g; Protein 25.2 g

Shredded Pork Ragu

Preparation Time: 10 minutes; Cooking Time: 45 minutes; Serve: 10
Ingredients:
- 18 oz pork tenderloin
- 7 oz jar roasted red peppers, drained
- 28 oz can tomato, crushed
- 5 garlic cloves, smashed
- 1 tsp olive oil
- 1 tbsp fresh parsley, chopped
- 2 bay leaves
- 2 fresh thyme sprigs
- 1/4 tsp black pepper
- 1 tsp kosher salt

Directions:
1. Season pork with pepper and salt.
2. Add olive oil into the instant pot and set the pot on sauté mode.
3. Add garlic into the pot and sauté for a minute.
4. Add pork and cook until lightly brown.
5. Add remaining ingredients and stir well.
6. Seal pot with lid and cook on high for 45 minutes.
7. Allow to release pressure naturally then open the lid.
8. Shred the pork using a fork.
9. Serve and enjoy.

Nutritional Value (Amount per Serving):
Calories 112; Fat 3.5 g; Carbohydrates 6 g; Sugar 3.4 g; Protein 14.5 g

Asian Pork

Preparation Time: 10 minutes; Cooking Time: 25 minutes; Serve: 6
Ingredients:
- 2 lbs pork belly, cut into 1.5-inch cubes
- 1 tbsp blackstrap molasses
- 3 tbsp sherry
- 2 tbsp swerve
- 1 tbsp ginger, grated
- 1/3 cup bone broth
- 2 tbsp coconut aminos
- 1 tsp sea salt

Directions:
1. Add all ingredients into the instant pot and stir well.
2. Seal pot with lid and select manual and set timer for 25 minutes.
3. Allow to release pressure naturally then open the lid.
4. Cook on sauté mode until sauce is thickened.
5. Stir well and serve.

Nutritional Value (Amount per Serving):
Calories 722; Fat 40.8 g; Carbohydrates 4.8 g; Sugar 1.9 g; Protein 71 g

Delicious Pork Chile Verde

Preparation Time: 10 minutes; Cooking Time: 30 minutes; Serve: 8
Ingredients:
- 2 lbs pork butt roast, cut into pieces
- 2 tsp cumin powder
- 1 tomato, chopped
- 1 tbsp fish sauce
- 1/4 cup cilantro
- 6 garlic cloves
- 2 Poblano peppers
- 3 jalapeno peppers
- 3 tomatillos, husk removed

Directions:
1. Add all ingredients except fish sauce and cilantro into the instant pot and stir well.
2. Seal pot with lid and cook on high for 30 minutes.
3. Allow to release pressure naturally then open the lid.
4. Remove pork from pot and place on a plate.
5. Add fish sauce and cilantro into the pot and stir well.
6. Puree the veggies using a blender.
7. Return pork into the pot and stir well.
8. Serve and enjoy.

Nutritional Value (Amount per Serving):
Calories 229; Fat 14.4 g; Carbohydrates 3.6 g; Sugar 1.1 g; Protein 20.9 g

Wine Rosemary Pork Belly

Preparation Time: 10 minutes; Cooking Time: 40 minutes; Serve: 4
Ingredients:
- 1 lb pork belly
- 1 garlic clove
- 1 rosemary sprig
- ½ cup white wine
- 3 tbsp olive oil
- Pepper
- Salt

Directions:
1. Add olive oil into the instant pot and set the pot on sauté mode.
2. Add meat to the pot and sauté for 3 minutes on each side.
3. Add remaining ingredients over the meat.
4. Seal pot with lid and cook on high for 40 minutes.
5. Release pressure using quick release method than open the lid.
6. Serve and enjoy.

Nutritional Value (Amount per Serving):
Calories 639; Fat 41 g; Carbohydrates 1.1 g; Sugar 0.2 g; Protein 52.4 g

Butter Braised Pork Loin

Preparation Time: 10 minutes; Cooking Time: 30 minutes; Serve: 6
Ingredients:
- 2 lbs pork loin
- 1 bay leaf
- 1 tsp pepper
- 2 tbsp olive oil
- 2 tbsp butter
- 2 ½ cups coconut milk
- 2 tsp salt

Directions:
1. Add oil into the instant pot and set the pot on sauté mode.
2. Season meat with pepper and salt.
3. Add meat to the pot and sauté until browned from all the sides.
4. Add remaining ingredients over the meat.
5. Seal pot with lid and cook on high for 30 minutes.
6. Release pressure using quick release method than open the lid.
7. Serve and enjoy.

Nutritional Value (Amount per Serving):
Calories 671; Fat 53.4 g; Carbohydrates 5.8 g; Sugar 3.3 g; Protein 43.7 g

Simple Creamy Pork Chops

Preparation Time: 10 minutes; Cooking Time: 20 minutes; Serve: 4
Ingredients:
- 4 pork chops
- ½ cup sour cream
- 10 oz chicken stock
- 10 oz French onion soup

Directions:
1. Add stock and pork chops into the instant pot.
2. Seal pot with lid and cook on high for 12 minutes.
3. Allow to release pressure naturally then open the lid.
4. Add remaining ingredients and stir well.
5. Set pot on sauté mode and cook for 7 minutes.
6. Serve and enjoy.

Nutritional Value (Amount per Serving):
Calories 356; Fat 26.6 g; Carbohydrates 7.4 g; Sugar 2.7 g; Protein 20.3 g

Tasty Pork Butt

Preparation Time: 10 minutes; Cooking Time: 65 minutes; Serve: 6
Ingredients:
- 4 lbs pork butt
- 1 ½ cups water
- 1 tbsp olive oil
- 1 tsp thyme

- 1 tsp oregano
- 1 tsp cayenne pepper
- 2 tsp pepper
- 2 tsp swerve
- 2 tsp cumin
- 2 tsp chili powder
- 2 tsp paprika

Directions:
1. Rub oil all over the meat.
2. In a small bowl, combine together all spices and rub all over the meat.
3. Pour water into the instant pot.
4. Place meat into the pot.
5. Seal pot with lid and cook on high for 65 minutes.
6. Release pressure using quick release method than open the lid.
7. Serve and enjoy.

Nutritional Value (Amount per Serving):
Calories 617; Fat 23 g; Carbohydrates 2.7 g; Sugar 0.2 g; Protein 94.6 g

Tomatillo Sirloin Pork

Preparation Time: 10 minutes; Cooking Time: 45 minutes; Serve: 4
Ingredients:
- 2 lbs pork sirloin, sliced
- 2 tsp cumin
- 16 oz tomatillo salsa
- 2 tsp garlic powder
- 1 tbsp olive oil
- ¼ tsp salt

Directions:
1. Add oil into the instant pot and set the pot on sauté mode.
2. Season meat with spices.
3. Add meat to the pot and sauté until browned.
4. Pour salsa over the meat.
5. Seal pot with lid and cook on high for 45 minutes.
6. Release pressure using quick release method than open the lid.
7. Serve and enjoy.

Nutritional Value (Amount per Serving):
Calories 457; Fat 23.8 g; Carbohydrates 9 g; Sugar 4.1 g; Protein 46.6 g

Simple Jerk Pork

Preparation Time: 10 minutes; Cooking Time: 45 minutes; Serve: 16
Ingredients:
- 4 lbs pork shoulder
- ½ cup chicken stock
- ¼ cup Jamaican jerk spice blend
- 1 tbsp olive oil

Directions:
1. Brush oil all over the meat.
2. Rub Jamaican spice blend all over the meat.

3. Set pot on sauté mode. Place meat into the pot and sauté until browned.
4. Pour stock over the meat.
5. Seal pot with lid and cook on high for 45 minutes.
6. Release pressure using quick release method than open the lid.
7. Shred the meat using a fork.
8. Serve and enjoy.

Nutritional Value (Amount per Serving):
Calories 339; Fat 25.2 g; Carbohydrates 0 g; Sugar 0 g; Protein 26.4 g

Tangy Pork

Preparation Time: 10 minutes; Cooking Time: 80 minutes; Serve: 10
Ingredients:
- 3 lbs pork shoulder
- 1 bay leaf
- ½ tbsp cumin
- ½ tbsp oregano
- 1/3 cup fresh lime juice
- 2/3 cup grapefruit juice
- 5 garlic cloves
- 1 tbsp salt

Directions:
1. Add all ingredients except meat and bay leaf into the blender and blend until smooth.
2. Cut meat into the four pieces and place in a large bowl.
3. Pour marinade over the meat. Mix well and place in refrigerator for overnight.
4. Add marinated meat into the pot with marinade. Add bay leaf.
5. Seal pot with lid and cook on high for 89 minutes.
6. Allow to release pressure naturally then open the lid.
7. Remove meat from pot and shred using a fork.
8. Return shredded meat to the pot and stir well.
9. Serve and enjoy.

Nutritional Value (Amount per Serving):
Calories 407; Fat 29.2 g; Carbohydrates 2.1 g; Sugar 1.1 g; Protein 32 g

Shredded Asian Pork

Preparation Time: 10 minutes; Cooking Time: 60 minutes; Serve: 6
Ingredients:
- 2 lbs pork shoulder
- 1 tsp paprika
- 2 tsp ginger, grated
- 5 drops liquid stevia
- 4 tbsp soy sauce
- 2 tbsp garlic paste
- 1 tbsp tomato paste
- 4 tbsp tomato sauce
- 1 cup chicken stock

Directions:
1. Add all ingredients except meat into the large bowl and mix well.
2. Add meat to the bow and coat well.

3. Transfer meat to the bowl and pour remaining sauce over the meat.
4. Seal pot with lid and cook on high for 60 minutes.
5. Allow to release pressure naturally then open the lid.
6. Shred the meat using a fork and stir well in the sauce.
7. Serve and enjoy.

Nutritional Value (Amount per Serving):
Calories 461; Fat 32.6 g; Carbohydrates 3.5 g; Sugar 1.2 g; Protein 36.5 g

Lime Pork Chops

Preparation Time: 10 minutes; Cooking Time: 15 minutes; Serve: 8
Ingredients:
- 3 ½ lbs pork chops
- ¾ tsp pepper
- ¾ tsp garlic powder
- ½ tsp ground cumin
- ¼ cup fresh lime juice
- ½ cup salsa
- 3 tbsp butter
- ¾ tsp salt

Directions:
1. Mix together lemon juice and salsa and set aside.
2. In a small bowl, mix together garlic powder, cumin, pepper, and salt and rub all over the pork chops.
3. Add butter into the instant pot and set the pot on sauté mode.
4. Add pork chops in the pot and sauté for 2-3 minutes on each side.
5. Pour salsa over the pot chops.
6. Seal pot with lid and cook on high for 15 minutes.
7. Release pressure using quick release method than open the lid.
8. Serve and enjoy.

Nutritional Value (Amount per Serving):
Calories 680; Fat 53.7 g; Carbohydrates 1.5 g; Sugar 0.6 g; Protein 45 g

Leek Pork

Preparation Time: 10 minutes; Cooking Time: 8 hours; Serve: 6
Ingredients:
- 2 lbs pork butt, cut into pieces
- 2 bay leaves
- ½ tsp pepper
- 2 tsp cayenne pepper
- 5 cups chicken broth
- 1 bell pepper, sliced
- ¼ cup olive oil
- 1 cup cherry tomatoes, sliced
- 2 leeks, chopped
- 1 tsp salt

Directions:
1. Add all ingredients into the instant pot and stir well to combine.
2. Seal pot with lid and cook on low for 8 hours.
3. Allow to release pressure naturally then open the lid.

4. Serve and enjoy.

Nutritional Value (Amount per Serving):
Calories 428; Fat 19.9 g; Carbohydrates 8.1 g; Sugar 3.6 g; Protein 52.1 g

Olive Capers Pork

Preparation Time: 10 minutes; Cooking Time: 15 minutes; Serve: 4

Ingredients:
- 1 lb pork neck, cut into the pieces
- ¼ tsp chili flakes
- 1 tsp dried rosemary
- 4 tbsp olive oil
- 2 tbsp parsley, chopped
- 4 olives
- 2 tbsp capers
- 2 tomatoes, chopped
- 2 tbsp apple cider vinegar
- 1 cup chicken stock
- 2 garlic cloves, crushed
- 1 onion, chopped
- ½ tsp pepper
- ½ tsp salt

Directions:
1. Add oil into the instant pot and set the pot on sauté mode.
2. Add garlic and onion to the pot and sauté for 3-4 minutes.
3. Add tomatoes and cook until softened.
4. Add meat, vinegar, chili, rosemary, pepper, and salt. Stir well and cook for 5 minutes.
5. Add olives, capers, and stock. Stir well.
6. Seal pot with lid and cook on high for 15 minutes.
7. Allow to release pressure naturally then open the lid.
8. Sprinkle with parsley and serve.

Nutritional Value (Amount per Serving):
Calories 506; Fat 44.8 g; Carbohydrates 7.5 g; Sugar 3.9 g; Protein 20.2 g

Chapter 11: Lamb Recipes

Quick Leg of Lamb

Preparation Time: 10 minutes; Cooking Time: 35 minutes; Serve: 8
Ingredients:
- 4 lbs leg of lamb, boneless
- 2 tbsp rosemary, chopped
- 3 garlic cloves, crushed
- 2 cups water
- 2 tbsp olive oil
- Pepper
- Salt

Directions:
1. Season meat with pepper and salt.
2. Add oil into the instant pot and set the pot on sauté mode.
3. Add meat to the pot and sauté until browned.
4. Remove meat from pot and spread the rosemary and garlic on top of meat.
5. Pour water into the instant pot then place rack into the pot.
6. Place meat on the rack.
7. Seal pot with lid and cook on meat/stew mode for 35 minutes.
8. Allow to release pressure naturally then open the lid.
9. Remove meat from pot and broil in a preheated broiler until brown.
10. Slice and serve.

Nutritional Value (Amount per Serving):
Calories 456; Fat 20.3 g; Carbohydrates 0.9 g; Sugar 0 g; Protein 63.8 g

Classic Lamb Curry

Preparation Time: 10 minutes; Cooking Time: 35 minutes; Serve: 4
Ingredients:
- 1 1/2 lbs lamb chunks
- 1 ½ cups can tomatoes, chopped
- ¾ tsp fennel powder
- ½ tsp coriander powder
- ½ tsp garam masala
- ½ tsp chili powder
- ¾ tsp cumin powder
- 1 ½ tsp ginger garlic paste
- 2 bay leaves
- 2 onions, chopped
- 1 tbsp vegetable oil
- Salt

Directions:
1. Add oil into the instant pot and set the pot on sauté mode.
2. Add bay leaves and onion to the pot and sauté until softened.
3. Add ginger garlic paste, meat, and all spices and stir well.
4. Add remaining ingredients and stir well to combine.
5. Seal pot with lid and cook on high for 5 minutes.
6. Allow to release pressure naturally then open the lid.
7. Stir well and serve.

Nutritional Value (Amount per Serving):
Calories 390; Fat 16.1 g; Carbohydrates 10 g; Sugar 5.4 g; Protein 49.3 g

Indian Lamb Korma

Preparation Time: 10 minutes; Cooking Time: 20 minutes; Serve: 4
Ingredients:
- 1 lb lamb leg, cut into pieces
- ½ tsp fresh lime juice
- 2 tbsp cilantro, chopped
- ½ tsp cardamom powder
- 1 tsp paprika
- ¼ tsp cayenne pepper
- ½ tsp turmeric
- 3 tsp garam masala
- ¾ cup water
- ½ cup coconut milk
- 2 tbsp tomato paste
- 2 tbsp ginger garlic paste
- 1 onion, chopped
- 1 tbsp olive oil
- 1 tsp salt

Directions:
1. Add oil into the instant pot and set the pot on sauté mode.
2. Add ginger garlic paste to the pot and sauté for a minute.
3. Add ¼ cup water, tomato paste, and all spices. Stir well.
4. Add coconut milk, remaining water and meat. Stir well.
5. Seal pot with lid and cook on high for 15 minutes.
6. Allow to release pressure naturally then open the lid.
7. Add lime juice and stir well.
8. Garnish with cilantro and serve.

Nutritional Value (Amount per Serving):
Calories 324; Fat 18.4 g; Carbohydrates 6.5 g; Sugar 3.2 g; Protein 33.5 g

Simple Lamb Curry

Preparation Time: 10 minutes; Cooking Time: 20 minutes; Serve: 4
Ingredients:
- 1 lb lamb shoulder, cut into cubes
- 2 tbsp cilantro, chopped
- 1 scallion, chopped
- ¼ cup water
- 1 ½ cups chicken stock
- 2 tsp dried thyme
- 2 garlic cloves, minced
- 2 tbsp curry powder
- 2 carrots, chopped
- 1 onion, chopped
- ½ tsp salt

Directions:
1. Add meat, curry powder, and onion to the pot and cook on sauté mode for 3-4 minutes.
2. Add stock and stir well.
3. Add remaining ingredients to the pot and stir well.
4. Seal pot with lid and cook on high for 20 minutes.

5. Allow to release pressure naturally then open the lid.
6. Stir well and serve.

Nutritional Value (Amount per Serving):
Calories 253; Fat 9.1 g; Carbohydrates 8.8 g; Sugar 3.2 g; Protein 33.3 g

Goat Curry

Preparation Time: 10 minutes; Cooking Time: 45 minutes; Serve: 6

Ingredients:
- 2 lbs lamb, cut into pieces
- 3 garlic cloves, minced
- 1 tbsp ginger, minced
- 2 onions, diced
- 2 tbsp olive oil
- ½ cup water
- 14 oz can tomato, diced
- ½ tsp cayenne
- 1 tsp turmeric
- 1 tsp paprika
- 1 tsp garam masala
- 1 tsp ground cumin
- 1 tbsp coriander powder
- 1 bay leaf
- 3 cardamom pods
- 2 whole cloves
- 2 tsp salt

Directions:
1. Add oil into the instant pot and set the pot on sauté mode.
2. Add meat to the pot and sauté until browned.
3. Add garlic, onion, spices, and ginger and sauté for 2-3 minutes.
4. Add water and tomatoes and stir well.
5. Seal pot with lid and cook on high for 45 minutes.
6. Allow to release pressure naturally then open the lid.
7. Stir well and serve.

Nutritional Value (Amount per Serving):
Calories 360; Fat 16.1 g; Carbohydrates 8.6 g; Sugar 3.9 g; Protein 43.8 g

Tender Lamb Curry

Preparation Time: 10 minutes; Cooking Time: 20 minutes; Serve: 6

Ingredients:
- 1 ½ lbs lamb stew meat, cut into cubed
- 1 zucchini, diced
- 2 carrots, sliced
- 1 onion, diced
- ¾ tsp turmeric
- 1 ½ tbsp garam masala
- 14 oz can tomato, diced
- 1 tbsp olive oil
- ½ cup coconut milk
- 1 tbsp ginger, grated
- 3 garlic cloves, minced
- ½ fresh lime juice
- ¼ tsp pepper
- ¼ tsp salt

Directions:

1. Add meat, lime juice, coconut milk, ginger, garlic, pepper, and salt into the large bowl. Stir well and place in refrigerator for overnight.
2. Add marinated meat into the instant pot with marinade.
3. Add carrot, onion, garam masala, oil, and tomatoes to the pot and stir well.
4. Seal pot with lid and cook on high for 20 minutes.
5. Allow to release pressure naturally then open the lid.
6. Add zucchini and cook on sauté mode for 5 minutes.
7. Garnish with cilantro and serve.

Nutritional Value (Amount per Serving):
Calories 319; Fat 15.6 g; Carbohydrates 11 g; Sugar 5.4 g; Protein 33.9 g

Lamb with Gravy

Preparation Time: 10 minutes; Cooking Time: 20 minutes; Serve: 4
Ingredients:
- 2 lbs lamb shanks
- 8 garlic cloves, peeled
- ½ tsp thyme
- 1 tsp vinegar
- 1 tbsp tomato paste
- 1 tbsp butter
- ½ cup chicken stock
- ½ cup wine
- 1 tbsp olive oil

Directions:
1. Add oil into the instant pot and set the pot on sauté mode.
2. Add garlic and cook until browned.
3. Add wine, thyme, stock, and tomato paste. Stir well.
4. Add meat and stir to combine.
5. Seal pot with lid and cook on high for 20 minutes.
6. Allow to release pressure naturally then open the lid.
7. Transfer meat to a plate.
8. Add vinegar and butter to the pot and stir well.
9. Pour sauce over the meat and serve.

Nutritional Value (Amount per Serving):
Calories 516; Fat 23.1 g; Carbohydrates 3.7 g; Sugar 0.9 g; Protein 64.4 g

Delicious Sage Lamb

Preparation Time: 10 minutes; Cooking Time: 60 minutes; Serve: 8
Ingredients:
- 6 lbs leg of lamb
- 1 ½ cups chicken stock
- 2 tbsp arrowroot
- 2 tsp garlic, minced
- 1 bay leaf
- ¼ tsp thyme
- 1 ½ tsp marjoram
- 1 ½ tsp sage
- Pepper
- Salt

Directions:
1. Add oil into the instant pot and set the pot on sauté mode.
2. Combine together garlic, herbs, pepper, and salt and rub over meat.
3. Add meat to the pot and sauté until browned.
4. Add bay leaf and stock. Stir well.
5. Seal pot with lid and cook on meat/stew mode for 60 minutes.
6. Release pressure using quick release method than open the lid.
7. Remove meat from pot and place to a plate.
8. Add arrowroot and whisk well and cook on sauté mode until sauce thickened.
9. Drizzle sauce over meat and serve.

Nutritional Value (Amount per Serving):
Calories 638; Fat 25.1 g; Carbohydrates 0.8 g; Sugar 0.1 g; Protein 95.8 g

Coconut Zucchini Lamb Curry

Preparation Time: 10 minutes; Cooking Time: 25 minutes; Serve: 4

Ingredients:
- 1 lb lamb, cut into cubes
- 1 ½ tbsp curry powder
- 1 carrot, sliced
- 1 onion, diced
- 1 zucchini, diced
- ½ cup coconut milk
- 1 cup tomatoes, diced
- 1 tsp ginger, grated
- 2 tsp garlic, minced
- 1 tbsp olive oil

Directions:
1. In a bowl, mix together meat, coconut milk, garlic, and ginger. Cover bowl and place in refrigerator for overnight.
2. Transfer meat to the instant pot along with the marinade.
3. Add oil, tomatoes, onion, and carrot. Stir well.
4. Seal pot with lid and cook on high for 20 minutes.
5. Allow to release pressure naturally then open the lid.
6. Add zucchini and cook on sauté mode for 5 minutes.
7. Serve and enjoy.

Nutritional Value (Amount per Serving):
Calories 354; Fat 19.5 g; Carbohydrates 11 g; Sugar 5.1 g; Protein 34.4 g

Flavorful Lamb Ragu

Preparation Time: 10 minutes; Cooking Time: 20 minutes; Serve: 8

Ingredients:
- 4 lbs leg of lamb, cut into cubes
- 1 tbsp olive oil
- 1 tsp oregano, chopped
- 1 tbsp rosemary, chopped
- 2 bay leaves
- 1 cup chicken stock
- 2 cups tomato passata
- 6 garlic cloves, sliced

- 2 carrots, diced
- 2 celery stalks, diced
- 1 onion, diced
- Pepper
- Salt

Directions:
1. Add oil into the instant pot and set the pot on sauté mode.
2. Season meat with pepper and salt. Add meat to the pot and sauté until browned.
3. Remove meat from pot and place on a plate.
4. Add onion, carrots, celery, and salt to the pot and sauté until softened.
5. Add bay leaves, oregano, rosemary, garlic, pepper, and salt and sauté for a minute.
6. Return meat to the pot along with stock and tomato passata. Stir well.
7. Seal pot with lid and cook on high for 60 minutes.
8. Release pressure using quick release method than open the lid.
9. Shred the meat using a fork.
10. Stir well and serve.

Nutritional Value (Amount per Serving):
Calories 456; Fat 18.6 g; Carbohydrates 4.1 g; Sugar 1.5 g; Protein 64.3 g

Thai Green Lamb Curry

Preparation Time: 10 minutes; Cooking Time: 20 minutes; Serve: 6
Ingredients:
- 2 lbs lamb meat, bone-in
- ¼ cup cilantro, chopped
- ½ tbsp lime juice
- 6 oz green beans, chopped
- ½ tbsp soy sauce
- ½ tbsp fish sauce
- 2 garlic cloves, crushed
- ½ cup chicken broth
- 4 oz unsweetened coconut milk
- 2 tbsp green curry paste
- ½ cup coconut cream
- 1 small onion, minced
- 1 tbsp olive oil
- Pepper
- Salt

Directions:
1. Season meat with pepper and salt.
2. Add oil into the instant pot and set the pot on sauté mode.
3. Add garlic and onion to the pot and sauté for 3-4 minutes.
4. Add curry paste and coconut cream and cook for 5 minutes.
5. Add meat, fish sauce, soy sauce, broth, and coconut milk. Stir well.
6. Seal pot with lid and cook on high for 8 minutes.
7. Release pressure using quick release method than open the lid.
8. Add lime juice and green beans and cook on sauté mode for 3 minutes.
9. Garnish with cilantro and serve.

Nutritional Value (Amount per Serving):
Calories 545; Fat 41.5 g; Carbohydrates 10.8 g; Sugar 1.7 g; Protein 31.3 g

Indian Lamb Rogan Josh

Preparation Time: 10 minutes; Cooking Time: 20 minutes; Serve: 4
Ingredients:
- 1 lb leg of lamb, cut into cubes
- 1 onion, diced
- 1 tbsp tomato paste
- 1/4 cup yogurt
- 1/4 cup water
- 1/4 tsp cayenne pepper
- 1 tsp turmeric
- 1 tsp paprika
- 2 tsp garam masala
- 1/4 cup cilantro, chopped
- 4 garlic cloves, minced
- 1/2 tsp ground cinnamon
- 2 tsp ginger, minced
- 1 tsp salt

Directions:
1. Add all ingredients into the large bowl and mix well. Place bowl in refrigerator for 2 hours.
2. Add marinated meat with marinade into the instant pot.
3. Seal pot with lid and cook on high for 20 minutes.
4. Allow to release pressure naturally then open the lid.
5. Serve and enjoy.

Nutritional Value (Amount per Serving):
Calories 248; Fat 8.8 g; Carbohydrates 7 g; Sugar 2.9 g; Protein 33.6 g

Cheese Herb Lamb Chops

Preparation Time: 10 minutes; Cooking Time: 18 minutes; Serve: 3
Ingredients:
- 3 lamb chops
- 1 cup water
- 1 tbsp olive oil
- ½ cup parmesan cheese
- ¼ tsp dried basil, crushed
- ¼ tsp dried oregano, crushed
- ½ tsp garlic powder
- Pepper
- Salt

Directions:
1. Season lamb chops with pepper, garlic powder, and salt.
2. Place seasoned lamb chops into the instant pot and cook o sauté mode for 4 minutes per side.
3. Remove lamb chops from pot and place on a dish.
4. Pour water into the instant pot then place a trivet in the pot.
5. Place lamb chops on top of the trivet.
6. Seal pot with lid and cook on high for 10 minutes.
7. Release pressure using quick release method than open the lid.
8. Serve and enjoy.

Nutritional Value (Amount per Serving):
Calories 413; Fat 27 g; Carbohydrates 6.4 g; Sugar 0.1 g; Protein 35.2 g

Garlic Ginger Lamb Shanks

Preparation Time: 10 minutes; Cooking Time: 27 minutes; Serve: 6
Ingredients:
- 4 lamb shanks
- 2 garlic cloves, minced
- 2 tbsp olive oil
- 1 ½ cups chicken broth
- 2 tbsp coconut aminos
- 2 tbsp apple cider vinegar
- 1 ½ tsp ground ginger
- 1 onion, sliced
- ½ tsp pepper

Directions:
1. Add oil into the instant pot and set the pot on sauté mode.
2. Add meat to the pot sauté until browned.
3. Add onion to the pot and sauté for 2 minutes.
4. Add ginger and garlic to the pot and sauté for a minute.
5. Add remaining ingredients and stir well.
6. Seal pot with lid and cook on high for 7 minutes.
7. Allow to release pressure naturally then open the lid.
8. Serve and enjoy.

Nutritional Value (Amount per Serving):
Calories 265; Fat 17.1 g; Carbohydrates 12.4 g; Sugar 2.3 g; Protein 14.7 g

Ginger Apple Lamb

Preparation Time: 10 minutes; Cooking Time: 10 minutes; Serve: 4
Ingredients:
- 1 lb lamb, boneless and cubed
- 1 tbsp vinegar
- ½ onion, sliced
- 1 ½ cups chicken broth
- 2 tbsp ginger, grated
- 2 tsp garlic, minced
- 1 tsp rosemary
- 2 tbsp olive oil
- 2 tbsp coconut aminos
- 1 apple, sliced

Directions:
1. Add 1 tablespoon of oil into the instant pot and set the pot on sauté mode.
2. Add meat to the pot and sauté until browned. Remove meat from pot and place on a plate.
3. Add remaining oil and onion and sauté until onion is softened.
4. Add garlic and ginger and sauté for a minute.
5. Add coconut aminos, broth, and vinegar and stir well.
6. Add meat and apple.
7. Seal pot with lid and cook on high for 10 minutes.
8. Allow to release pressure naturally then open the lid.
9. Serve and enjoy.

Nutritional Value (Amount per Serving):

Calories 333; Fat 16.2 g; Carbohydrates 11.9 g; Sugar 6.8 g; Protein 34.3 g

Almond Lamb Patties

Preparation Time: 10 minutes; Cooking Time: 10 minutes; Serve: 6
Ingredients:
- 2 lbs lamb minced
- 1 tbsp olive oil
- 1 tsp dried mint
- ½ tsp garam masala
- ½ tsp chili powder
- ½ cup ground almonds
- 4 eggs, beaten
- 1 green chili, chopped
- 2 garlic cloves, minced
- 1 onion, chopped
- 1 tsp salt

Directions:
1. In a large bowl, combine together meat, all spices, 3 eggs, green chili pepper, and garlic.
2. Make small patties from mixture. Roll patties in remaining egg then coat with ground almonds. Set aside.
3. Add oil into the instant pot and set the pot on sauté mode.
4. Place patties it the pot and cook for 5-6 minutes on each side.
5. Serve and enjoy.

Nutritional Value (Amount per Serving):
Calories 458; Fat 35.4 g; Carbohydrates 4.1 g; Sugar 1.4 g; Protein 31.5 g

Creamy Yogurt Lamb

Preparation Time: 10 minutes; Cooking Time: 40 minutes; Serve: 4
Ingredients:
- 2 lbs lamb shoulder, boneless and cut into pieces
- ¼ tsp saffron
- 1 tbsp ginger, grated
- 1 tsp chili powder
- 1 tbsp parsley, chopped
- 1 tbsp lime juice
- 2 tbsp olive oil
- 1 cup yogurt
- 1 tsp salt

Directions:
1. In a bowl, combine together yogurt, saffron, ginger, chili powder, and salt. Stir well and set aside.
2. Add meat into the yogurt mixture and stir well. Cover bowl with foil and place in refrigerator for 30 minutes.
3. Add oil into the instant pot and set the pot on sauté mode.
4. Add meat with marinade into the pot and stir well.
5. Pour 1 cup water into the pot and stir well.
6. Seal pot with lid and cook on high for 30 minutes.
7. Release pressure using quick release method than open the lid.
8. Set pot on sauté mode and sauté until sauce thickens, about 10 minutes.

9. Add lime juice and stir well.
10. Garnish with parsley and serve.

Nutritional Value (Amount per Serving):
Calories 533; Fat 24.6 g; Carbohydrates 6 g; Sugar 4.5 g; Protein 67.4 g

Veggie Lamb Chops

Preparation Time: 10 minutes; Cooking Time: 25 minutes; Serve: 5
Ingredients:
- 5 lamb chops
- 2 bay leaves
- 1 cup chicken stock
- 1 bell pepper, chopped
- 1 cup cauliflower, cut into florets
- 1 cup onions, chopped
- 2 tbsp olive oil
- ½ tsp pepper
- 1 tsp salt

Directions:
1. Add oil into the instant pot and set the pot on sauté mode.
2. Season lamb chops with pepper and salt. Place lamb chops into the instant pot.
3. Add onion, pepper, and cauliflower on top. Pour stock.
4. Seal pot with lid and cook on high for 15 minutes.
5. Release pressure using quick release method than open the lid.
6. Preheat the oven to 176 C/ 400 F.
7. Transfer lamb chops and vegetables on a baking tray and roast in preheated oven for 10 minutes on each side.
8. Serve and enjoy.

Nutritional Value (Amount per Serving):
Calories 124; Fat 10.1 g; Carbohydrates 5.3 g; Sugar 2.8 g; Protein 4.4 g

Balsamic Lamb Shoulder

Preparation Time: 10 minutes; Cooking Time: 35 minutes; Serve: 5
Ingredients:
- 2 lbs lamb shoulder
- 1 tsp dried sage
- 1 tbsp Dijon mustard
- 2 tbsp soy sauce
- 2 garlic cloves, crushed
- ¼ cup balsamic vinegar
- ¼ cup Swerve
- 1 cup chicken stock
- 2 tbsp butter
- ½ tsp pepper
- 1 tsp salt

Directions:
1. Add butter into the instant pot and set the pot on sauté mode.
2. Add garlic to the pot and sauté for a minute.
3. Add swerve, Dijon, balsamic vinegar, and soy sauce. Stir for 2-3 minutes.
4. Season meat with pepper, sage, and salt.

5. Place meat to the pot and pour in the stock.
6. Seal pot with lid and cook on high for 35 minutes.
7. Allow to release pressure naturally then open the lid.
8. Serve and enjoy.

Nutritional Value (Amount per Serving):
Calories 391; Fat 18.2 g; Carbohydrates 1.6 g; Sugar 0.3 g; Protein 51.8 g

Zucchini Lamb Curry

Preparation Time: 10 minutes; Cooking Time: 25 minutes; Serve: 4
Ingredients:
- 1 lb lamb stew meat, cubed
- 2 tsp turmeric
- 2 tbsp ginger, grated
- ¼ cup cilantro, chopped
- 2 tbsp garam masala
- 3 tbsp butter
- 2 tbsp apple cider vinegar
- 1 cup coconut milk
- 3 garlic cloves, minced
- 1 cup zucchini, cut into chunks
- 2 cups cauliflower florets
- 1 tsp pepper

Directions:
1. Season meat with ginger, garlic, pepper, and salt. Place meat in the large bowl.
2. Add apple cider vinegar and coconut milk over the meat. Place in refrigerator for 1 hour.
3. Add marinated meat to the instant pot along with the marinade.
4. Add turmeric, garam masala, butter, and cauliflower. Stir well.
5. Seal pot with lid and cook on high for 20 minutes.
6. Release pressure using quick release method than open the lid.
7. Add zucchini and stir well.
8. Seal pot again and cook on high for 5 minutes.
9. Release pressure using quick release method than open the lid.
10. Add cilantro and stir well.
11. Serve and enjoy.

Nutritional Value (Amount per Serving):
Calories 462; Fat 31.7 g; Carbohydrates 10.7 g; Sugar 3.9 g; Protein 35.3 g

Spinach Lamb Dish

Preparation Time: 10 minutes; Cooking Time: 15 minutes; Serve: 4
Ingredients:
- 4 cup lamb meat, boneless, cooked, and shredded
- ¼ tsp red pepper flakes
- ½ tbsp fresh lemon juice
- 2 cups chicken broth
- 1 tbsp olive oil
- ½ tbsp garlic, minced
- 1 onion, chopped
- ¼ cup tomato puree
- ½ cup tomatoes, chopped
- 5 cup fresh spinach, chopped
- Pepper

- Salt

Directions:
1. Add oil into the instant pot and set the pot on sauté mode.
2. Add onion to the pot and sauté for 3 minutes.
3. Add red pepper flakes and garlic and sauté for a minute.
4. Add spinach and sauté for 2 minutes.
5. Add remaining ingredients and stir well.
6. Seal pot with lid and cook on high for 9 minutes.
7. Release pressure using quick release method than open the lid.
8. Serve warm and enjoy.

Nutritional Value (Amount per Serving):
Calories 311; Fat 19.5 g; Carbohydrates 7.1 g; Sugar 3.1 g; Protein 25.4 g

Lamb Mushroom Stew

Preparation Time: 10 minutes; Cooking Time: 20 minutes; Serve: 3

Ingredients:
- 10 oz lamb shanks
- ½ cup fresh parsley, chopped
- ¼ cup chicken broth
- 1 cup cherry tomatoes
- ½ cup olives, pitted and halved
- 2 garlic cloves, minced
- ½ tbsp tomato paste
- ½ lb cremini mushrooms, stemmed and quartered
- ½ small onion, chopped
- ½ tbsp olive oil
- Pepper
- Salt

Directions:
1. Add oil into the instant pot and set the pot on sauté mode.
2. Add onion and mushrooms and sauté for 4-5 minutes.
3. Add garlic and tomato paste and cook for a minute.
4. Add meat, broth, tomatoes, and olives. Stir well.
5. Seal pot with lid and cook on high for 15 minutes.
6. Release pressure using quick release method than open the lid.
7. Add parsley and stir well.
8. Serve and enjoy.

Nutritional Value (Amount per Serving):
Calories 269; Fat 12.1 g; Carbohydrates 9.8 g; Sugar 3.9 g; Protein 30.2 g

Mongolian Lamb

Preparation Time: 10 minutes; Cooking Time: 18 minutes; Serve: 6

Ingredients:
- 2 lbs lamb steak, cut into strips
- 2 scallions, chopped
- 3 tbsp water
- 2 tbsp arrowroot

- ½ cup soy sauce, low-sodium
- ½ cup water
- 3 garlic cloves, minced
- 1 tbsp olive oil

Directions:
1. Add oil into the instant pot and set the pot on sauté mode.
2. Add meat to the pot and cook for 5 minutes.
3. Add the ginger and garlic and cook for a minute.
4. Add remaining ingredients and stir well.
5. Seal pot with lid and cook on high for 12 minutes.
6. Release pressure using quick release method than open the lid.
7. Serve and enjoy.

Nutritional Value (Amount per Serving):
Calories 318; Fat 13.5 g; Carbohydrates 2.8 g; Sugar 0.5 g; Protein 44.1 g

Mushroom Lamb Chops

Preparation Time: 10 minutes; Cooking Time: 21 minutes; Serve: 4
Ingredients:
- 4 lamb chops
- ½ cup water
- 1 cup tomato sauce, sugar-free
- 1 ½ cups button mushrooms, chopped
- 1 onion, chopped
- 2 garlic cloves
- 1 tbsp olive oil
- Pepper
- Salt

Directions:
1. Add oil into the instant pot and set the pot on sauté mode.
2. Add garlic to the pot and sauté for a minute.
3. Add lamb chops, pepper, and salt and cook for 5 minutes.
4. Add remaining ingredients and stir well.
5. Seal pot with lid and cook on high for 15 minutes.
6. Release pressure using quick release method than open the lid.
7. Serve and enjoy.

Nutritional Value (Amount per Serving):
Calories 672; Fat 27.7 g; Carbohydrates 7.3 g; Sugar 4.2 g; Protein 93.9 g

Delicious Lamb Ribs

Preparation Time: 10 minutes; Cooking Time: 19 minutes; Serve: 10
Ingredients:
- 4 lbs lamb ribs
- 2 tsp Worcestershire sauce
- 2 tbsp fresh lemon juice
- 1 cup chicken broth
- 2 cups sugar-free ketchup
- 1 onion, sliced
- 3 tsp butter
- 2 tsp paprika
- Pepper
- Salt

Directions:
1. In a bowl, mix together ketchup, Worcestershire sauce, lemon juice, and broth.
2. Season meat with paprika, pepper, and salt.
3. Add butter in the pot and set the pot on sauté mode.
4. Add ribs to the pot and cook until browned, about 3-4 minutes.
5. Add onion on top of meat. Pour sauce mixture over the meat and onion.
6. Seal pot with lid and cook on high for 15 minutes.
7. Allow to release pressure naturally then open the lid.
8. Serve and enjoy.

Nutritional Value (Amount per Serving):
Calories 458; Fat 25.5 g; Carbohydrates 4.8 g; Sugar 4 g; Protein 48.2 g

Asian Lamb Steaks

Preparation Time: 10 minutes; Cooking Time: 23 minutes; Serve: 3
Ingredients:
- 1 lb lamb steak, trimmed and cut into strips
- 2 tbsp parsley, chopped
- 1 ½ tbsp water
- 1 tbsp arrowroot
- 2 tbsp fresh lemon juice
- ¼ cup soy sauce, low-sodium
- ¼ cup water
- 2 garlic cloves, minced
- ½ tbsp olive oil
- Pepper
- Salt

Directions:
1. Season meat with pepper and salt.
2. Add oil into the instant pot and set the pot on sauté mode.
3. Add meat to the pot and sauté until browned, about 5 minutes.
4. Remove meat from pot and place on a plate.
5. Add garlic to the pot and sauté for a minute.
6. Add meat, lemon juice, soy sauce, and ¼ cup of water and stir well.
7. Seal pot with lid and cook on high for 12 minutes.
8. Release pressure using quick release method than open the lid.
9. In a small bowl, mix together water and arrowroot. Pour in the pot and cook on sauté mode for 4-5 minutes.
10. Garnish with parsley and serve.

Nutritional Value (Amount per Serving):
Calories 321; Fat 13.5 g; Carbohydrates 3 g; Sugar 0.6 g; Protein 44.2 g

Red Wine Lamb

Preparation Time: 10 minutes; Cooking Time: 15 minutes; Serve: 4
Ingredients:

- 2 lbs leg of lamb, boneless and cut into chunks
- 2 tbsp tomato paste
- ½ cup beef stock
- 1 tsp oregano
- 2 tsp fresh thyme, chopped
- 1 tsp fresh rosemary, chopped
- 2 carrots, peeled and chopped
- 1 cup red wine
- 4 garlic cloves, sliced
- 1 tbsp olive oil
- Pepper
- Salt

Directions:
1. Season meat with pepper and salt.
2. Add oil into the instant pot and set the pot on sauté mode.
3. Add meat to the pot and sauté until browned. Remove meat from pot and set aside.
4. Add garlic to the pot and sauté for 30 seconds. Add wine and stir well.
5. Add meat to the pot with remaining ingredients and stir to combine.
6. Seal pot with lid and cook on high for 15 minutes.
7. Allow to release pressure naturally then open the lid.
8. Serve and enjoy.

Nutritional Value (Amount per Serving):
Calories 530; Fat 20.4 g; Carbohydrates 7.9 g; Sugar 3 g; Protein 65 g

Spicy & Creamy Lamb

Preparation Time: 10 minutes; Cooking Time: 25 minutes; Serve: 6

Ingredients:
- 2 lbs leg of lamb, boneless and cut into pieces
- 2 bay leaves
- 1 cinnamon stick
- 2 garlic cloves
- 1 ½ tsp cumin seeds
- 2 tsp fennel seeds
- ½ tsp garlic powder
- 1 tsp garam masala
- 2 tbsp chili powder
- 1 tsp cumin powder
- 1 tsp ginger powder
- 1 tbsp coriander powder
- 3 cups chicken stock
- 2 cups cherry tomatoes, chopped
- 2 tbsp butter
- ¼ cup heavy cream
- 1 tsp salt

Directions:
1. Add meat, garam masala, and heavy cream in a large bowl and stir well. Cover bowl with foil and place in refrigerator for overnight.
2. Add butter in the instant pot and set the pot on sauté mode.
3. Add bay leaves, fennel seeds, cumin seeds, cloves, cinnamon, cardamom, and bay leaves and cook for 1-2 minutes.
4. Add remaining spices and stir for a minute.
5. Add meat with heavy cream and stir well.
6. Add cherry tomatoes and stock. Stir well.
7. Seal pot with lid and cook on high for 25 minutes.

8. Allow to release pressure naturally then open the lid.
9. Serve and enjoy.

Nutritional Value (Amount per Serving):
Calories 365; Fat 17.9 g; Carbohydrates 5.7 g; Sugar 2.2 g; Protein 44.2 g

Delicious Italian Lamb

Preparation Time: 10 minutes; Cooking Time: 25 minutes; Serve: 4
Ingredients:
- 4 lamb shanks
- 1 tsp dried rosemary
- 1 tomato, chopped
- ¼ cup leeks, chopped
- 2 celery stalks, chopped
- 2 garlic cloves
- 1 onion, chopped
- ¼ cup apple cider vinegar
- 3 tbsp olive oil
- 3 cups chicken broth
- 8 oz mushrooms, sliced
- 2 tsp sea salt

Directions:
1. Add all ingredients into the instant pot and stir well.
2. Seal pot with lid and cook on high for 25 minutes.
3. Allow to release pressure naturally then open the lid.
4. Serve and enjoy.

Nutritional Value (Amount per Serving):
Calories 764; Fat 35.8 g; Carbohydrates 7.6 g; Sugar 3.5 g; Protein 97.9 g

Tomato Thyme Lamb Shanks

Preparation Time: 10 minutes; Cooking Time: 20 minutes; Serve: 4
Ingredients:
- 4 lamb shanks
- 2 bay leaves
- 1 tsp dried thyme
- 2 cups chicken broth
- 1 tbsp fish sauce
- 2 tbsp butter
- 2 tbsp balsamic vinegar
- 1 cup cherry tomatoes
- 3 garlic cloves, crushed
- 2 celery stalks, chopped
- 1 large onion, chopped
- 1 tsp sea salt

Directions:
1. Add butter into the instant pot and set the pot on sauté mode.
2. Add meat to the pot and sauté until browned. Remove meat from pot and place on a plate.
3. Add onion, celery, and garlic to the pot and sauté for 4-5 minutes.
4. Add vinegar and stir well.
5. Add meat to the pot along with remaining ingredients. Stir well.
6. Seal pot with lid and cook on stew mode.
7. Release pressure using quick release method than open the lid.
8. Serve and enjoy.

Nutritional Value (Amount per Serving):
Calories 710; Fat 30.6 g; Carbohydrates 7.1 g; Sugar 3.4 g; Protein 95.6 g

Cauliflower Lamb Meatballs

Preparation Time: 10 minutes; Cooking Time: 12 minutes; Serve: 4
Ingredients:
- 1 lb ground lamb
- 1 tsp marjoram
- 2 tbsp olive oil
- 3 tbsp butter
- 1 cup cauliflower, chopped
- 4 eggs
- 2 tbsp almond flour
- 3 garlic cloves, crushed
- ½ tsp pepper
- 1 tsp salt

Directions:
1. In a mixing bowl, combine together meat, marjoram, oil, eggs, almond flour, garlic, pepper, and salt.
2. Make small meatballs from the mixture and set aside.
3. Spray round baking dish with cooking spray. Add cauliflower into the baking dish and spread well.
4. Place meatballs on top of cauliflower layer. Cover dish with foil.
5. Pour 1 cup of water into the instant pot then place a trivet in the pot.
6. Place baking dish on top of the trivet.
7. Seal pot with lid and cook on high for 12 minutes.
8. Release pressure using quick release method than open the lid.
9. Remove dish from the pot.
10. Melt butter in a microwave.
11. Drizzle meatballs with melted butter and serve.

Nutritional Value (Amount per Serving):
Calories 501; Fat 35.4 g; Carbohydrates 5.7 g; Sugar 1.5 g; Protein 41.2 g

Buttery Lamb

Preparation Time: 10 minutes; Cooking Time: 45 minutes; Serve: 6
Ingredients:
- 2 lbs lamb shoulder, cut into pieces
- 2 rosemary sprigs
- ¼ cup balsamic vinegar
- 3 tbsp butter
- 4 cups chicken broth
- 1 tsp pepper
- 2 tsp salt

Directions:
1. Season meat with pepper and salt and place in the pot.
2. Add rosemary, vinegar, and broth into the pot.
3. Seal pot with lid and cook on high for 25 minutes.
4. Release pressure using quick release method than open the lid.

5. Preheat the oven to 232 C/ 450 F.
6. Remove meat from pot and brush with butter. Place on a baking tray.
7. Roast in preheated oven for 20 minutes.
8. Serve and enjoy.

Nutritional Value (Amount per Serving):
Calories 361; Fat 17.8 g; Carbohydrates 0.9 g; Sugar 0.5 g; Protein 45.8 g

Coconut Ginger Lamb

Preparation Time: 10 minutes; Cooking Time: 30 minutes; Serve: 5
Ingredients:
- 2 lbs lamb shoulder
- ½ tsp white pepper
- 1 tsp cumin powder
- 1 tsp coriander powder
- 3 cups vegetable stock
- ½ cup coconut milk
- 1 onion, cut into wedges
- 3 garlic cloves, chopped
- 1 tbsp ginger, chopped
- 2 tbsp olive oil
- 1 tsp salt

Directions:
1. Place meat in the pot.
2. Pour stock over the meat.
3. Seal pot with lid and cook on high for 30 minutes.
4. Release pressure using quick release method than open the lid.
5. Remove meat from pot and set aside.
6. Remove stock from the pot.
7. Add oil into the instant pot and set the pot on sauté mode.
8. Add ginger, onion, and garlic to the pot and sauté for 5-6 minutes.
9. Meanwhile, rub the meat with cumin, coriander, pepper, and salt.
10. Place meat into the pot and pour coconut milk over the meat.
11. Cook on sauté mode for 4-5 minutes.
12. Place meat on serving dish and drizzle with sauce.
13. Serve and enjoy.

Nutritional Value (Amount per Serving):
Calories 464; Fat 26 g; Carbohydrates 6.3 g; Sugar 3 g; Protein 52 g

Spicy Pepper Lamb Curry

Preparation Time: 10 minutes; Cooking Time: 40 minutes; Serve: 4
Ingredients:
- 2 lbs leg of lamb
- 1 tsp cumin seeds
- 1 tsp chili powder
- 1 tsp fennel seeds
- 2 tsp ginger, grated
- 1 tsp garam masala
- 1 tbsp olive oil
- ½ cup coriander, chopped

- 2 cups chicken stock
- 1 cup tomatoes, diced
- 1 bell pepper, chopped
- 1 onion, chopped
- 3 garlic cloves, chopped
- ½ tsp pepper
- 1 tsp salt

Directions:
1. Add oil into the instant pot and set the pot on sauté mode.
2. Add fennel seeds, cumin seeds, and onion and sauté for 3-4 minutes or until onion softened.
3. Add tomatoes and bell pepper. Stir well.
4. Add chili powder, ginger, and garam masala. Stir well.
5. Add meat to the pot then pour stock over the meat.
6. Add coriander and stir well.
7. Seal pot with lid and cook on high for 40 minutes.
8. Release pressure using quick release method than open the lid.
9. Set pot on sauté mode and cook for 10 minutes.
10. Serve and enjoy.

Nutritional Value (Amount per Serving):
Calories 499; Fat 21 g; Carbohydrates 9.4 g; Sugar 4.3 g; Protein 65.6 g

Sprout with Lamb

Preparation Time: 10 minutes; Cooking Time: 15 minutes; Serve: 4
Ingredients:
- 2 racks of lamb
- 1 tsp dried rosemary
- ½ tsp dried sage
- ½ tsp chili powder
- 1 cup sour cream
- 3 cups chicken stock
- 2 tbsp olive oil
- 2 celery stalks
- ½ cup mushrooms
- 1 cup cherry tomatoes
- 1 cup Brussels sprouts
- ½ tsp pepper
- 1 tsp salt

Directions:
1. Season meat with sage, rosemary, and salt.
2. Place meat into the instant pot and pour stock over the meat.
3. Seal pot with lid and cook on high for 15 minutes.
4. Release pressure using quick release method than open the lid.
5. Add sprouts, oil, celery, mushrooms, and tomatoes. Season with chili powder and salt.
6. Seal pot again and cook on high for 5 minutes.
7. Release pressure using quick release method than open the lid.
8. Serve and enjoy.

Nutritional Value (Amount per Serving):
Calories 309; Fat 24.8 g; Carbohydrates 7.9 g; Sugar 2.6 g; Protein 15.4 g

Spicy Lamb Leg

Preparation Time: 10 minutes; Cooking Time: 20 minutes; Serve: 4
Ingredients:
- 2 lbs lamb leg, boneless and chopped
- 1 thyme sprig
- 2 tsp chili powder
- 2 cup chicken stock
- 2 red chili peppers, chopped
- 3 garlic cloves, crushed
- 3 tbsp olive oil
- ½ tsp pepper
- 1 tsp salt

Directions:
1. Rub garlic and oil over the meat.
2. Season meat with chili powder, pepper, and salt. Wrap meat with foil and place in refrigerator for 30 minutes.
3. Place meat in instant pot and pour stock over meat.
4. Add chili peppers thyme.
5. Seal pot with lid and cook on high for 20 minutes.
6. Allow to release pressure naturally then open the lid.
7. Serve and enjoy.

Nutritional Value (Amount per Serving):
Calories 512; Fat 26.2 g; Carbohydrates 2.2 g; Sugar 0.6 g; Protein 64.6 g

Lemon Coconut Lamb

Preparation Time: 10 minutes; Cooking Time: 15 minutes; Serve: 4
Ingredients:
- 1 lb lamb tenderloin, cut into pieces
- 1 tbsp cumin powder
- 2 tsp turmeric powder
- 2 tsp garam masala
- 3 tbsp chili powder
- 2 tbsp apple cider
- 2 tbsp fresh lemon juice
- 1 cup cilantro, chopped
- 2 onions, chopped
- 2 cups chicken broth
- 1 cup coconut milk
- 3 tbsp butter
- 1 cup cherry tomatoes, chopped
- 1 tsp salt

Directions:
1. Season meat with pepper and salt and place into the instant pot.
2. Set pot on sauté mode and cook for 4-5 minutes.
3. Add remaining ingredients on top of meat.
4. Seal pot with lid and cook on high for 15 minutes.
5. Allow to release pressure naturally then open the lid.
6. Stir well and serve.

Nutritional Value (Amount per Serving):
Calories 420; Fat 25 g; Carbohydrates 13.8 g; Sugar 5.4 g; Protein 35.3 g

Lamb Garlic Eggplant Curry

Preparation Time: 10 minutes; Cooking Time: 30 minutes; Serve: 4
Ingredients:
- 2 lamb shanks
- 2 bay leaves
- 1 cinnamon stick
- 2 tbsp cumin seeds
- 1 tbsp oregano
- 1 tbsp paprika
- ½ eggplant, cubed
- ¼ cup yogurt
- 4 cups chicken broth
- 4 tbsp butter
- 3 garlic cloves
- 2 green chili peppers
- 2 tsp salt

Directions:
1. Add meat in a large mixing bowl. Season meat with cumin seeds, oregano, paprika, garlic, pepper, and salt.
2. Add meat into the pot and set the pot on sauté mode and cook for 3-4 minutes.
3. Once meat is browned then add eggplants and cook for 5 minutes.
4. Add chili peppers, yogurt, and broth and stir well.
5. Seal pot with lid and cook on high for 30 minutes.
6. Allow to release pressure naturally then open the lid.
7. Serve and enjoy.

Nutritional Value (Amount per Serving):
Calories 493; Fat 26.2 g; Carbohydrates 9.3 g; Sugar 3.9 g; Protein 53.4 g

Gluten-Free Lamb Curry

Preparation Time: 10 minutes; Cooking Time: 30 minutes; Serve: 4
Ingredients:
- 1 ½ lbs lamb chunks, boneless
- 1 cup coconut milk
- 1 cup tomatoes, crushed
- 1 tsp garam masala
- 1 tsp turmeric
- 1 red chili, chopped
- 1 tbsp coriander
- 1 tbsp cumin
- 1 zucchini, chopped
- 1 carrot, chopped
- 1 tbsp ginger, grated
- 2 garlic cloves, crushed
- 1 onion, chopped
- Pepper
- Salt

Directions:
1. Add oil into the instant pot and set the pot on sauté mode.
2. Add ginger, garlic, and onion to the pot and sauté until softened.
3. Add spices, lamb, zucchini, and carrot and stir to coat.
4. Add coconut milk, tomatoes, and chili. Stir well.
5. Seal pot with lid and cook on high for 20 minutes.

6. Allow to release pressure naturally then open the lid.
7. Season with coriander, pepper, and salt.
8. Serve and enjoy.

Nutritional Value (Amount per Serving):
Calories 502; Fat 27.5 g; Carbohydrates 13.3 g; Sugar 6.1 g; Protein 51.1 g

Squash Lamb Curry

Preparation Time: 10 minutes; Cooking Time: 40 minutes; Serve: 10

Ingredients:
- 4 cups butternut squash, diced
- 13.5 oz coconut milk
- ¼ cup tomato paste
- ¼ tsp cayenne pepper
- 1 tsp paprika
- 1 tsp turmeric
- 1 tsp ground ginger
- 1 tbsp ground cumin
- 1 tbsp ground coriander
- 2 ½ tsp real salt
- 3 garlic cloves, minced
- 1 onion, chopped
- 1 ½ lbs lamb, cut into pieces
- 2 tbsp butter

Directions:
1. Add butter into the instant pot and set the pot on sauté mode.
2. Add meat to the pot and cook until browned.
3. Add onion and sauté until browned.
4. Add garlic and stir for a minute.
5. Add all seasoning and stir to combine.
6. Add squash, coconut milk, and tomato paste. Stir well.
7. Seal pot with lid and cook on high for 10 minutes.
8. Allow to release pressure naturally then open the lid.
9. Stir well and serve.

Nutritional Value (Amount per Serving):
Calories 276; Fat 16.7 g; Carbohydrates 11.9 g; Sugar 3.9 g; Protein 21.2 g

Jamaican Goat Curry

Preparation Time: 10 minutes; Cooking Time: 10 minutes; Serve: 6

Ingredients:
- 2 lbs goat chops
- 2 green onions, chopped
- 2 thyme sprigs
- 3 tbsp curry powder
- 3 cups onion, diced
- 4 garlic cloves
- 3 tbsp olive oil
- 2 cloves
- 2 tsp peppercorns
- 2 tsp ground ginger
- 1 tsp fenugreek seeds
- 2 tsp mustard seeds
- 1 tbsp coriander seeds
- 1 tbsp cumin seeds
- 3 tsp turmeric
- 2 tsp chili powder

- Salt

Directions:
1. Lightly toast whole spices in a pan over medium heat.
2. Grind the toasted spices until get nice ground spice mixture.
3. Add oil into the instant pot and set the pot on sauté mode.
4. Add meat to the pot and sauté until browned.
5. Add onion and sauté until softened.
6. Add green onion, thyme, garlic, curry powder, and ground spice mixture. Stir well.
7. Add 2 cups of water and salt. Stir well.
8. Seal pot with lid and cook on high for 25 minutes.
9. Allow to release pressure naturally then open the lid.
10. Stir well and serve.

Nutritional Value (Amount per Serving):
Calories 400; Fat 19.5 g; Carbohydrates 11.5 g; Sugar 2.9 g; Protein 44.6 g

Flavorful Indian Goat Curry

Preparation Time: 10 minutes; Cooking Time: 25 minutes; Serve: 4

Ingredients:
- 1 lb mutton, cut into pieces
- 1 tbsp lemon juice
- 1 tomato, chopped
- ½ tbsp garlic, minced
- ½ tbsp ginger, minced
- 1 onion, chopped
- 1 green chili, chopped
- 3 tbsp olive oil
- 1 tsp garam masala
- 2 tsp coriander powder
- 1 tsp cayenne
- ¼ tsp turmeric
- 2 black cardamom
- 1 bay leaf
- 1-inch cinnamon stick
- 4 cloves
- 6 black peppercorns
- ½ tsp cumin seeds
- 1 tsp salt

Directions:
1. Add oil into the instant pot and set the pot on sauté mode.
2. Add whole spices to the pot and sauté for 30 seconds.
3. Add green chili, garlic, ginger, and onion and sauté for 4 minutes.
4. Add tomatoes and spices and cook for 2 minutes.
5. Add meat and stir well and sauté for 2 minutes.
6. Seal pot with lid and cook on high for 20 minutes.
7. Allow to release pressure naturally then open the lid.
8. Add lemon juice and stir well.
9. Serve and enjoy.

Nutritional Value (Amount per Serving):
Calories 346; Fat 21.6 g; Carbohydrates 4.7 g; Sugar 1.8 g; Protein 32.7 g

Perfect North-Indian Mutton Curry

Preparation Time: 10 minutes; Cooking Time: 45 minutes; Serve: 6
Ingredients:
- 2 lbs mutton, cut into pieces
- 1 tbsp butter
- 1 tsp garam masala
- 4 tbsp curry powder
- 5 large tomatoes, chopped
- 1 tbsp ginger garlic paste
- 3 onions, chopped
- 1 green chili, split lengthwise
- 3 cloves
- 3 cardamom pods
- 1-inch cinnamon stick
- 1 bay leaf
- 1 tsp fennel seeds
- 3 tbsp olive oil
- 1 tsp turmeric
- 1 tbsp salt

Directions:
1. Rub turmeric all over the meat and set aside.
2. Add oil into the instant pot and set the pot on sauté mode.
3. Add cloves, cardamom, cinnamon, bay leaf, and fennel seeds to the pot and sauté for a minute.
4. Add ginger garlic paste, onion, and green chili and sauté for 8 minutes.
5. Add tomatoes, curry powder, coriander powder, and salt and cook for 5 minutes.
6. Add meat and 1 cup of water and stir well.
7. Seal pot with lid and cook on high for 25 minutes.
8. Allow to release pressure naturally then open the lid.
9. Add butter and stir well.
10. Serve and enjoy.

Nutritional Value (Amount per Serving):
Calories 458; Fat 24.5 g; Carbohydrates 13 g; Sugar 6.5 g; Protein 45.4 g

Quick Lamb Rogan Josh

Preparation Time: 10 minutes; Cooking Time: 30 minutes; Serve: 4
Ingredients:
- 1 lb leg of lamb, cut into cubes
- ¼ cup water
- 1 tsp cayenne pepper
- ½ tsp cinnamon
- 1 tsp turmeric
- 1 tsp paprika
- 2 tsp garam masala
- ¼ cup cilantro, chopped
- 1 tbsp tomato paste
- ¼ cup yogurt
- 2 tsp ginger, minced
- 3 garlic cloves, minced
- 1 onion, diced
- 1 tsp salt

Directions:
1. Add all ingredients into the large bowl and mix well. Place in refrigerator for overnight.
2. Pour marinated meat into the instant pot along with the marinade. Stir well.

3. Seal pot with lid and cook on high for 20 minutes.
4. Allow to release pressure naturally then open the lid.
5. Stir well and serve.

Nutritional Value (Amount per Serving):
Calories 248; Fat 8.8 g; Carbohydrates 7 g; Sugar 2.9 g; Protein 33.6 g

Delicious Jordanian Lamb

Preparation Time: 10 minutes; Cooking Time: 20 minutes; Serve: 4
Ingredients:
- 1 lb leg of lamb, cut into chunks
- 2 cups onions, sliced
- 4 tbsp butter
- 2 tsp arrowroot
- ½ cup water
- 1 cup yogurt
- 1/8 tsp cardamom seeds
- 1/8 tsp ground nutmeg
- ¼ tsp cloves
- 1-inch cinnamon stick
- ½ tsp black peppercorns
- 1 tsp coriander
- 1 tsp cumin seeds
- 1 tsp salt

Directions:
1. Grind all the whole spices in the grinder.
2. Add yogurt, arrowroot, water, and ground spice mixture to the blender and blend for a minute.
3. Add butter into the instant pot and set the pot on sauté mode.
4. Add meat and onion to the pot and cook for 2-3 minutes.
5. Pour yogurt mixture over the meat and stir well.
6. Seal pot with lid and cook on soup mode for 10 minutes.
7. Allow to release pressure naturally then open the lid.
8. Stir well and serve.

Nutritional Value (Amount per Serving):
Calories 384; Fat 20.8 g; Carbohydrates 10.4 g; Sugar 6.8 g; Protein 36.3 g

Chapter 12: Seafood & Fish Recipes

Lemon Butter Shrimp Scampi

Preparation Time: 10 minutes; Cooking Time: 1 minute; Serve: 4
Ingredients:
- 1 lb shrimp, peeled and deveined
- ½ cup vegetable stock
- ¼ cup dry white wine
- 2 garlic cloves, minced
- 2 tbsp butter
- ½ lemon juice
- ¼ tbsp fresh parsley, chopped
- Pepper
- Salt

Directions:
1. Add butter into the instant pot and set the pot on sauté mode.
2. Add garlic and sauté for 30 seconds.
3. Add remaining ingredients except for parsley and lemon juice and stir well.
4. Seal pot with lid and cook on high pressure for 1 minute.
5. Release pressure using quick release method than open the lid.
6. Add lemon juice and garnish with parsley.
7. Serve and enjoy.

Nutritional Value (Amount per Serving):
Calories 203; Fat 8 g; Carbohydrates 3 g; Sugar 0.5 g; Protein 26.1 g

Quick Shrimp Scampi

Preparation Time: 10 minutes; Cooking Time: 2 minutes; Serve: 2
Ingredients:
- 1 lb shrimp, peeled and deveined
- ½ lemon juice
- 1 cup water
- ½ tsp red pepper flakes
- 1 ½ tbsp garlic, minced
- 2 tbsp butter
- Pepper
- Salt

Directions:
1. Add butter into the instant pot and set the pot on sauté mode.
2. Add garlic, pepper, red pepper flakes, and salt to the pot and sauté for 2 minutes.
3. Add shrimp and water. Stir well.
4. Seal pot with lid and cook on high pressure for 2 minutes.
5. Release pressure using quick release method than open the lid.
6. Add lemon juice.
7. Stir well and serve.

Nutritional Value (Amount per Serving):
Calories 385; Fat 15.6 g; Carbohydrates 6.1 g; Sugar 0.4 g; Protein 52.3 g

Flavorful Shrimp Curry

Preparation Time: 10 minutes; Cooking Time: 15 minutes; Serve: 4
Ingredients:
- 1 lb shrimp, deveined
- ¼ cup fresh cilantro, chopped
- 1 tbsp fresh lime juice
- 3.5 oz coconut milk
- 1 cup tomato, chopped
- ½ tbsp garlic, minced
- ½ tbsp ginger, minced
- 1 cup onion, chopped
- 1 green chili, chopped
- 1 tsp mustard seeds
- 1 tbsp olive oil
- Spices:
- 1 tsp coriander powder
- ½ tsp garam masala
- ½ tsp chili powder
- ½ tsp turmeric
- ½ tsp salt

Directions:
1. Add oil into the instant pot and set the pot on sauté mode.
2. Add mustard seeds and sauté until mustard seeds are pop up.
3. Add green chili, garlic, ginger, and onion and sauté for 5 minutes.
4. Add tomato and spices and sauté for 2-3 minutes.
5. Add shrimp and coconut milk to the pot. Stir well.
6. Seal pot with lid and cook on low pressure for 3 minutes.
7. Release pressure using quick release method than open the lid.
8. Add lime juice and stir well. Garnish with freshly chopped cilantro.
9. Serve and enjoy.

Nutritional Value (Amount per Serving):
Calories 252; Fat 11.8 g; Carbohydrates 9.1 g; Sugar 3.4 g; Protein 27.6 g

Thai Prawns

Preparation Time: 10 minutes; Cooking Time: 1 minute; Serve: 4
Ingredients:
- 2 lbs prawns, remove shells
- 1 tsp cumin
- 1 tbsp coriander
- 1 tbsp Thai curry paste
- 3 tbsp coconut oil
- 1 tbsp garlic cloves, grated
- 2 lime juice
- Pepper
- Salt

Directions:
1. Pour 1 cup of water into the instant pot.
2. Add all ingredients into the large mixing bowl and mix well.
3. Add bowl mixture into the instant pot steamer basket.
4. Seal pot with lid and cook on high for 1 minute.
5. Release pressure using quick release method than open the lid.

6. Stir well and serve.

Nutritional Value (Amount per Serving):
Calories 372; Fat 14.2 g; Carbohydrates 7 g; Sugar 0.7 g; Protein 52 g

Garlic Butter Mussels

Preparation Time: 15 minutes; Cooking Time: 3 minutes; Serve: 2

Ingredients:
- 1 lb mussels, rinsed and clean
- 1 cup vegetable stock
- 2 tbsp olive oil
- 2 tbsp butter
- 2 scallions, chopped
- 3 tbsp fresh parsley, chopped
- 1 small onion, minced
- 2 garlic cloves, minced
- Pepper
- Salt

Directions:
1. Add oil and butter to the instant pot and set the pot on sauté mode.
2. Add onion and sauté for 2 minutes.
3. Add garlic and sauté for 1 minute.
4. Add stock, scallions, and parsley and stir well.
5. Seal pot with lid and cook on high for 3 minutes.
6. Release pressure using quick release method than open the lid.
7. Serve and enjoy.

Nutritional Value (Amount per Serving):
Calories 447; Fat 31.7 g; Carbohydrates 15.1 g; Sugar 2.9 g; Protein 28.1 g

Lemon Garlic Shrimp Scampi

Preparation Time: 10 minutes; Cooking Time: 10 minutes; Serve: 4

Ingredients:
- 1 ½ lbs jumbo shrimp, peeled and deveined
- 2 tsp fresh lemon juice
- ¼ cup fresh parsley, chopped
- 6 tbsp butter
- 3 garlic cloves, chopped
- ¼ cup dry white wine
- ¼ tsp black pepper
- 2 tsp kosher salt

Directions:
1. Add shrimp, garlic, and wine into the instant pot and stir well. Season with pepper and salt.
2. Seal pot with lid and cook on high for 1 minute.
3. Release pressure using quick release method than open the lid.
4. Transfer shrimp to a bowl. Set pot on sauté mode and cook for 6 minutes or until liquid reduced half.
5. Add butter and stir until sauce thickened.
6. Return shrimp to the pot. Add lemon juice and parsley. Stir well.

7. Serve and enjoy.

Nutritional Value (Amount per Serving):
Calories 292; Fat 17.3 g; Carbohydrates 1.5 g; Sugar 3.3 g; Protein 30.9 g

Wild-Caught Crab Legs

Preparation Time: 5 minutes; Cooking Time: 3 minutes; Serve: 4

Ingredients:
- 2 lbs wild-caught crab legs
- 1 lemon, cut into slices
- 1/3 cup butter, melted
- 1 cup water

Directions:
1. Pour 1 cup of water into the instant pot then place a trivet in the pot.
2. Place crab legs on top of the trivet.
3. Seal pot with lid and cook on high for 3 minutes.
4. Release pressure using quick release method than open the lid.
5. Transfer cooked crab legs on serving platter and top with lemon and butter.
6. Serve and enjoy.

Nutritional Value (Amount per Serving):
Calories 407; Fat 19.4 g; Carbohydrates 1.4 g; Sugar 0.4 g; Protein 53.7 g

Shrimp Coconut Curry

Preparation Time: 10 minutes; Cooking Time: 25 minutes; Serve: 6

Ingredients:
- 2 lbs shrimp, peeled and deveined
- 1 garlic clove, minced
- 1 tsp ginger, grated
- 3 tbsp fresh lime juice
- 2 tsp curry spice
- 1 tsp paprika
- 1 tsp cumin
- ¼ cup coconut milk
- For sauce:
- 1/3 cup fresh cilantro, chopped
- 14 oz coconut milk
- 3 tbsp curry paste
- 28 oz can tomato, diced
- 2 garlic cloves, minced
- 2 tsp ginger, grated
- 1 small onion, diced
- 2 tbsp olive oil
- 1 tsp sea salt

Directions:
1. In a large bowl, mix together coconut milk, garlic, ginger, sea salt, lime juice, and spices. Add shrimp to the bowl and stir well to coat.
2. Add oil into the instant pot and set the pot on sauté mode.
3. Add garlic, ginger, and onion to the pot and sauté for 2-3 minutes.
4. Add tomatoes, coconut milk, curry paste, and salt. Stir well.
5. Seal pot with lid and cook on high for 7 minutes.
6. Release pressure using quick release method than open the lid.
7. Set pot on sauté mode. Add marinated shrimp to the pot and stir well.

8. Cook shrimp on sauté mode for 2-5 minutes.
9. Stir well and serve.

Nutritional Value (Amount per Serving):
Calories 308; Fat 11 g; Carbohydrates 13 g; Sugar 5.1 g; Protein 36.4 g

Lemon Garlic Mussels

Preparation Time: 10 minutes; Cooking Time: 3 minutes; Serve: 4
Ingredients:
- 2 lbs mussels
- ½ fresh lemon juice
- ½ cup chicken broth
- ½ cup dry white wine
- 3 garlic cloves, minced
- 1 tbsp olive oil
- 3 shallots, minced

Directions:
1. Add oil into the instant pot and set the pot on sauté mode.
2. Add garlic and shallots and sauté for 2 minutes.
3. Add mussels, red pepper flakes, broth, and wine. Stir well.
4. Seal pot with lid and cook on low for 3 minutes.
5. Release pressure using quick release method than open the lid.
6. Add lemon juice and stir well.
7. Garnish with parsley and serve.

Nutritional Value (Amount per Serving):
Calories 265; Fat 8.8 g; Carbohydrates 11.4 g; Sugar 0.5 g; Protein 28 g

Crab Legs with Butter Sauce

Preparation Time: 10 minutes; Cooking Time: 3 minutes; Serve: 4
Ingredients:
- 2 lbs crab legs
- 1 lemon juice
- ¼ cup butter
- 1 garlic clove, minced
- 1 tsp olive oil
- 1 cup water

Directions:
1. Pour water into the instant pot.
2. Add crab legs into the instant pot steamer basket.
3. Seal pot with lid and cook on high for 3 minutes.
4. Release pressure using quick release method than open the lid.
5. Meanwhile, heat oil in a saucepan over medium heat.
6. Add garlic to the pan and sauté for a minute.
7. Add butter and stir until butter is melted.
8. Add lemon juice and stir.
9. Pour sauce over crab legs and serve.

Nutritional Value (Amount per Serving):

Calories 346; Fat 16.2 g; Carbohydrates 1.6 g; Sugar 0.4 g; Protein 43.9 g

Chili Herb Mussels

Preparation Time: 10 minutes; Cooking Time: 5 minutes; Serve: 4
Ingredients:
- 2 lbs mussels, scrubbed
- ½ cup chicken broth
- 2 garlic cloves, minced
- 2 tsp dried oregano
- ½ tsp red pepper flakes
- 14 oz tomatoes, chopped
- 1 onion, chopped
- 2 tbsp olive oil

Directions:
1. Add oil into the instant pot and set the pot on sauté mode.
2. Add onion, garlic, and red pepper flakes and sauté for 2-3 minutes.
3. Add mussels, broth, oregano, and tomatoes. Stir well.
4. Seal pot with lid and cook on high for 2 minutes.
5. Allow to release pressure naturally then open the lid.
6. Stir well and serve.

Nutritional Value (Amount per Serving):
Calories 297; Fat 12.4 g; Carbohydrates 14 g; Sugar 1.3 g; Protein 29.1 g

Garlic Tomato Swordfish

Preparation Time: 10 minutes; Cooking Time: 5 minutes; Serve: 2
Ingredients:
- 1 lb swordfish steaks
- ½ tsp black pepper
- 14 oz can tomato, crushed
- ½ tsp red pepper flakes
- 3 garlic cloves, minced
- 2 tbsp olive oil
- ½ tsp salt

Directions:
1. Add oil into the instant pot and set the pot on sauté mode.
2. Add tomatoes, garlic, red pepper flakes, pepper, and salt. Stir well.
3. Add fish and coat well.
4. Seal pot with lid and cook on high for 3 minutes.
5. Release pressure using quick release method than open the lid.
6. Serve and enjoy.

Nutritional Value (Amount per Serving):
Calories 523; Fat 25.8 g; Carbohydrates 12.2 g; Sugar 6.9 g; Protein 59.8 g

Salmon with Vegetable

Preparation Time: 10 minutes; Cooking Time: 4 minutes; Serve: 4
Ingredients:

- 4 salmon fillets
- 10 oz Bok Choy, cut into slices
- 1 tsp vinegar
- 2 garlic cloves, minced
- 2 tbsp gingerroot, grated
- 1 ½ cups chicken stock

Directions:
1. Add bok choy, vinegar, garlic, gingerroot, and broth to the instant pot and stir well.
2. Place steamer rack in the instant pot and place fish on the rack.
3. Seal pot with lid and cook o high for 4 minutes.
4. Release pressure using quick release method than open the lid.
5. Transfer fish on a plate. Using slotted spoon remove bok choy from pot and place around the salmon.
6. Serve and enjoy.

Nutritional Value (Amount per Serving):
Calories 260; Fat 11.5 g; Carbohydrates 4.2 g; Sugar 1.2 g; Protein 36.2 g

Salmon with Sauce

Preparation Time: 10 minutes; Cooking Time: 4 minutes; Serve: 4
Ingredients:
- 4 salmon fillets
- ¼ tsp paprika
- ¼ cup dry white wine
- 1 ¼ cups chicken stock
- 1 garlic clove, minced
- ¾ tsp lemon juice
- 1 tsp fresh dill weed
- ¼ cup cucumber, peeled, seeded, and shredded
- 1/3 cup yogurt

Directions:
1. In a small bowl, mix together yogurt, garlic, lemon juice, dill weed, cucumber, pepper, and salt.
2. Add stock, lemon juice, and wine to the instant pot and stir well.
3. Place steamer rack in the instant pot.
4. Place salmon fish fillets on steamer rack. Season with paprika.
5. Seal pot with lid and cook on high for 4 minutes.
6. Release pressure using quick release method than open the lid.
7. Transfer fish on a plate.
8. Pour yogurt mixture over the fish and serve.

Nutritional Value (Amount per Serving):
Calories 268; Fat 11.5 g; Carbohydrates 2.7 g; Sugar 1.9 g; Protein 36 g

Lemon Butter Crabs

Preparation Time: 10 minutes; Cooking Time: 3 minutes; Serve: 2
Ingredients:
- 1 ½ lbs crabs
- ¼ cup garlic, minced
- 1 tbsp fresh lemon juice
- ½ cup water

- ¼ cup butter, melted
- 2 tbsp fish sauce
- ¼ tsp salt

Directions:
1. Add crabs into the instant pot and season with garlic and salt.
2. Mix together butter and fish sauce. Pour over crabs.
3. Add water and stir well.
4. Seal pot with lid and cook on high for 3 minutes.
5. Release pressure using quick release method than open the lid.
6. Add lemon juice and stir well.
7. Serve and enjoy.

Nutritional Value (Amount per Serving):
Calories 584; Fat 29.2 g; Carbohydrates 6.5 g; Sugar 1 g; Protein 71 g

Jerk Fish with Vegetable

Preparation Time: 10 minutes; Cooking Time: 5 minutes; Serve: 4

Ingredients:
- 4 cod fish fillets
- 1 tsp fresh lime juice
- ½ tsp lime zest
- ¼ cup yogurt
- 1 cup vegetable stock
- 1 tbsp jerk seasoning
- 4 asparagus spears
- ½ bell pepper, chopped
- 1 cup cremini mushrooms, sliced
- 1 onion, chopped
- 2 tsp olive oil

Directions:
1. Add oil into the instant pot and set the pot on sauté mode.
2. Add onion to the pot and sauté for 3 minutes.
3. Add bell pepper and mushrooms and cook for 3 minutes.
4. Turn off the sauté mode.
5. Place steaming rack over the veggies.
6. Place fish fillets on the steamer rack. Arrange the asparagus on top of fish.
7. Sprinkle jerks seasoning over the fish fillets.
8. Pour stock around the fish.
9. Seal pot with lid and cook on high for 3 minutes.
10. Release pressure using quick release method than open the lid.
11. In a small bowl, whisk together yogurt, lime juice, and lime zest.
12. Top fish fillets with yogurt mixture and serve.

Nutritional Value (Amount per Serving):
Calories 248; Fat 4.7 g; Carbohydrates 7 g; Sugar 4.3 g; Protein 43.4 g

Ginger Onion Haddock

Preparation Time: 10 minutes; Cooking Time: 8 minutes; Serve: 2

Ingredients:
- 4 haddock fillets
- 1 tbsp ginger, chopped
- 2 tbsp olive oil
- 2 fresh lemon juice
- 1 cup white wine
- 4 green onions, chopped
- Pepper
- Salt

Directions:
1. Rub oil over the fish fillets and season with pepper and salt.
2. Add all ingredients except fish fillets in the instant pot and stir well.
3. Place a steamer basket in the instant pot.
4. Place fish in a steamer basket.
5. Seal pot with lid and cook on high for 8 minutes.
6. Release pressure using quick release method than open the lid.
7. Serve and enjoy.

Nutritional Value (Amount per Serving):
Calories 295; Fat 8.6 g; Carbohydrates 6.4 g; Sugar 1.6 g; Protein 37.1 g

Tomato Parsley Mussels

Preparation Time: 10 minutes; Cooking Time: 3 minutes; Serve: 4

Ingredients:
- 2 lbs mussels, clean and rinsed
- 1 cup tomatoes, diced
- ½ tsp pepper
- ½ tbsp parsley, dried
- ½ cup white wine
- Salt

Directions:
1. Add parsley, tomatoes, wine, pepper, and salt into the instant pot and stir well.
2. Add mussels in a steamer basket.
3. Seal pot with lid and cook on high for 3 minutes.
4. Release pressure using quick release method than open the lid.
5. Serve and enjoy.

Nutritional Value (Amount per Serving):
Calories 230; Fat 5.2 g; Carbohydrates 11.5 g; Sugar 1.4 g; Protein 27.5 g

Lemon Garlic Steamed Tilapia

Preparation Time: 10 minutes; Cooking Time: 3 minutes; Serve: 4

Ingredients:
- 4 tilapia fillets
- 3 sprigs dill
- 3 garlic cloves
- ½ tbsp olive oil
- 1 fresh lemon juice
- ½ tsp pepper
- ½ tsp salt

Directions:
1. Place fish fillets on top of foil. Season with lemon juice, oil, pepper, and salt.

2. Place dill and garlic o top of fish fillets.
3. Cover fish fillets with another foil piece.
4. Pour 2 cups of water into the instant pot and place trivet in the pot.
5. Place fish packet on top of the trivet.
6. Seal pot with lid and cook on high for 3 minutes.
7. Release pressure using quick release method than open the lid.
8. Serve and enjoy.

Nutritional Value (Amount per Serving):
Calories 324; Fat 7.7 g; Carbohydrates 2.3 g; Sugar 0.5 g; Protein 64.5 g

Garlic Cajun Fish Fillet

Preparation Time: 5 minutes; Cooking Time: 1 minute; Serve: 8
Ingredients:
- 1 1/2 lbs fish filets
- 1/2 tbsp garlic powder
- 1 tbsp Cajun seasoning
- 2 tbsp olive oil

Directions:
1. Pour 1 cup water into the instant pot than place trivet into the pot.
2. Place fish filets on top of the trivet. Season with Cajun seasoning and garlic powder.
3. Seal pot with lid and cook on high for 1 minute.
4. Release pressure using quick release method than open the lid.
5. Heat oil into the pan over medium heat.
6. Place fish fillets in the pan and cook for 2 minutes.
7. Serve and enjoy.

Nutritional Value (Amount per Serving):
Calories 165; Fat 9.8 g; Carbohydrates 12 g; Sugar 0.8 g; Protein 7.4 g

Lemon Salmon Fish Fillet

Preparation Time: 5 minutes; Cooking Time: 5 minutes; Serve: 3
Ingredients:
- 3 wild Alaskan salmon fillets
- 1 cup chicken stock
- 2 lemons, sliced
- Pepper
- Salt

Directions:
1. Pour stock into the instant pot then place steamer rack into the pot.
2. Place fish fillets on a steamer rack and season with pepper and salt.
3. Place lemon slices on salmon fillets.
4. Seal pot with lid and cook on high for 5 minutes.
5. Release pressure using quick release method than open the lid.
6. Serve and enjoy.

Nutritional Value (Amount per Serving):

Calories 147; Fat 5.9 g; Carbohydrates 0.3 g; Sugar 0.2 g; Protein 21.9 g

Quick & Simple Fish Fillet

Preparation Time: 5 minutes; Cooking Time: 2 minutes; Serve: 2

Ingredients:
- 2 salmon fillets
- 2 tbsp olive oil
- 1 cup water
- Pepper
- Kosher salt

Directions:
1. Pour water into the instant pot and place trivet in the pot.
2. Place salmon fillets on top of the trivet.
3. Seal pot with lid and cook on low for 2 minutes.
4. Release pressure using quick release method than open the lid.
5. Heat oil into the pan over medium heat.
6. Season fish fillet with pepper and salt and place skin side down in the pan and cook for 2 minutes.
7. Serve and enjoy.

Nutritional Value (Amount per Serving):
Calories 353; Fat 24.6 g; Carbohydrates 0 g; Sugar 0 g; Protein 34.5 g

Tomato Lemon Fish Fillet

Preparation Time: 10 minutes; Cooking Time: 13 minutes; Serve: 6

Ingredients:
- 1 1/2 lbs cod fillet
- 3 tbsp olive oil
- 1 tsp oregano
- 1 onion, sliced
- 28 oz can tomato, diced
- 1 fresh lemon juice
- 1/2 tsp pepper
- 1 tsp salt

Directions:
1. Add oil into the instant pot and set the pot on sauté mode.
2. Add remaining ingredients into the pot and sauté for 8 minutes.
3. Seal pot with lid and cook on high for 5 minutes.
4. Release pressure using quick release method than open the lid.
5. Serve and enjoy.

Nutritional Value (Amount per Serving):
Calories 186; Fat 7.9 g; Carbohydrates 8.7 g; Sugar 5.3 g; Protein 21.7 g

Orange Ginger Fish Fillets

Preparation Time: 5 minutes; Cooking Time: 7 minutes; Serve: 4

Ingredients:
- 4 white fish fillets
- 1 orange juice
- 1 tbsp olive oil
- 1 cup chicken stock
- 1 tbsp ginger, chopped
- Pepper
- Salt

Directions:
1. Add all ingredients except fish into the instant pot stir well.
2. Place a steamer basket into the instant pot.
3. Place fish fillets into the steamer basket.
4. Seal pot with lid and cook on high for 7 minutes.
5. Allow to release pressure naturally then open the lid.
6. Serve and enjoy.

Nutritional Value (Amount per Serving):
Calories 312; Fat 15.3 g; Carbohydrates 3.4 g; Sugar 2 g; Protein 38.1 g

Simple 3 Ingredients Fish Fillets

Preparation Time: 5 minutes; Cooking Time: 2 minutes; Serve: 4
Ingredients:
- 1 lb fish fillets, cut in half
- 1 1/2 cup chicken stock
- 1/2 cup green chutney

Directions:
1. Place fish fillets on foil piece.
2. Pour green chutney over fish fillets and wrap foil around the fish fillets.
3. Pour stock into the instant pot then place a trivet in the pot.
4. Place fish wrap on top of the trivet.
5. Seal pot with lid and cook on low for 2 minutes.
6. Allow to release pressure naturally then open the lid.
7. Serve and enjoy.

Nutritional Value (Amount per Serving):
Calories 178; Fat 9.4 g; Carbohydrates 13 g; Sugar 0.2 g; Protein 11 g

Chili Lemon Fish Fillets

Preparation Time: 10 minutes; Cooking Time: 5 minutes; Serve: 4
Ingredients:
- 4 salmon fillets
- 1 fresh lemon juice
- 1 cup water
- 2 tbsp chili pepper
- Pepper
- Salt

Directions:
1. Season fish fillet with chili pepper, lemon juice, pepper, and salt.

2. Pour 1 cup of water into the instant pot then place a trivet in the pot.
3. Place salmon fillets on top of the trivet.
4. Seal pot with lid and cook on high for 5 minutes.
5. Release pressure using quick release method than open the lid.
6. Serve and enjoy.

Nutritional Value (Amount per Serving):
Calories 239; Fat 11 g; Carbohydrates 0.8 g; Sugar 0.5 g; Protein 34 g

Butter Shrimp Grits

Preparation Time: 10 minutes; Cooking Time: 7 minutes; Serve: 6
Ingredients:
- 1 lb shrimp, thawed
- 1/2 cup quick grits
- 1 tsp paprika
- 2 tbsp cilantro, chopped
- 1/2 cup cheddar cheese, shredded
- 1 tbsp olive oil
- 1 tbsp butter
- 1 1/2 cups chicken broth
- 1/4 tsp red pepper flakes
- 1/2 tsp kosher salt

Directions:
1. Add oil into the pot and set the pot on sauté mode.
2. Add shrimp into the pot and cook until it turns to pink. Season with red pepper flakes and salt.
3. Remove shrimp from the pot and set aside.
4. Add remaining ingredients into the pot and stir well.
5. Seal pot with lid and cook on high for 7 minutes.
6. Allow to release pressure naturally then open the lid.
7. Add cheese and stir until cheese melted.
8. Top with shrimp and serve.

Nutritional Value (Amount per Serving):
Calories 222; Fat 9 g; Carbohydrates 12 g; Sugar 0.3 g; Protein 21 g

Frozen Shrimp

Preparation Time: 5 minutes; Cooking Time: 1 minute; Serve: 6
Ingredients:
- 28 oz frozen shrimp, deveined
- 1/2 cup apple cider vinegar
- 1/2 cup chicken stock

Directions:
1. Add all ingredients into the instant pot and stir well.
2. Seal pot with lid and cook on high for 1 minute.
3. Release pressure using quick release method than open the lid.
4. Serve and enjoy.

Nutritional Value (Amount per Serving):

Calories 146; Fat 2.4 g; Carbohydrates 1.4 g; Sugar 0.1 g; Protein 27 g

Coconut Cayenne Shrimp

Preparation Time: 10 minutes; Cooking Time: 4 minutes; Serve: 4
Ingredients:
- 1 lb shrimp, deveined
- 7 oz coconut milk, unsweetened
- 1 tsp garam masala
- 1 tbsp ginger, minced
- 1/2 tsp cayenne pepper
- 1/2 tsp turmeric
- 1 tbsp garlic, minced
- 1 tsp salt

Directions:
1. Add all ingredients into the microwave safe bowl. Stir well and cover the bowl with foil.
2. Pour 1 cup water into the instant pot then place trivet into the pot.
3. Place bowl on top of the trivet.
4. Seal pot with lid and cook on low for 4 minutes.
5. Release pressure using quick release method than open the lid.
6. Serve and enjoy.

Nutritional Value (Amount per Serving):
Calories 250; Fat 13 g; Carbohydrates 6.2 g; Sugar 1.6 g; Protein 27 g

Cajun Fish Fillet

Preparation Time: 5 minutes; Cooking Time: 1 minute; Serve: 6
Ingredients:
- 1 1/2 lbs mahi mahi fish fillets
- 1/2 tbsp garlic powder
- 1 tbsp Cajun seasoning
- 2 tbsp olive oil

Directions:
1. Pour 1 cup water into the instant pot than place trivet into the pot.
2. Place fish fillets on top of trivet and sprinkle with Cajun seasoning and garlic powder.
3. Seal pot with lid and cook on high for 1 minute.
4. Release pressure using quick release method than open the lid.
5. Heat oil in a pan over medium heat.
6. Place fish fillets in the pan and cook for 2 minutes.
7. Serve and enjoy.

Nutritional Value (Amount per Serving):
Calories 142; Fat 5.7 g; Carbohydrates 1.5 g; Sugar 0.2 g; Protein 21.1 g

Creamy Salmon Casserole

Preparation Time: 10 minutes; Cooking Time: 8 minutes; Serve: 6
Ingredients:

- 1/4 cup olive oil
- 2 frozen salmon pieces
- 2 cups milk
- 2 cups chicken broth
- 14 oz can cream of celery soup
- 2 cups frozen vegetables
- 1 tsp garlic, minced
- Pepper
- Salt

Directions:
1. Add all ingredients into the instant pot and stir well.
2. Seal pot with lid and cook on high for 8 minutes.
3. Release pressure using quick release method than open the lid.
4. Stir well and serve.

Nutritional Value (Amount per Serving):
Calories 289; Fat 19.2 g; Carbohydrates 13.3 g; Sugar 2.1 g; Protein 16.9 g

Orange Ginger Fish Fillets

Preparation Time: 5 minutes; Cooking Time: 7 minutes; Serve: 4
Ingredients:
- 4 white fish fillets
- 1 tbsp ginger, chopped
- 1 orange juice
- 1 tbsp olive oil
- 1 cup chicken stock
- 3 spring onions
- Pepper
- Salt

Directions:
1. Add fish fillets into the steamer basket.
2. Add remaining ingredients into the instant pot stir well.
3. Place a steamer basket into the instant pot.
4. Seal pot with lid and cook on high for 7 minutes.
5. Allow to release pressure naturally then open the lid.
6. Place fish fillets on dish and drizzle sauce over fish fillets.
7. Serve and enjoy.

Nutritional Value (Amount per Serving):
Calories 315; Fat 15.4 g; Carbohydrates 4.2 g; Sugar 2.3 g; Protein 38.3 g

Shrimp with Crumbled Cheese

Preparation Time: 10 minutes; Cooking Time: 1 minute; Serve: 6
Ingredients:
- 1 lb frozen shrimp
- 1/2 tsp red pepper flakes
- 1 tbsp garlic
- 2 tbsp butter
- 14.5 oz can tomato
- 1 1/2 cups onion, chopped
- 1/4 cup parsley, chopped
- 1/2 cup black olives, sliced
- 1 cup feta cheese, crumbled
- 1 tsp oregano
- 1 tsp salt

Directions:
1. Add butter into the instant pot and set the pot on sauté mode.
2. Add garlic and red pepper flakes to the pot and stir well.
3. Add oregano, tomatoes, onion, and salt. Stir well.
4. Add frozen shrimp and stir well.
5. Seal pot with lid and cook on low for 1 minute.
6. Release pressure using quick release method than open the lid.
7. Stir in parsley, olives, and crumbled feta cheese.
8. Serve and enjoy.

Nutritional Value (Amount per Serving):
Calories 223; Fat 11.8 g; Carbohydrates 9.4 g; Sugar 4.6 g; Protein 20.3 g

Shrimp with Asparagus

Preparation Time: 5 minutes; Cooking Time: 2 minutes; Serve: 4
Ingredients:
- 1 lb shrimp, peeled and deveined
- 15 asparagus spears, trimmed
- 1 tsp olive oil
- 1/2 tbsp Cajun seasoning

Directions:
1. Pour 1 cup water into the instant pot then place a trivet in the pot.
2. Arrange asparagus on trivet then place shrimp on asparagus.
3. Drizzle with olive oil and season with Cajun seasoning.
4. Seal pot with lid and cook on high for 2 minutes.
5. Allow to release pressure naturally then open the lid.
6. Serve and enjoy.

Nutritional Value (Amount per Serving):
Calories 157; Fat 3.2 g; Carbohydrates 4.1 g; Sugar 1.1 g; Protein 27.2 g

Tomato Jalapeno Shrimp

Preparation Time: 10 minutes; Cooking Time: 5 minutes; Serve: 4
Ingredients:
- 1 lb frozen shrimp, peeled and deveined
- 1 fresh lemon juice
- 1 jalapeno pepper, minced
- 15 oz can tomato, diced
- 1 onion, minced
- 2 garlic cloves, minced
- 1 tsp cayenne pepper
- 1 tsp white pepper
- 1 tsp black pepper

Directions:
1. Add all ingredients into the instant pot and stir well.
2. Seal pot with lid and cook on high for 5 minutes.
3. Release pressure using quick release method than open the lid.
4. Stir well and serve.

Nutritional Value (Amount per Serving):
Calories 164; Fat 2.3 g; Carbohydrates 10.9 g; Sugar 5.2 g; Protein 24.8 g

Delicious Adobo Shrimp

Preparation Time: 10 minutes; Cooking Time: 10 minutes; Serve: 4
Ingredients:
- 1 lb shrimps, peeled and deveined
- 1 tsp swerve
- 1 tbsp peppercorn
- 2 cups chicken stock
- 1 red chili pepper, chopped
- 1 onion, chopped
- 2 tbsp fish sauce
- 4 garlic cloves, crushed
- 2 tbsp green onion, chopped
- ¼ cup soy sauce
- ¼ cup vinegar
- ¼ cup olive oil
- 2 tsp salt

Directions:
1. In a large bowl, whisk together oil, swerve, peppercorn, chili pepper, onion, fish sauce, garlic, green onion, soy sauce, vinegar, and salt.
2. Add shrimp to the bowl and stir well. Cover bowl and place in refrigerator for 1 hour.
3. Add marinated shrimp into the instant pot with marinade and stir well.
4. Seal pot with lid and cook on high for 10 minutes.
5. Release pressure using quick release method than open the lid.
6. Stir well and serve.

Nutritional Value (Amount per Serving):
Calories 285; Fat 14.9 g; Carbohydrates 9.2 g; Sugar 2.3 g; Protein 28.4 g

Parmesan Salmon

Preparation Time: 10 minutes; Cooking Time: 5 minutes; Serve: 4
Ingredients:
- 1 lb salmon fillets, sliced in four pieces
- 1 tsp white pepper
- 2 cups chicken stock
- ¼ cup parmesan cheese, grated
- ¼ cup butter
- 2 fresh lemon juice
- 1 tsp salt

Directions:
1. Pour stock into the instant pot.
2. Drizzle salmon with fresh lemon juice and place into the instant pot steamer basket.
3. Season salmon with pepper and salt.
4. Seal pot with lid and cook on high for 5 minutes.
5. Release pressure using quick release method than open the lid.
6. Remove salmon from the pot and set aside.
7. Remove stock from the pot.
8. Add butter into the pot and set the pot on sauté mode.

9. Add salmon to the pot and cook for 2-3 minutes.
10. Sprinkle with grated cheese and serve.

Nutritional Value (Amount per Serving):
Calories 414; Fat 28g; Carbohydrates 1.2 g; Sugar 0.9 g; Protein 34.7 g

Mussels with Asparagus

Preparation Time: 10 minutes; Cooking Time: 5 minutes; Serve: 4
Ingredients:
- 1 lb mussels, cleaned
- 1 ½ tsp paprika
- ½ tsp garlic powder
- ½ tsp pepper
- 4 cups chicken stock
- 2 tsp fresh lemon juice
- 3 tbsp olive oil
- 1 bell pepper, chopped
- 1 cup sun-dried tomatoes
- 7 oz asparagus, cut into pieces
- 1 tsp sea salt

Directions:
1. Add oil into the instant pot and set the pot on sauté mode.
2. Add asparagus to the pot and sauté for 2-3 minutes.
3. Add mussels and sun-dried tomatoes. Season with paprika, garlic powder, pepper, and salt.
4. Cook on sauté for 4-5 minutes.
5. Add stock and bell pepper. Stir well.
6. Seal pot with lid and cook on high for 5 minutes.
7. Release pressure using quick release method than open the lid.
8. Serve and enjoy.

Nutritional Value (Amount per Serving):
Calories 230; Fat 14 g; Carbohydrates 11.7 g; Sugar 4.5 g; Protein 16.2 g

Bacon Lemon Pepper Shrimp

Preparation Time: 10 minutes; Cooking Time: 7 minutes; Serve: 5
Ingredients:
- 1 lb shrimp, peeled and deveined
- ¼ tsp chili powder
- 1 tsp old bay seasoning
- 1/8 tsp lemon pepper
- 5 cups chicken stock
- 2 tbsp soy sauce
- 6 tbsp butter
- 3 garlic cloves, crushed
- 1 onion, chopped
- 10 bacon slices, chopped

Directions:
1. Add butter into the instant pot and set the pot on sauté mode.
2. Add garlic and sauté for a minute.
3. Add remaining ingredients and stir well.
4. Seal pot with lid and cook on high for 5 minutes.
5. Allow to release pressure naturally then open the lid

6. Stir well and serve.

Nutritional Value (Amount per Serving):
Calories 461; Fat 31.9 g; Carbohydrates 5.9 g; Sugar 1.8 g; Protein 36.3 g

Teriyaki Shrimp

Preparation Time: 10 minutes; Cooking Time: 4 minutes; Serve: 4

Ingredients:
- 1 lb shrimp, peeled and deveined
- 2 tsp swerve
- 1 tsp garlic powder
- 1 tbsp fresh ginger, grated
- 1 cup chicken stock
- 2 tbsp olive oil
- 1 tbsp vinegar
- ¼ cup soy sauce
- 1 tsp sea salt

Directions:
1. Pour chicken stock and shrimp into the instant pot and stir well.
2. Seal pot with lid and cook on high for 4 minutes.
3. Release pressure using quick release method than open the lid.
4. Set pot on sauté mode. Once stock starts to boil then add vinegar, oil, and soy sauce, and stir well.
5. Sprinkle with ginger, garlic, swerve, and salt and cook for 10 minutes.
6. Serve and enjoy.

Nutritional Value (Amount per Serving):
Calories 216; Fat 9.2 g; Carbohydrates 5.6 g; Sugar 0.7 g; Protein 27.2 g

Ginger Garlic Fish Fillets

Preparation Time: 10 minutes; Cooking Time: 6 minutes; Serve: 2

Ingredients:
- 1 lb tilapia fillets, chopped
- 1 tsp garlic powder
- 1 tbsp ginger, grated
- 1 cup chicken stock
- 1 tbsp vinegar
- 3 tbsp soy sauce
- 2 tbsp olive oil
- 1 green onion, chopped
- ¼ cup celery, chopped
- 1 tsp sea salt

Directions:
1. In a large mixing bowl, whisk together oil, garlic powder, ginger, vinegar, soy sauce, and sea salt.
2. Add fish in a bowl and coat well with marinade. Cover bowl and place in refrigerator for 1 hour.
3. Add fish with marinade into the instant pot.
4. Add celery on top of fish.
5. Seal pot with lid and cook on high for 6 minutes.
6. Release pressure using quick release method than open the lid.

7. Stir well and serve.

Nutritional Value (Amount per Serving):
Calories 344; Fat 16.5 g; Carbohydrates 6.1 g; Sugar 1.6 g; Protein 44.8 g

Cauliflower Shrimp Risotto

Preparation Time: 10 minutes; Cooking Time: 6 minutes; Serve: 4

Ingredients:
- 1 lb fresh shrimp, peeled and deveined
- 2 tbsp parsley, chopped
- 2 tsp paprika
- ¼ cup butter
- 2 tbsp olive oil
- 2 garlic cloves, crushed
- ¾ cup chicken stock
- ¼ cup tomato puree, sugar-free
- 1 cup cherry tomatoes, chopped
- 2 cups cauliflower florets
- ½ tsp pepper
- 1 tsp salt

Directions:
1. Add oil into the instant pot and set the pot on sauté mode.
2. Add shrimp to the pot and sauté for 1-2 minutes.
3. Add tomatoes, garlic, and cauliflower. Stir well and season with pepper, paprika, and salt.
4. Add tomato puree and stock. Stir well.
5. Seal pot with lid and cook on high for 6 minutes.
6. Release pressure using quick release method than open the lid.
7. Garnish with parleys and serve.

Nutritional Value (Amount per Serving):
Calories 331; Fat 20.9 g; Carbohydrates 9.1 g; Sugar 3.4 g; Protein 28.1 g

Cheese Thyme Mussels

Preparation Time: 10 minutes; Cooking Time: 5 minutes; Serve: 4

Ingredients:
- 1 lb mussels, cleaned
- 2 tbsp parsley, chopped
- ½ tsp chili flakes
- 1 tsp dried thyme
- ¼ cup parmesan cheese, grated
- 3 tbsp butter
- 2 tbsp fresh lemon juice
- 4 garlic cloves, crushed
- 2 cups chicken stock

Directions:
1. Add butter into the instant pot and set the pot on sauté mode.
2. Add garlic and sauté for 2-3 minutes.
3. Add parsley, chili flakes, thyme, lemon juice, and stock to the pot and stir well.
4. Add mussels in the instant pot steamer basket and place basket in the pot.
5. Seal pot with lid and cook on high for 5 minutes.
6. Release pressure using quick release method than open the lid.
7. Serve and enjoy.

Nutritional Value (Amount per Serving):
Calories 224; Fat 13.8 g; Carbohydrates 6 g; Sugar 0.6 g; Protein 17.3 g

Lemon Butter Scallops

Preparation Time: 10 minutes; Cooking Time: 8 minutes; Serve: 4
Ingredients:
- 5 scallops
- ½ tsp white pepper
- ½ tsp garlic powder
- 1 tbsp fresh lemon juice
- 3 tbsp butter
- 2 tbsp olive oil
- 1 cup chicken stock
- ¼ cup apple cider vinegar
- 1 onion, chopped
- 1 tsp salt

Directions:
1. Add oil into the instant pot and set the pot on sauté mode.
2. Add onion to the pot and sauté for 3-4 minutes.
3. Add vinegar, stock, and scallops and stir well. Season with white pepper, garlic powder, and salt.
4. Seal pot with lid and cook on high for 8 minutes.
5. Release pressure using quick release method than open the lid.
6. Add lemon juice and butter and stir until butter is melted.
7. Serve and enjoy.

Nutritional Value (Amount per Serving):
Calories 189; Fat 16.1 g; Carbohydrates 4.3 g; Sugar 1.6 g; Protein 7 g

Creamy Celery Crabmeat

Preparation Time: 10 minutes; Cooking Time: 3 minutes; Serve: 4
Ingredients:
- 1 lb lump crabmeat
- ½ celery stalk, chopped
- ¼ cup butter
- ½ onion, chopped
- ¼ cup chicken stock
- ½ cup heavy cream

Directions:
1. Add butter into the instant pot and set the pot on sauté mode.
2. Add celery and onion and sauté for 4 minutes.
3. Add crab meat and stock. Stir well to combine.
4. Seal pot with lid and cook on high for 3 minutes.
5. Release pressure using quick release method than open the lid.
6. Add heavy cream and stir well.
7. Serve and enjoy.

Nutritional Value (Amount per Serving):
Calories 207; Fat 17.8 g; Carbohydrates 3.2 g; Sugar 2 g; Protein 9.9 g

Chapter 13: Vegan & Vegetarian Recipes

Cilantro Lime Cauliflower Rice

Preparation Time: 10 minutes; Cooking Time: 15 minutes; Serve: 4
Ingredients:
- 1 medium cauliflower head, cut into florets
- ¼ tsp paprika
- ¼ tsp turmeric
- ¼ tsp cumin
- ½ tsp dried parsley
- 2 tbsp olive oil
- ¼ tsp salt

Directions:
1. Pour 1 cup of water into the instant pot.
2. Add cauliflower florets into the instant pot steamer basket.
3. Seal pot with lid and cook on manual high pressure for 1 minute.
4. Release pressure using quick release method than open the lid.
5. Remove cauliflower from pot and place onto a dish.
6. Remove water from the instant pot.
7. Add olive oil into the pot and set the pot on sauté mode.
8. Add cooked cauliflower florets to the instant pot and stir well.
9. Using potato masher break cauliflower into the small pieces.
10. Add remaining ingredients and stir for 1-2 minutes.
11. Serve and enjoy.

Nutritional Value (Amount per Serving):
Calories 97; Fat 7.2 g; Carbohydrates 7.9 g; Sugar 3.5 g; Protein 2.9 g

Fried Cabbage

Preparation Time: 10 minutes; Cooking Time: 3 minutes; Serve: 6
Ingredients:
- 1 cabbage head, chopped
- ½ tsp chili powder
- 3 tbsp low sodium soy sauce
- ½ onion, diced
- ½ tsp paprika
- ½ tsp garlic salt
- 1 cup vegetable stock
- 2 tbsp olive oil
- ½ tsp salt

Directions:
1. Add olive oil into the instant pot and set the pot on sauté mode.
2. Add chopped cabbage into the instant pot and stir well.
3. Add remaining ingredients and stir well to combine.
4. Seal pot with lid and cook on high for 3 minutes.
5. Release pressure using quick release method.
6. Stir well and serve.

Nutritional Value (Amount per Serving):

Calories 82; Fat 5.2 g; Carbohydrates 9.3 g; Sugar 4.8 g; Protein 2.2 g

Flavors Southern Cabbage

Preparation Time: 10 minutes; Cooking Time: 10 minutes; Serve: 8
Ingredients:
- 1 cabbage head, chopped
- 1 cup vegetable broth
- 1 tbsp apple cider vinegar
- 1 bay leaf
- 5 thyme sprigs
- 1 tbsp garlic, minced
- 2 tbsp olive oil
- 1 ½ cups onions, sliced
- 1 tsp sea salt

Directions:
1. Add oil into the instant pot and set the pot on sauté mode.
2. Add onion to the pan and sauté for 2-3 minutes.
3. Add vinegar, bay leaf, thyme, and garlic and stir well.
4. Add cabbage, broth, and salt to the pot and stir to mix.
5. Seal pot with lid and cook on high pressure for 3 minutes.
6. Release pressure using quick release method than open the lid.
7. Discard thyme and bay leaf.
8. Serve and enjoy.

Nutritional Value (Amount per Serving):
Calories 68; Fat 3.8 g; Carbohydrates 7.7 g; Sugar 3.9 g; Protein 2.1 g

Parmesan Lemon Butter Brussel Sprouts

Preparation Time: 5 minutes; Cooking Time: 6 minutes; Serve: 4
Ingredients:
- 1 lb Brussels sprouts, trimmed and washed
- 1 lemon juice
- 2 tbsp butter
- 1 cup water
- ¼ cup parmesan cheese, grated

Directions:
1. Pour water into the instant pot.
2. Add Brussels sprouts into the instant pot steamer basket.
3. Seal pot with lid and cook on high for 2 minutes.
4. Release pressure using quick release method than open the lid.
5. Remove Brussels sprouts from instant pot and place on a dish.
6. Drain water from the pot.
7. Add butter into the instant pot and set the pot on sauté mode.
8. Add cooked Brussels sprouts and lemon juice and sauté until browned.
9. Garnish with parmesan cheese and serve.

Nutritional Value (Amount per Serving):
Calories 253; Fat 15.2 g; Carbohydrates 10.6 g; Sugar 2.7 g; Protein 16 g

Creamy Cheese Brussels sprouts

Preparation Time: 10 minutes; Cooking Time: 2 minutes; Serve: 5
Ingredients:
- 1 lb Brussels sprouts, trim and rinse
- 1/3 cup parmesan cheese, grated
- 3 oz cream cheese
- 2 garlic cloves, minced
- ¾ cup vegetable broth
- ¼ tsp pepper
- 1 tbsp butter

Directions:
1. Add all ingredients except parmesan cheese into the instant pot and stir well.
2. Seal pot with lid and cook on high pressure for 2 minutes.
3. Release pressure using quick release method than open the lid.
4. Add parmesan cheese and stir well.
5. Serve and enjoy.

Nutritional Value (Amount per Serving):
Calories 167; Fat 11.2 g; Carbohydrates 9.3 g; Sugar 2.1 g; Protein 8.4 g

Artichoke Spinach Dip

Preparation Time: 10 minutes; Cooking Time: 10 minutes; Serve: 6
Ingredients:
- 10 oz frozen spinach, chopped
- 1 tsp Worcestershire sauce
- 14 oz can artichoke hearts, drained and chopped
- 1 cup mozzarella cheese, shredded
- ½ cup parmesan cheese, grated
- 8 oz cream cheese, cut into cubes
- ½ cup onion, chopped
- 2 garlic cloves, minced
- Pepper
- Salt

Directions:
1. Add all ingredients into the large mixing bowl and mix until well combined.
2. Transfer bowl mixture into the baking dish and cover with aluminum foil.
3. Pour 1 cup water into the instant pot and place trivet in the pot.
4. Place dish on top of the trivet.
5. Seal pot with lid and cook on high pressure for 10 minutes.
6. Release pressure using quick release method than open the lid.
7. Remove dish carefully from the instant pot.
8. Uncover the dish. Stir well and serve.

Nutritional Value (Amount per Serving):
Calories 232; Fat 17.2 g; Carbohydrates 7.6 g; Sugar 1.4 g; Protein 10.8 g

Spinach Cheese Dip

Preparation Time: 10 minutes; Cooking Time: 5 minutes; Serve: 8
Ingredients:
- 1 lb fresh spinach
- 1 tsp onion powder
- 1 cup mozzarella cheese, shredded
- 8 oz cream cheese, cubed
- ½ cup mayonnaise
- ½ cup sour cream
- ½ cup vegetable broth
- 1 tbsp olive oil
- 3 garlic cloves, minced
- ¼ tsp pepper
- ½ tsp salt

Directions:
1. Add oil into the instant pot and set the pot on sauté mode.
2. Add spinach and garlic to the pot and sauté until cooked. Drain excess liquid.
3. Add remaining ingredients to the pot and stir well.
4. Seal pot with lid and cook on high pressure for 4 minutes.
5. Release pressure using quick release method than open the lid.
6. Stir well and serve.

Nutritional Value (Amount per Serving):
Calories 230; Fat 20.5 g; Carbohydrates 7.8 g; Sugar 1.4 g; Protein 5.8 g

Creamy Ranch Cauliflower Mashed

Preparation Time: 10 minutes; Cooking Time: 15 minutes; Serve: 4
Ingredients:
- 1 head cauliflower, cut into florets
- 2 tbsp cream
- 4 tbsp butter
- 3 tbsp dry ranch dressing mix
- 1 cup water

Directions:
1. Pour water into the instant pot.
2. Add cauliflower florets into the instant pot steamer basket.
3. Seal pot with lid and cook on high pressure for 15 minutes.
4. Release pressure using quick release method than open the lid.
5. Remove cauliflower florets from pot and place into the large mixing bowl.
6. Add remaining ingredients into the bowl and mash cauliflower using the potato masher until smooth and creamy.
7. Serve and enjoy.

Nutritional Value (Amount per Serving):
Calories 126; Fat 12 g; Carbohydrates 4.3 g; Sugar 2 g; Protein 1.6 g

Garlic Cheese Artichokes

Preparation Time: 10 minutes; Cooking Time: 10 minutes; Serve: 4
Ingredients:
- 4 artichokes, wash and trim
- ½ cup vegetable stock
- ¼ cup parmesan cheese, grated
- 4 tsp olive oil
- 2 tsp garlic, minced

Directions:
1. Discard top of artichoke and stem and outer leaves.
2. Top each artichoke with garlic and drizzle with oil.
3. Sprinkle each artichoke with grated cheese.
4. Place artichoke into the instant pot insert. Pour in ½ cup water.
5. Seal pot with lid and cook on steam mode and set the timer for 10 minutes.
6. Release pressure using quick release method than open the lid.
7. Serve and enjoy.

Nutritional Value (Amount per Serving):
Calories 93; Fat 6.2 g; Carbohydrates 6.7 g; Sugar 1.1 g; Protein 4.6 g

Cheese Garlic Asparagus

Preparation Time: 10 minutes; Cooking Time: 8 minutes; Serve: 4
Ingredients:
- 15 asparagus spears
- 3 tbsp parmesan cheese, grated
- 3 tbsp butter
- 1 cup water
- 2 garlic cloves, minced

Directions:
1. Pour 1 cup of water into the instant pot then place trivet into the pot.
2. Place asparagus spears on a piece of aluminum foil with butter and garlic. Curve the all the edges of foil.
3. Place asparagus with foil on top of the trivet.
4. Seal pot with lid and cook on high pressure for 8 minutes.
5. Release pressure using quick release method than open the lid.
6. Sprinkle with grated cheese and serve.

Nutritional Value (Amount per Serving):
Calories 94; Fat 9 g; Carbohydrates 2.5 g; Sugar 0.9 g; Protein 1.7 g

Delicious Cajun Zucchini

Preparation Time: 10 minutes; Cooking Time: 1 minute; Serve: 4
Ingredients:
- 4 zucchinis, sliced
- 1 tsp garlic powder

- 1 tsp paprika
- 2 tbsp Cajun seasoning
- ½ cup water
- 1 tbsp butter

Directions:
1. Add all ingredients into the instant pot and stir well.
2. Seal pot with lid and cook on low pressure for 1 minute.
3. Release pressure using quick release method than open the lid.
4. Stir well and serve.

Nutritional Value (Amount per Serving):
Calories 61; Fat 3.3 g; Carbohydrates 7.4 g; Sugar 3.6 g; Protein 2.7 g

Perfect Herbed Carrots

Preparation Time: 10 minutes; Cooking Time: 18 minutes; Serve: 4
Ingredients:
- 1 lb baby carrots
- ½ tsp oregano
- ½ tsp thyme
- 1 tsp garlic powder
- 2 tbsp butter
- 1 cup water
- Pepper
- Salt

Directions:
1. Pour 1 cup of water into the instant pot.
2. Add baby carrots into the instant pot steamer basket.
3. Seal pot with lid and select steam mode and set timer for 2 minutes.
4. Release pressure using quick release method than open the lid.
5. Transfer carrots on the plate and remove instant pot water.
6. Add butter into the pot and set the pot on sauté mode.
7. Add steamed carrots in the pot with remaining ingredients and cook for 2-3 minutes.
8. Stir well and serve.

Nutritional Value (Amount per Serving):
Calories 94; Fat 6 g; Carbohydrates 10.1 g; Sugar 5.6 g; Protein 0.9 g

Cheese Zucchini Noodles

Preparation Time: 10 minutes; Cooking Time: 5 minutes; Serve: 2
Ingredients:
- 2 zucchinis, spiralized into noodles
- 4 tbsp parmesan cheese, grated
- 1 tbsp mint, sliced
- 1/3 fresh lemon juice
- ½ lemon zest
- 2 garlic cloves, chopped
- 2 tbsp olive oil
- ½ tsp sea salt

Directions:
1. Add oil into the instant pot and set the pot on sauté mode.
2. Add lemon zest, garlic, and salt in the pot and stir for 30 seconds.
3. Add zucchini noodles and lemon juice and sauté for 20-30 seconds.

4. Once zucchini noodles are warmed then sprinkle parmesan cheese and mint leaves on top.
5. Stir well and serve.

Nutritional Value (Amount per Serving):
Calories 234; Fat 19 g; Carbohydrates 8 g; Sugar 3.6 g; Protein 8.7 g

Lemon Garlic Kale

Preparation Time: 10 minutes; Cooking Time: 5 minutes; Serve: 4
Ingredients:
- 1 lb kale, wash and stems trimmed
- ½ lemon juice
- ½ cup water
- 3 garlic cloves, sliced
- 1 tbsp olive oil
- ½ tsp kosher salt

Directions:
1. Add oil into the instant pot and set the pot on sauté mode.
2. Add garlic sauté for 30 seconds.
3. Add kale, salt, and water into the pot and stir well.
4. Seal pot with lid and cook on high pressure for 5 minutes.
5. Release pressure using quick release method than open the lid.
6. Add lemon juice and pepper. Stir well.
7. Serve and enjoy.

Nutritional Value (Amount per Serving):
Calories 91; Fat 3.6 g; Carbohydrates 12 g; Sugar 0.1 g; Protein 3.6 g

Garlicky Green Beans

Preparation Time: 10 minutes; Cooking Time: 5 minutes; Serve: 4
Ingredients:
- 1 lb fresh green beans
- 1 cup water
- 1 garlic clove, minced
- 2 tbsp butter
- Pepper
- Salt

Directions:
1. Add all ingredients into the instant pot and stir well.
2. Seal pot with lid and cook on low pressure for 5 minutes.
3. Release pressure using quick release method than open the lid.
4. Stir well and serve.

Nutritional Value (Amount per Serving):
Calories 87; Fat 5.9 g; Carbohydrates 8.4 g; Sugar 1.6 g; Protein 2.2 g

Coconut Green Beans

Preparation Time: 10 minutes; Cooking Time: 5 minutes; Serve: 4
Ingredients:

- 4 cups green beans, chopped
- 2 tbsp fresh coconut, grated
- ¼ tsp turmeric
- 2 garlic cloves, minced
- ¼ cup onion, chopped
- 2 green chilies, chopped
- 3-4 curry leaves
- ¼ tsp mustard seeds
- 2 tbsp coconut oil
- Salt

Directions:
1. Add oil into the instant pot and set the pot on sauté mode.
2. Once the oil is hot then add mustard seeds and sauté until mustard seeds pop up.
3. Add curry leaves and green chilies and sauté for 20 seconds.
4. Add garlic and onion and sauté until onion is softened.
5. Add beans, turmeric, and salt. Stir well.
6. Add grated coconut and stir well.
7. Seal pot with lid and cook on low for 1 minute.
8. Release pressure using quick release method than open the lid.
9. Stir well and serve.

Nutritional Value (Amount per Serving):
Calories 108; Fat 7.9 g; Carbohydrates 9.6 g; Sugar 2 g; Protein 2.3 g

Spicy Eggplant

Preparation Time: 10 minutes; Cooking Time: 15 minutes; Serve: 4
Ingredients:
- 1 eggplant, cut into cubes
- ½ cup water
- ¼ cup tomato paste
- ½ tsp Italian seasoning
- 1 tsp paprika
- ½ tsp red pepper
- 1 tsp garlic powder
- 2 tbsp olive oil
- 1 tsp salt

Directions:
1. Pour ½ cup of water into the instant pot.
2. Add eggplant into the instant pot steamer basket.
3. Seal pot with lid and cook on high pressure for 5 minutes.
4. Release pressure using quick release method than open the lid.
5. Remove eggplant from the pot and drain all liquid from the pot.
6. Add olive oil into the instant pot and set the pot on sauté mode.
7. Add tomato paste, Italian seasoning, paprika, red pepper, and garlic powder to the pot and sauté for 3-4 minutes.
8. Add cooked eggplant pieces to pot and stir well. Season with salt.
9. Cook for 5 minutes more on sauté mode.
10. Serve and enjoy.

Nutritional Value (Amount per Serving):
Calories 114; Fat 7.5 g; Carbohydrates 11.7 g; Sugar 6 g; Protein 2 g

Balsamic Garlic Mushrooms

Preparation Time: 10 minutes; Cooking Time: 6 minutes; Serve: 4
Ingredients:
- 1 lb fresh mushrooms, sliced
- 3 garlic cloves, minced
- 1/3 cup olive oil
- 3 tbsp white wine
- Pepper
- Salt

Directions:
1. Add oil into the instant pot and set the pot on sauté mode
2. Add garlic and mushrooms to the pot and sauté for 2-3 minutes.
3. Add vinegar and white wine. Stir well and cook for 1-2 minutes.
4. Season with pepper and salt.
5. Serve and enjoy.

Nutritional Value (Amount per Serving):
Calories 181; Fat 17.1 g; Carbohydrates 4.8 g; Sugar 2.1 g; Protein 3.7 g

Easy Herbed Mushrooms

Preparation Time: 10 minutes; Cooking Time: 3 hours 10 minutes; Serve: 4
Ingredients:
- 28 oz cremini mushrooms
- 2 tbsp parsley, chopped
- 2 tbsp butter
- ¼ cup half and half
- 1 cup vegetable stock
- 1 bay leaf
- ¼ tsp dried thyme
- ½ tsp dried oregano
- ½ tsp dried basil
- 3 garlic cloves, minced
- Pepper
- Salt

Directions:
1. Add mushrooms, bay leaf, thyme, oregano, basil, and garlic into the instant pot.
2. Add stock, pepper, and salt to the pot and stir well.
3. Seal pot with lid and select slow cooker mode and cook on low for 3 hours.
4. Add butter and half and half. Stir well.
5. Set pot on sauté mode and cook for 10 minutes.
6. Garnish with parsley and serve.

Nutritional Value (Amount per Serving):
Calories 132; Fat 8.3 g; Carbohydrates 10.4 g; Sugar 4 g; Protein 5.7 g

Mushroom with Green Beans

Preparation Time: 10 minutes; Cooking Time: 10 minutes; Serve: 4
Ingredients:

- 1 lb green beans, washed and trimmed
- 1 tsp balsamic vinegar
- 1 garlic clove, minced
- 8 oz mushrooms, sliced
- ½ onion, diced
- 2 tbsp olive oil
- Pepper
- Salt

Directions:
1. Pour ½ cup of water into the instant pot.
2. Add green beans into the instant pot steamer basket.
3. Seal pot with lid and cook on high pressure for 1 minute.
4. Release pressure using quick release method than open the lid.
5. Remove beans from pot and place on a plate. Drain all liquid from the pot.
6. Add olive oil into the pot and set the pot on sauté mode.
7. Add garlic and onion to the pot and sauté for 1-2 minutes.
8. Add sliced mushrooms and sauté until softened.
9. Add cooked garlic beans, balsamic vinegar, pepper, and salt. Stir well.
10. Serve and enjoy.

Nutritional Value (Amount per Serving):
Calories 114; Fat 7.3 g; Carbohydrates 11 g; Sugar 3.2 g; Protein 4 g

Stir Fried Cabbage

Preparation Time: 10 minutes; Cooking Time: 10 minutes; Serve: 4
Ingredients:
- 6 cups red cabbage, sliced
- 1 cup water
- 2 garlic cloves, minced
- 1 onion, chopped
- 1 tbsp olive oil
- 1 tbsp apple cider vinegar
- 1/2 cup unsweetened applesauce
- Pepper
- Salt

Directions:
1. Add oil in instant pot and set the pot on sauté mode.
2. Add onion and garlic and sauté for 2 minutes.
3. Add remaining ingredients and stir well.
4. Seal pot with lid and cook on high for 10 minutes.
5. Release pressure using quick release method than open lid carefully.
6. Stir well and serve.

Nutritional Value (Amount per Serving):
Calories 83; Fat 3.7 g; Carbohydrates 12.7 g; Sugar 7.7 g; Protein 1.8 g

Healthy Beets Salad

Preparation Time: 10 minutes; Cooking Time: 20 minutes; Serve: 8
Ingredients:
- 1 ½ lbs beetroots
- ¼ tsp black pepper

- ¼ cup balsamic vinegar
- ¼ cup olive oil
- ½ tsp dried oregano
- ½ tsp dill
- 1 tsp parsley, chopped
- ¼ tsp sea salt

Directions:
1. Pour 2 cups water into the instant pot then place a trivet in the pot.
2. Place beetroots on top of the trivet.
3. Seal pot with lid and cook on high for 15 minutes.
4. Release pressure using quick release method than open the lid.
5. Remove beets from the pot and set aside to cool completely.
6. Remove the skin of beetroots.
7. Cut beetroot into the small pieces and place in a large bowl.
8. Add remaining ingredients to the bowl and mix well.
9. Serve and enjoy.

Nutritional Value (Amount per Serving):
Calories 93; Fat 6.5 g; Carbohydrates 8.6 g; Sugar 6.8 g; Protein 1.4 g

Broccoli Garlic Mash

Preparation Time: 10 minutes; Cooking Time: 5 minutes; Serve: 4

Ingredients:
- 1 lb broccoli, chopped
- ¼ tsp red pepper flakes
- 4 oz cream cheese
- ½ cup water
- 2 garlic cloves, crushed
- 1 tbsp butter
- ¼ tsp pepper
- ¼ tsp salt

Directions:
1. Add butter into the pot and set the pot on sauté mode.
2. Add garlic and sauté for 30 seconds.
3. Add remaining ingredients and stir well.
4. Seal pot with lid and cook on high for 1 minute.
5. Release pressure using quick release method than open the lid.
6. Mash the broccoli mixture using potato masher until smooth.
7. Season with pepper and salt.
8. Serve and enjoy.

Nutritional Value (Amount per Serving):
Calories 302; Fat 26 g; Carbohydrates 7 g; Sugar 2.3 g; Protein 7 g

Asian Bok Choy

Preparation Time: 10 minutes; Cooking Time: 4 minutes; Serve: 4

Ingredients:
- 1 medium Bok Choy head, leaves separated
- 2 tsp sesame seeds
- ½ tsp sesame oil

- 1 tsp soy sauce
- 1 cup water
- Pepper
- Salt

Directions:
1. Pour water into the pot and place steamer basket on top.
2. Add bok choy into the steamer basket.
3. Seal pot with lid and cook on high for 4 minutes.
4. Release pressure using quick release method than open the lid.
5. Transfer boy choy to a bowl and toss with remaining ingredients.
6. Serve and enjoy.

Nutritional Value (Amount per Serving):
Calories 27; Fat 1.6 g; Carbohydrates 2.7 g; Sugar 0.5 g; Protein 1.9 g

Nutritious Beets with Cheese

Preparation Time: 10 minutes; Cooking Time: 20 minutes; Serve: 4
Ingredients:
- 4 medium beets
- ½ lemon juice
- ½ cup goat cheese, crumbled
- 1 cup water
- 1 tbsp olive oil
- Pepper
- Salt

Directions:
1. Pour 2 cups of water into the instant pot then place the steamer basket on top.
2. Add beets in the steamer basket.
3. Seal pot with lid and cook on high for 20 minutes.
4. Release pressure using quick release method than open the lid.
5. Remove beets from the pot and set aside to cool completely.
6. Cut beets into the small pieces and place in large bowl.
7. Add remaining ingredients to the bowl and toss well.
8. Serve and enjoy.

Nutritional Value (Amount per Serving):
Calories 115; Fat 6.2 g; Carbohydrates 10.3 g; Sugar 8.1 g; Protein 3.7 g

Steamed Garlic Broccoli

Preparation Time: 5 minutes; Cooking Time: 1 minute; Serve: 2
Ingredients:
- 3 cups broccoli head, cut into florets
- 1 cup water
- 2 garlic cloves, peeled and crushed
- Pepper
- Salt

Directions:
1. Pour 1 cup of water into the instant pot.
2. Add all ingredients into the instant pot steamer basket and place in the pot.

3. Seal pot with lid and cook on low for 1 minute.
4. Release pressure using quick release method than open the lid.
5. Serve and enjoy.

Nutritional Value (Amount per Serving):
Calories 51; Fat 0.5 g; Carbohydrates 10.1 g; Sugar 2.4 g; Protein 4 g

Tomato Green Beans

Preparation Time: 10 minutes; Cooking Time: 3 minutes; Serve: 6

Ingredients:
- 14 oz can tomato, crushed
- 1 ½ lbs green beans, trimmed
- ½ cup vegetable stock
- 3 garlic cloves, sliced
- 2 tbsp olive oil
- ¼ cup fresh basil
- Pepper
- Salt

Directions:
1. Add oil into the instant pot and set the pot on sauté mode.
2. Add garlic and sauté until lightly golden.
3. Add tomatoes, green beans, stock, pepper, and salt. Stir well.
4. Seal pot with lid and cook on low for 3 minutes.
5. Allow to release pressure naturally then open the lid.
6. Add basil and stir well.
7. Serve and enjoy.

Nutritional Value (Amount per Serving):
Calories 93; Fat 5.2 g; Carbohydrates 12.3 g; Sugar 4.2 g; Protein 2.8 g

Delicious Parmesan Broccoli

Preparation Time: 10 minutes; Cooking Time: 2 minutes; Serve: 6

Ingredients:
- 1 ½ lbs broccoli, cut into florets
- ½ cup parmesan cheese, grated
- ½ cup vegetable stock
- ¼ tsp red pepper flakes
- 4 garlic cloves, minced
- ¼ cup olive oil
- Pepper
- Salt

Directions:
1. Add oil into the instant pot and set the pot on sauté mode.
2. Add red pepper flakes and garlic and sauté for 30 seconds.
3. Add broccoli and stock and stir well.
4. Seal pot with lid and cook o low for 2 minutes.
5. Release pressure using quick release method than open the lid.
6. Set pot on sauté mode and cook until liquid is thickened.
7. Add parmesan cheese and stir well. Season with pepper and salt.
8. Serve and enjoy.

Nutritional Value (Amount per Serving):
Calories 166; Fat 12.1 g; Carbohydrates 8.6 g; Sugar 2.3 g; Protein 7.3 g

Healthy Butternut Squash

Preparation Time: 10 minutes; Cooking Time: 5 minutes; Serve: 6
Ingredients:
- 2 lbs butternut squash, cubed
- ¼ cup heavy cream
- 1 tsp fresh thyme, minced
- 2 tbsp butter
- Pepper
- Salt

Directions:
1. Pour 2 cups of water into the instant pot then place steamer basket in the pot.
2. Add squash into the steamer basket.
3. Seal pot with lid and cook on high for 5 minutes.
4. Allow to release pressure naturally then open the lid.
5. Transfer squash to a bowl and mash using masher until smooth.
6. Add remaining ingredients to the bowl and stir well to combine.
7. Serve and enjoy.

Nutritional Value (Amount per Serving):
Calories 65; Fat 5.7 g; Carbohydrates 3.9 g; Sugar 0.7 g; Protein 0.5 g

Healthy Sautéed Veggies

Preparation Time: 10 minutes; Cooking Time: 10 minutes; Serve: 3
Ingredients:
- ¼ cup dried mushrooms
- 1 onion, sliced
- 1 small zucchini, cut into cubes
- 2 bell pepper, sliced
- ¼ tsp dried oregano
- ½ tsp dried thyme
- 2 tbsp olive oil
- 2 tbsp tamari sauce
- ½ cup sour cream
- ¼ cup feta cheese
- 1 tsp sea salt

Directions:
1. Add oil into the instant pot and set the pot on sauté mode.
2. Add zucchini and sauté for 5-6 minutes.
3. Add onion and bell peppers. Season with salt.
4. Add tamari sauce and stir well.
5. Add oregano, thyme, and salt and cook for 2-3 minutes.
6. Add mushrooms and feta cheese and cook for 3-4 minutes.
7. Turn off the instant pot sauté mode.
8. Add sour cream and stir well.
9. Serve and enjoy.

Nutritional Value (Amount per Serving):

Calories 251; Fat 20.4 g; Carbohydrates 13 g; Sugar 7.1 g; Protein 6.1 g

Spinach with Cheese

Preparation Time: 10 minutes; Cooking Time: 6 minutes; Serve: 4
Ingredients:
- 3 cups spinach, chopped
- 2 tbsp parmesan cheese, grated
- ½ cup yogurt
- ½ cup feta cheese, crumbled
- 4 tbsp olive oil
- 2 garlic cloves, crushed
- 1 medium onion, chopped
- 1 leek, chopped
- 1 cup kale, chopped
- ½ tsp dried mint
- ½ tsp salt

Directions:
1. Add oil into the instant pot and set the pot on sauté mode.
2. Add leek and onion and sauté for 3-4 minutes.
3. Add garlic and sauté for a minute.
4. Add kale and spinach. Season with mint and salt and cook until spinach wilted.
5. Add feta cheese and half yogurt. Stir well and cook for 3 minutes.
6. Sprinkle with parmesan cheese and top with remaining yogurt.
7. Serve and enjoy.

Nutritional Value (Amount per Serving):
Calories 241; Fat 19.1 g; Carbohydrates 11.7 g; Sugar 5.1 g; Protein 7 g

Greens with Tofu

Preparation Time: 10 minutes; Cooking Time: 10 minutes; Serve: 4
Ingredients:
- 1 lb collard greens, chopped
- ¼ tsp red chili flakes
- ½ tsp paprika
- 2 tsp balsamic vinegar
- 1 tbsp butter
- 2 tsp olive oil
- 1 cup vegetable stock
- ¼ cup walnuts, chopped
- 3 garlic cloves, chopped
- 1 cup tofu, cut into cubes
- ¼ tsp pepper
- ½ tsp sea salt

Directions:
1. Add oil into the instant pot and set the pot on sauté mode.
2. Add tofu, garlic, pepper, and salt and sauté for 2-3 minutes. Remove from pot and set aside.
3. Add butter and collard green and cook for 2-3 minutes.
4. Add stock, chili flakes, paprika, and salt. Stir well.
5. Seal pot with lid and cook on high for 2 minutes.
6. Release pressure using quick release method than open the lid.
7. Add walnuts and vinegar and stir well.

8. Transfer collard greens on serving plate and top with tofu.
9. Serve and enjoy.

Nutritional Value (Amount per Serving):
Calories 176; Fat 13.8 g; Carbohydrates 9.6 g; Sugar 1 g; Protein 9.8 g

Creamy Basil Broccoli

Preparation Time: 10 minutes; Cooking Time: 10 minutes; Serve: 4
Ingredients:
- 1 lb broccoli, chopped
- ¼ tsp dried oregano
- ¼ tsp dried parsley
- 1 tbsp fresh lemon juice
- 1 tbsp olive oil
- 2 garlic cloves, peeled
- ½ cup avocado, chopped
- ½ cup cottage cheese
- ½ cup fresh basil, chopped
- ½ tsp red pepper
- 1 tsp salt

Directions:
1. Pour 1 cup of water into the instant pot.
2. Add broccoli into the steamer basket and place in the pot.
3. Season broccoli with pepper and salt.
4. Seal pot with lid and select steam mode and cook for 10 minutes.
5. Meanwhile, add basil, oregano, parsley, red pepper, lemon juice, olive oil, garlic, avocado, and cottage cheese in a food processor and process until smooth.
6. Once instant pot timer is over then allow to release pressure naturally then open the lid.
7. Transfer broccoli to a serving plate and top with basil mixture.
8. Serve and enjoy.

Nutritional Value (Amount per Serving):
Calories 136; Fat 8.1 g; Carbohydrates 11 g; Sugar 2.2 g; Protein 7.7 g

Lime Sauce Mushrooms

Preparation Time: 10 minutes; Cooking Time: 10 minutes; Serve: 4
Ingredients:
- 1 lb Portobello mushrooms, sliced
- 1 tsp apple cider vinegar
- 1 tsp fresh ginger, grated
- 1 tbsp butter
- 1 cup heavy cream
- 1 tsp lime zest
- 1 fresh lime juice
- 1 small onion, chopped
- 3 garlic cloves, minced
- 1 tsp pepper
- 1 tsp sea salt

Directions:
1. Add garlic, pepper, vinegar, ginger, heavy cream, lime juice, onion, and onion to the food processor and process until smooth. Set aside.
2. Add butter into the instant pot and set the pot on sauté mode.

3. Add mushrooms to the pot and sauté for 5 minutes. Remove mushrooms from pot and place on a plate. Set aside.
4. Pour blended mixture into the pot and cook on sauté mode 4-5 minutes.
5. Turn off the sauté mode of the instant pot.
6. Place mushrooms on a plate and drizzle with sauce.
7. Garnish with lime zest and serve.

Nutritional Value (Amount per Serving):
Calories 178; Fat 14.1 g; Carbohydrates 8.1 g; Sugar 1 g; Protein 4.4 g

Stir Fried Leek Swiss chard

Preparation Time: 10 minutes; Cooking Time: 10 minutes; Serve: 4
Ingredients:
- 2 cups Swiss chard, chopped
- ¼ tsp cayenne pepper
- 2 tbsp parmesan cheese, grated
- ½ cup cream cheese
- 1 tbsp olive oil
- 2 garlic cloves, chopped
- 1 small onion, chopped
- 2 cups leeks, chopped
- ½ tsp pepper
- 1 tsp sea salt

Directions:
1. Add oil into the instant pot and set the pot on sauté mode.
2. Add garlic and onion to the pot and sauté for 5 minutes.
3. Add greens and season with cayenne, pepper, and salt. Stir for 10-12 minutes.
4. Add parmesan cheese and cream cheese and cook for 2-3 minutes.
5. Serve and enjoy.

Nutritional Value (Amount per Serving):
Calories 191; Fat 15 g; Carbohydrates 10.1 g; Sugar 2.8g; Protein 5 g

Stir Fried Broccoli Cauliflower

Preparation Time: 10 minutes; Cooking Time: 13 minutes; Serve: 3
Ingredients:
- 1 cup broccoli, chopped
- 2 cups cauliflower, chopped
- ¼ tsp onion powder
- ¼ tsp red pepper flakes
- 2 eggs
- 1 tbsp olive oil
- 2 garlic cloves, chopped
- ¼ tsp pepper
- ½ tsp salt

Directions:
1. Add oil into the instant pot and set the pot on sauté mode.
2. Add broccoli and cauliflower to the pot and sauté for 2 minutes. Season with onion powder, red pepper flakes, pepper, and salt.
3. Add ¼ cup of water and cook on sauté mode for 5 minutes.
4. Add the egg on top and season with salt. Cook for 2-3 minutes.

5. Serve and enjoy.

Nutritional Value (Amount per Serving):
Calories 114; Fat 7.8 g; Carbohydrates 6.8 g; Sugar 2.5 g; Protein 6.1 g

Asian Mushroom Curry

Preparation Time: 10 minutes; Cooking Time: 27 minutes; Serve: 4

Ingredients:
- 3 cups mushrooms, sliced
- ¼ cup yogurt
- ½ cup unsweetened coconut milk
- ¼ tsp chili powder
- ¼ tsp turmeric powder
- ¼ tsp cumin powder
- ¼ tsp coriander powder
- ½ tsp garlic, minced
- Salt

Directions:
1. In a baking dish add all ingredients and stir until well combined.
2. Pour 1 cup of water into the instant pot then place a trivet in the pot.
3. Place dish on top of the trivet.
4. Seal pot with lid and cook on high for 27 minutes.
5. Allow to release pressure naturally then open the lid.
6. Serve and enjoy.

Nutritional Value (Amount per Serving):
Calories 93; Fat 7.6 g; Carbohydrates 4.8 g; Sugar 3 g; Protein 3.3 g

Cauliflower Mac & Cheese

Preparation Time: 10 minutes; Cooking Time: 5 minutes; Serve: 4

Ingredients:
- 2 cups cauliflower, grated
- 2 tbsp cream cheese
- ½ cup half and half
- ½ cup cheddar cheese, shredded
- Pepper
- Salt

Directions:
1. Add all ingredients into the baking dish and stir to combine.
2. Cover dish with aluminum foil.
3. Pour 1 ½ cups of water into the instant pot then place a trivet in the pot.
4. Place baking dish on top of the trivet.
5. Seal pot with lid and cook on low for 5 minutes.
6. Preheat the broiler.
7. Remove dish from the instant pot and uncover the dish.
8. Place dish in preheated broiler and broil for 2-3 minutes.
9. Serve and enjoy.

Nutritional Value (Amount per Serving):
Calories 126; Fat 10 g; Carbohydrates 4.3 g; Sugar 1.3 g; Protein 5.8 g

Chili Turmeric Cauliflower

Preparation Time: 10 minutes; Cooking Time: 7 minutes; Serve: 4
Ingredients:
- 1 small cauliflower head, cut into florets
- 1 tbsp fresh cilantro, chopped
- ½ cup water
- ½ tsp paprika
- ½ tsp turmeric
- 1 tsp ground cumin
- 1 tsp olive oil
- 1 green chili, chopped
- ½ small onion, chopped
- 2 tomatoes, chopped
- Pepper
- Salt

Directions:
1. Add tomato, green chili, and onion to the food processor and process until smooth.
2. Add oil into the instant pot and set the pot on sauté mode.
3. Add blended tomato mixture to the pot and sauté for 2-3 minutes.
4. Add spices and stir for a minute.
5. Add cauliflower and water and stir well.
6. Seal pot with lid and cook on low for 2-3 minutes.
7. Release pressure using quick release method than open the lid.
8. Serve and enjoy.

Nutritional Value (Amount per Serving):
Calories 45; Fat 1.6 g; Carbohydrates 7.3 g; Sugar 3.6 g; Protein 2.1 g

Yogurt Butter Cauliflower Mash

Preparation Time: 10 minutes; Cooking Time: 3 minutes; Serve: 8
Ingredients:
- 1 cauliflower head, chopped
- 2 tbsp fresh chives, chopped
- 2 tsp butter, melted
- 2 tbsp yogurt
- ½ cup vegetable broth
- Pepper
- Salt

Directions:
1. Pour broth into the instant pot and place steamer basket in the pot.
2. Add cauliflower into the steamer basket.
3. Seal pot with lid and cook on high for 3 minutes.
4. Release pressure using quick release method than open the lid.
5. Transfer cauliflower into the food processor along with yogurt, pepper and salt and process until smooth.
6. Drizzle with butter and garnish with chives.
7. Serve and enjoy.

Nutritional Value (Amount per Serving):

Calories 22; Fat 1.1 g; Carbohydrates 2.1 g; Sugar 1.1 g; Protein 1.2 g

Almond Cheese Broccoli

Preparation Time: 10 minutes; Cooking Time: 10 minutes; Serve: 3
Ingredients:
- 2 cups broccoli florets
- ½ tbsp paprika
- 2 tsp garlic powder
- 1 tbsp olive oil
- Pepper
- Salt
- For sauce:
- 1 tsp garlic powder
- 1 cup cheddar cheese, shredded
- ½ cup unsweetened almond milk
- 2 tbsp almond flour
- 3 tbsp butter
- Salt

Directions:
1. Add broccoli, 2 tsp garlic powder, paprika, oil, pepper, and salt to the large bowl and toss well.
2. Pour 1 cup of water into the instant pot and place steamer basket in the pot.
3. Add broccoli into the steamer basket.
4. Seal pot with lid and cook on low for 10 minutes.
5. Allow to release pressure naturally then open the lid.
6. Meanwhile, for the sauce: Melt butter in a pan over medium heat.
7. Add almond flour and stir continuously.
8. Slowly pour almond milk and stir constantly. Cook for 2-3 minutes or until sauce thickens.
9. Add garlic powder, cheese, and salt and stir until smooth.
10. Remove lid and transfer broccoli to the plate.
11. Drizzle broccoli with sauce and serve.

Nutritional Value (Amount per Serving):
Calories 440; Fat 39 g; Carbohydrates 11.6 g; Sugar 2.7 g; Protein 16 g

Tomato Garlic Bell Pepper

Preparation Time: 10 minutes; Cooking Time: 10 minutes; Serve: 5
Ingredients:
- 5 green bell peppers, cut into strips
- 2 tbsp fresh parsley, chopped
- 2 garlic cloves, chopped
- 2 tomatoes, chopped
- 1 onion, sliced
- 1 tbsp olive oil
- Pepper
- Salt

Directions:
1. Add oil into the instant pot and set the pot on sauté mode.
2. Add onion to the pot and sauté for 3-4 minutes.
3. Add bell peppers, and garlic and cook for 5 minutes.
4. Add remaining ingredients and stir well.

5. Seal pot with lid and cook on high for 5 minutes.
6. Release pressure using quick release method than open the lid.
7. Serve and enjoy.

Nutritional Value (Amount per Serving):
Calories 82; Fat 3.2 g; Carbohydrates 13.5 g; Sugar 8.2 g; Protein 2 g

Sweet & Spicy Cinnamon Carrots

Preparation Time: 10 minutes; Cooking Time: 1 minute; Serve: 4
Ingredients:
- 1 lb carrots, halved and quartered
- 1/8 tsp cinnamon
- ¼ tsp red pepper flakes
- ½ tsp cayenne pepper
- 1 tsp ground cumin
- 3 tsp ground mustard
- 2 tbsp butter
- 1 tbsp swerve
- Pepper
- Salt

Directions:
1. Pour 1 cup of water into the instant pot and place steamer basket in the pot.
2. Add carrots in the steamer basket.
3. Seal pot with lid and cook on high for 1 minute.
4. Release pressure using quick release method than open the lid.
5. Transfer carrots to the bowl.
6. Remove water from the pot.
7. Add butter into the instant pot and set the pot on sauté mode.
8. Add remaining ingredients and stir well.
9. Add carrots and stir for 1 minute.
10. Turn off the instant pot.
11. Sprinkle cinnamon on top of carrots and serve.

Nutritional Value (Amount per Serving):
Calories 114; Fat 6.7 g; Carbohydrates 13 g; Sugar 5.8 g; Protein 1.7 g

Sweet Cinnamon Carrots

Preparation Time: 10 minutes; Cooking Time: 4 minutes; Serve: 8
Ingredients:
- 2 lbs baby carrots
- ½ cup water
- ½ tsp ground cinnamon
- 2 tbsp swerve
- 1/3 cup butter
- Salt

Directions:
1. Add all ingredients into the instant pot and stir to combine.
2. Seal pot with lid and cook on high for 4 minutes.
3. Allow to release pressure naturally then open the lid.
4. Serve and enjoy.

Nutritional Value (Amount per Serving):
   Calories 109; Fat 7.8 g; Carbohydrates 10 g; Sugar 5.4 g; Protein 0.8 g

Italian Seasoned Carrots

Preparation Time: 10 minutes; Cooking Time: 20 minutes; Serve: 16
Ingredients:
- 5 lbs baby carrots
- 1 tsp spike seasoning
- 1 tsp Italian seasoning
- ½ cup vegetable stock
- 3 garlic cloves
- 1 onion, chopped
- 2 tbsp olive oil

Directions:
1. Add oil into the instant pot and set the pot on sauté mode.
2. Add garlic and onion and sauté for 4-5 minutes.
3. Add carrots and cook for 5 minutes.
4. Add remaining ingredients and stir well.
5. Seal pot with lid and cook on high for 10 minutes.
6. Allow to release pressure naturally then open the lid.
7. Serve and enjoy.

Nutritional Value (Amount per Serving):
   Calories 70; Fat 2.2 g; Carbohydrates 12.7 g; Sugar 7.2 g; Protein 1 g

Chapter 14: Desserts Recipes

Creamy Chocolate Mousse

Preparation Time: 10 minutes; Cooking Time: 20 minutes; Serve: 5
Ingredients:
- 4 egg yolks
- ½ tsp vanilla
- ½ cup unsweetened almond milk
- 1 cup heavy whipping cream
- ¼ cup unsweetened cocoa powder
- ¼ cup water
- ½ cup Swerve
- Pinch of sea salt

Directions:
1. In a bowl, add egg yolks and whisk until well beaten.
2. In a medium saucepan, add swerve, cocoa powder, and water and whisk until well combined.
3. Add almond milk and heavy whipping cream to the saucepan and whisk to combine. Heat over medium-low heat until just heat up but not boil.
4. Add vanilla and salt and stir well.
5. Slowly add saucepan mixture to the eggs and whisk until well combined.
6. Pour batter into the ramekins.
7. Pour 1 1.2 cups of water into the instant pot then place trivet to the pot.
8. Place ramekins on top of the trivet.
9. Seal pot with lid and cook on manual high pressure for 6 minutes.
10. Release pressure using quick release method than open the lid.
11. Remove ramekins from the pot and set aside to cool completely.
12. Place ramekins in the refrigerator for 3-4 hours.
13. Serve chilled and enjoy.

Nutritional Value (Amount per Serving):
Calories 141; Fat 13.4 g; Carbohydrates 3.9 g; Sugar 0.2 g; Protein 3.6 g

Mini Chocó Cake

Preparation Time: 10 minutes; Cooking Time: 9 minutes; Serve: 2
Ingredients:
- 2 eggs
- ¼ cup unsweetened cocoa powder
- 1 tsp vanilla
- ½ tsp baking powder
- 2 tbsp heavy cream
- 2 tbsp swerve

Directions:
1. In a bowl, mix together all dry ingredients until well combined.
2. Add all wet ingredients to the dry mixture and whisk until smooth.
3. Spray two ramekins with cooking spray.
4. Pour batter into the prepared ramekins.
5. Pour 1 cup water into the instant pot then place trivet to the pot.

6. Place ramekins on top of the trivet.
7. Seal pot with lid and cook on manual high pressure for 9 minutes.
8. Release pressure using quick release method than open the lid.
9. Remove ramekins from the pot and set aside to cool completely.
10. Place ramekins in the refrigerator for 3-4 hours.
11. Serve chilled and enjoy.

Nutritional Value (Amount per Serving):
Calories 152; Fat 11 g; Carbohydrates 9 g; Sugar 0.8 g; Protein 8 g

Easy Pumpkin Pudding

Preparation Time: 10 minutes; Cooking Time: 30 minutes; Serve: 6
Ingredients:
- 2 eggs
- 1 tsp vanilla
- 1 tsp pumpkin pie spice
- 15 oz can pumpkin puree
- ¾ cup Swerve
- ½ cup heavy whipping cream

Directions:
1. In a large mixing bowl, whisk eggs with remaining ingredients until well combined.
2. Spray 6*3-inch baking dish with cooking spray and set aside.
3. Pour batter into the prepared baking dish.
4. Pour 1 ½ cups water into the instant pot then place a trivet in the pot.
5. Place baking dish on top of the trivet.
6. Seal pot with lid and cook on high pressure for 20 minutes.
7. Allow to release pressure naturally for 10 minutes then release using quick release method.
8. Remove baking dish from the instant pot and set aside to cool completely.
9. Place in refrigerator for 4-5 hours.
10. Serve chilled and enjoy.

Nutritional Value (Amount per Serving):
Calories 89; Fat 5.2 g; Carbohydrates 7.4 g; Sugar 2.6 g; Protein 3.3 g

Delicious Coconut Custard

Preparation Time: 5 minutes; Cooking Time: 30 minutes; Serve: 4
Ingredients:
- 3 eggs
- 1 tsp vanilla extract
- 1/3 cup Swerve
- 1 cup unsweetened coconut milk

Directions:
1. Spray 6" baking dish with cooking spray and set aside.
2. In a large mixing bowl, blend together eggs, vanilla, swerve, and coconut milk.
3. Pour blended mixture into the baking dish and cover dish with aluminum foil piece.
4. Pour 2 cups water into the instant pot than place trivet in the pot.
5. Place baking dish on top of the trivet.

6. Seal pot with lid and cook on high pressure for 30 minutes.
7. Allow to release pressure naturally then open the lid.
8. Remove dish from the pot and set aside to cool completely.
9. Place in refrigerator for 3-4 hours.
10. Serve chilled and enjoy.

Nutritional Value (Amount per Serving):
Calories 189; Fat 17.6 g; Carbohydrates 3.9 g; Sugar 2.4 g; Protein 5.5 g

Vanilla Egg Custard

Preparation Time: 10 minutes; Cooking Time: 7 minutes; Serve: 6
Ingredients:
- 6 eggs
- 1 tsp vanilla
- ¾ cup Swerve
- 4 cups cream
- Pinch of sea salt

Directions:
1. In a large mixing bowl, beat eggs. Add cream, vanilla, salt, and swerve and blend until well combined.
2. Pour blended mixture into the baking dish and cover with foil.
3. Pour 1 ½ cups of water into the instant pot then place a trivet in the pot.
4. Place baking dish on top of the trivet.
5. Seal pot with lid and cook o high pressure for 7 minutes.
6. Allow to release pressure naturally for 10 minutes then release using quick release method.
7. Serve and enjoy.

Nutritional Value (Amount per Serving):
Calories 168; Fat 13.3 g; Carbohydrates 5.7 g; Sugar 3.6 g; Protein 6.8 g

Almond Coconut Cake

Preparation Time: 10 minutes; Cooking Time: 40 minutes; Serve: 8
Ingredients:
- Dry ingredients:
- 1 tsp apple pie spice
- 1 tsp baking powder
- 1/3 cup Swerve
- ½ cup unsweetened shredded coconut
- 1 cup almond flour
- Wet ingredients:
- ½ cup heavy whipping cream
- ¼ cup butter, melted
- 2 eggs, lightly beaten

Directions:
1. In a large bowl, mix together all dry ingredients until well combined.
2. Add all wet ingredients into the dry mixture and beat until well combined.
3. Spray 6" baking dish with cooking spray. Pour batter into the prepared baking dish.
4. Pour 2 cups water into the instant pot then place a trivet in the pot.
5. Place baking dish on top of the trivet.

6. Seal pot with lid and cook on high pressure for 40 minutes.
7. Allow to release pressure naturally for 10 minutes then release using quick release method.
8. Remove baking dish from the pot and set aside to cool completely.
9. Serve and enjoy.

Nutritional Value (Amount per Serving):
Calories 159; Fat 15.4 g; Carbohydrates 3.1 g; Sugar 0.7 g; Protein 2.9 g

Perfect Carrot Almond Cake

Preparation Time: 10 minutes; Cooking Time: 40 minutes; Serve: 8

Ingredients:
- 3 eggs
- ½ cup walnuts, chopped
- 1 cup carrot, shredded
- ½ cup heavy whipping cream
- ¼ cup coconut oil
- 1 ½ tsp apple pie spice
- 1 tsp baking powder
- 2/3 cup Swerve
- 1 cup almond flour

Directions:
1. Spray 6" baking dish with cooking spray and set aside.
2. Add all ingredients into the large mixing bowl and mix with electric mixer until well combined.
3. Pour batter into the prepared dish and cover dish with foil.
4. Pour 2 cups of water into the instant pot then place a trivet in the pot.
5. Place baking dish on top of the trivet.
6. Seal pot with lid and cook on high pressure for 40 minutes.
7. Allow to release pressure naturally for 10 minutes then release using quick release method.
8. Remove dish from the pot and set aside to cool completely.
9. Serve and enjoy.

Nutritional Value (Amount per Serving):
Calories 184; Fat 17.6 g; Carbohydrates 3.9 g; Sugar 1.1 g; Protein 5 g

Yummy Chocó Pudding Cake

Preparation Time: 10 minutes; Cooking Time: 6 minutes; Serve: 6

Ingredients:
- 2 eggs
- 3 tbsp unsweetened cocoa powder
- ¼ cup arrowroot
- 1 tsp vanilla
- ½ cup applesauce
- 2/3 cup unsweetened dark chocolate, chopped
- Pinch of salt

Directions:
1. Pour 2 cups water into the instant pot then place a trivet in the pot.
2. Spray 6-inch baking dish with cooking spray and set aside.

3. Add chopped dark chocolate into the microwave safe bowl and microwave for 1 minute or until chocolate melted. Stir well.
4. In a large bowl, whisk together eggs, vanilla, and applesauce until well combined.
5. Add dry ingredients and mix well. Add melted chocolate and stir to combine.
6. Pour batter into the prepared baking dish and place on top of the trivet.
7. Seal pot with lid and cook on high pressure for 4 minutes.
8. Release pressure using quick release method than open the lid.
9. Remove dish from the pot and set aside to cool completely.
10. Serve and enjoy.

Nutritional Value (Amount per Serving):
Calories 219; Fat 16.1 g; Carbohydrates 11 g; Sugar 2.3 g; Protein 6.2 g

Gluten-Free Chocó Lava Cake

Preparation Time: 10 minutes; Cooking Time: 7 minutes; Serve: 2
Ingredients:
- 2 tbsp butter, melted
- 2 eggs
- ¼ tsp vanilla
- 2 tbsp heavy whipping cream
- ½ tsp baking powder
- 2 tbsp swerve
- 4 tbsp unsweetened cocoa powder
- Pinch of salt

Directions:
1. Spray two ramekins with cooking spray and set aside.
2. Pour 2 cups of water into the instant pot then place a trivet in the pot.
3. In a large mixing bowl, whisk together cocoa powder, baking powder, swerve, and sea salt.
4. In another bowl, whisk together eggs, vanilla, and heavy whipping cream.
5. Add melted butter and whisk well.
6. Pour egg mixture into the dry mixture and using electric mixer blend until smooth.
7. Pour batter into the prepared ramekins.
8. Place ramekins on top of the trivet.
9. Seal pot with lid and cook on high pressure for 4 minutes.
10. Release pressure using quick release method than open the lid.
11. Remove ramekins from the instant pot and set aside to cool for 5 minutes.
12. Serve and enjoy.

Nutritional Value (Amount per Serving):
Calories 249; Fat 22.9 g; Carbohydrates 9.3 g; Sugar 0.6 g; Protein 8.1 g

Flavorful Vanilla Cheesecake

Preparation Time: 10 minutes; Cooking Time: 20 minutes; Serve: 8
Ingredients:
- 2 eggs
- ½ cup Swerve
- 1 tsp vanilla
- 16 oz cream cheese

Directions:
1. Spray 7" spring-form pan with cooking spray and set aside.
2. Add all ingredients into the blender and blend until smooth.
3. Pour batter into the prepared pan and cover the pan with foil.
4. Pour 2 cups of water into the instant pot then place a trivet in the pot.
5. Place cake pan on top of the trivet.
6. Seal pot with lid and cook on high pressure for 20 minutes.
7. Allow to release pressure naturally then open the lid.
8. Remove cake pan from the pot and set aside to cool completely.
9. Place in refrigerator for 2-3 hours.
10. Serve chilled and enjoy.

Nutritional Value (Amount per Serving):
Calories 215; Fat 20.9 g; Carbohydrates 1.8 g; Sugar 0.3 g; Protein 5.7 g

Tasty Matcha Cheesecake

Preparation Time: 10 minutes; Cooking Time: 35 minutes; Serve: 6
Ingredients:
- 2 eggs
- 1 tbsp matcha powder
- 2 tbsp heavy whipping cream
- ½ tsp vanilla
- 2 tsp coconut flour
- ½ cup Swerve
- 16 oz cream cheese

Directions:
1. Spray 7-inch spring-form pan with cooking spray and set aside.
2. Pour 1 ½ cups of water into the instant pot then place a trivet in the pot.
3. In a mixing bowl, add cream cheese, matcha powder, whipping cream, vanilla, coconut flour, and swerve.
4. Using electric mixer mix cream cheese mixture until smooth and creamy.
5. Add eggs one by one and beat well with electric mixer.
6. Pour batter into the prepared pan and place pan on top of the trivet.
7. Seal pot with lid and cook on high pressure for 35 minutes.
8. Allow to release pressure naturally then open the lid.
9. Remove cake pan from the pot and set aside to cool completely.
10. Top with cream and serve.

Nutritional Value (Amount per Serving):
Calories 307; Fat 29.8 g; Carbohydrates 3 g; Sugar 0.3 g; Protein 7.8 g

Yummy Chocó Layer Cheesecake

Preparation Time: 10 minutes; Cooking Time: 15 minutes; Serve: 8
Ingredients:
- 2 eggs
- 1 tbsp coconut oil

- ¼ cup unsweetened chocolate chips
- 2 cups water
- 2 tsp vanilla
- ¼ cup sour cream
- ½ cup peanut flour
- 1 cup erythritol
- 16 oz cream cheese, softened

Directions:
1. In a large bowl, beat cream cheese and sweetener until smooth. Slowly fold in vanilla, sour cream, and peanut flour.
2. Add eggs one by one and fold well to combine.
3. Spray 4" spring-form pan with cooking spray.
4. Pour batter into the prepared pan and cover the pan with foil.
5. Pour 1 ½ cups of water into the instant pot then place a trivet in the pot.
6. Place pan on top of the trivet.
7. Seal pot with lid and cook on high for 15 minutes.
8. Allow to release pressure naturally then open the lid.
9. Remove cake pan from the pot and set aside to cool completely.
10. In a microwave safe bowl add coconut oil and chocolate chips and microwave for 30 seconds. Stir until smooth.
11. Drizzle melted chocolate over cheesecake and place in refrigerator for 1-2 hours.
12. Serve chilled and enjoy.

Nutritional Value (Amount per Serving):
Calories 313; Fat 28.9 g; Carbohydrates 5.2 g; Sugar 0.3 g; Protein 8.2 g

Delicious Peanut Butter Fudge

Preparation Time: 10 minutes; Cooking Time: 42 minutes; Serve: 12
Ingredients:
- 1 cup unsweetened chocolate chips
- 1 tsp vanilla
- ¼ cup unsweetened peanut butter
- ¼ cup erythritol
- 8 oz cream cheese

Directions:
1. Add all ingredients into the instant pot and stir well.
2. Seal pot with lid and cook on slow cooker for 1 hour. Release pressure using quick release method.
3. Stir until smooth and cook for 30 minutes more.
4. Pour mixture into the 8*8" baking pan and place in refrigerator for 2 hours or until set.
5. Slice and serve.

Nutritional Value (Amount per Serving):
Calories 230; Fat 19.9 g; Carbohydrates 6.9 g; Sugar 0.4 g; Protein 5.1 g

Choco Almond Cupcakes

Preparation Time: 10 minutes; Cooking Time: 10 minutes; Serve: 6

Ingredients:
- 2 eggs
- 1 tsp vanilla
- ¼ cup blueberries
- 2 tsp baking powder
- 3 tbsp butter
- 2 tbsp unsweetened cocoa powder
- ¼ cup Swerve
- 3 tbsp yogurt
- ¼ cup cream cheese
- 1 cup shredded coconut
- 1 ½ cusp almond flour

Directions:
1. In a large bowl, combine together butter and eggs and beat using a blender until fluffy.
2. Add swerve, yogurt, and cream cheese and stir well.
3. Add almond flour, baking powder, and shredded coconut. Mix well.
4. Add blueberries and fold well.
5. Pour batter into the six-silicone mold and set aside.
6. Pour 1 cup of water into the instant pot and place trivet in the pot.
7. Place silicon mold on top of the trivet.
8. Seal pot with lid and cook on high for 10 minutes.
9. Release pressure using quick release method than open the lid.
10. Serve and enjoy.

Nutritional Value (Amount per Serving):
Calories 210; Fat 18.9 g; Carbohydrates 7.2 g; Sugar 2.5 g; Protein 5.4 g

Cinnamon Pancakes

Preparation Time: 10 minutes; Cooking Time: 3 minutes; Serve: 4

Ingredients:
- 4 eggs
- 2 tbsp heavy cream
- 3 tbsp butter
- 3 tsp baking powder
- 3 tbsp coconut flour
- ¼ cup almond flour
- ¼ tsp nutmeg
- ½ tsp cinnamon
- 2 tsp vanilla extract
- ¼ tsp salt

Directions:
1. In a large bowl, combine together all ingredients. Using blender beat until smooth batter form.
2. Spray instant pot from inside with cooking spray.
3. Set instant pot on sauté mode.
4. Add ¼ cup of batter into the pot and cook for 2-3 minutes.
5. Gently remove pancake from the pot and make remaining batter pancake.
6. Serve and enjoy.

Nutritional Value (Amount per Serving):
Calories 231; Fat 18.2 g; Carbohydrates 9.3 g; Sugar 1.5 g; Protein 7.7 g

Yummy Chocolate Mousse

Preparation Time: 10 minutes; Cooking Time: 5 minutes; Serve: 8
Ingredients:
- 2 cups mascarpone cheese
- ¼ tsp agar powder
- 1 tsp vanilla
- 3 tbsp swerve
- 1 tbsp coconut oil, melted
- ½ cup coconut cream
- ¼ cup yogurt
- 1 cup whipping cream
- For sauce
- 2 tsp swerve
- ½ tsp vanilla extract
- ¼ cup coconut cream
- 2 tbsp unsweetened cocoa powder

Directions:
1. Add coconut oil into the instant pot and set the pot on sauté mode. Add mascarpone, yogurt, swerve, and vanilla. Stir well and warm up.
2. Add agar powder and cook for 2-3 minutes. Stir continuously.
3. Transfer pot mixture to the bowl.
4. Add coconut cream and whipping cream to the bowl and beat using a blender.
5. Divide mixture into the two serving bowls and set aside.
6. Again, set the instant pot on sauté mode. Add coconut cream to the pot.
7. Stir in swerve, vanilla, and cocoa powder and cook for 1-2 minutes.
8. Remove sauce from pot and drizzle over mousse.
9. Place in refrigerator for 1 hour.
10. Serve chilled and enjoy.

Nutritional Value (Amount per Serving):
Calories 266; Fat 23.3 g; Carbohydrates 6.9 g; Sugar 1.4 g; Protein 8.9 g

Simple Chocolate Mug Cake

Preparation Time: 10 minutes; Cooking Time: 5 minutes; Serve: 1
Ingredients:
- 3 tbsp almond flour
- 2 tsp swerve
- ¼ tsp vanilla
- ½ tsp baking powder
- 1 tbsp unsweetened chocolate chips
- 1 tbsp unsweetened cocoa powder
- 3 tbsp coconut oil

Directions:
1. In a small bowl, mix together all ingredients until well combined.
2. Pour batter into the heat-safe mug and cover mug with foil.
3. Pour 1 cup of water into the instant pot then place a trivet in the pot.
4. Place mug on top of the trivet.
5. Seal pot with lid and cook on high for 5 minutes.
6. Release pressure using quick release method than open the lid.

7. Serve and enjoy.

Nutritional Value (Amount per Serving):
Calories 607; Fat 59.8 g; Carbohydrates 15 g; Sugar 1 g; Protein 7.5 g

Chocolate Brownies

Preparation Time: 10 minutes; Cooking Time: 25 minutes; Serve: 6

Ingredients:
- 3 eggs
- 2 tsp vanilla
- 2 tsp baking powder
- ¼ cup Swerve
- ¼ cup almonds, chopped
- 1/3 cup coconut cream
- ¼ cup unsweetened cocoa powder
- 2 tbsp butter, melted
- ¼ cup flaxseed meal
- ¾ cup almond flour

Directions:
1. In a large bowl, mix together almond flour, baking powder, swerve, cocoa powder, and flaxseed meal.
2. Add eggs, coconut cream, almond, vanilla, and butter. Beat using a blender until well combined.
3. Spray baking pan with cooking spray.
4. Pour batter into the pan and cover the pan with foil. Set aside.
5. Pour 2 cups of water into the instant pot then place a trivet in the pot.
6. Place pan on top of the trivet.
7. Seal pot with lid and cook on high for 25 minutes.
8. Release pressure using quick release method than open the lid.
9. Cut into the slices and serve.

Nutritional Value (Amount per Serving):
Calories 178; Fat 14.9 g; Carbohydrates 6.8 g; Sugar 1.2 g; Protein 6.3 g

Almond Cheesecake

Preparation Time: 10 minutes; Cooking Time: 35 minutes; Serve: 6

Ingredients:
- For crust:
- 1 tsp swerve
- 2 tbsp butter, melted
- ¾ cup ground almonds
- For cake:
- ¼ cup sour cream
- 1 tsp vanilla
- 2 eggs
- ¼ tsp liquid stevia
- 8 oz cream cheese, softened

Directions:
1. In a bowl, combine together almonds, butter, and swerve. Transfer the mixture into the 7" baking dish and spread evenly.
2. In another bowl beat together, liquid stevia and cream cheese until smooth.
3. Add egg one at a time.

4. Add sour cream and vanilla and beat until smooth.
5. Pour cheese mixture into the baking dish on top of the crust.
6. Cover dish with foil.
7. Pour 2 cups of water into the instant pot and place trivet in the pot.
8. Place baking pan on top of the trivet.
9. Seal pot with lid and cook on high for 12 minutes.
10. Allow to release pressure naturally then open the lid.
11. Slice and serve.

Nutritional Value (Amount per Serving):
Calories 279; Fat 26.4 g; Carbohydrates 4.5 g; Sugar 0.8 g; Protein 7.6 g

Hazelnuts Coconut Cake

Preparation Time: 10 minutes; Cooking Time: 20 minutes; Serve: 10
Ingredients:
- 2 cups coconut flour
- 2 tsp vanilla
- 3 tbsp hazelnuts, chopped
- 2 cups heavy whipping cream
- ¼ cup Swerve
- 5 eggs
- 1 cup coconut cream
- 3 tsp baking powder
- 3 tbsp shredded coconut
- ¼ cup almond flour

Directions:
1. Pour 1 cup of water into the instant pot then place a trivet in the pot.
2. In a large bowl, mix together all dry ingredients.
3. Add egg one by one ad beat using a blender until well combined.
4. Add vanilla and coconut cream and beat for 2 minutes.
5. Spray cake pan with cooking spray.
6. Pour batter into the cake pan and place pan on top of the trivet.
7. Seal pot with lid and cook on high for 20 minutes.
8. Release pressure using quick release method than open the lid.
9. Remove cake pan from the pot and set aside to cool completely.
10. Meanwhile, beat heavy cream until fluffy. Add hazelnuts and stir well.
11. Remove cake from pan and top with whipped cream. Place in refrigerator for 1-2 hours.
12. Serve and enjoy.

Nutritional Value (Amount per Serving):
Calories 204; Fat 18.9 g; Carbohydrates 5.3 g; Sugar 1.5 g; Protein 4.6 g

Hazelnuts Brownies

Preparation Time: 10 minutes; Cooking Time: 25 minutes; Serve: 6
Ingredients:
- 4 eggs
- 1 tsp vanilla
- 3 tbsp hazelnuts, chopped
- ¼ cup Swerve

- 2 tbsp butter
- ½ cup mascarpone
- ½ cup flaxseed meal
- ¾ cup almond flour
- ¼ tsp salt

Directions:
1. In a large bowl, add all ingredients and beat until smooth.
2. Spray baking dish with cooking spray.
3. Pour batter into the prepared pan.
4. Pour 1 cup of water into the instant pot then place a trivet in the pot.
5. Place dish on top of the trivet.
6. Seal pot with lid and cook on high for 25 minutes.
7. Release pressure using quick release method than open the lid.
8. Cut into pieces and serve.

Nutritional Value (Amount per Serving):
Calories 198; Fat 15.5 g; Carbohydrates 4.8 g; Sugar 0.7 g; Protein 8.9 g

Almond Coconut Bars

Preparation Time: 10 minutes; Cooking Time: 15 minutes; Serve: 6
Ingredients:
- 3 eggs
- 1 tsp vanilla
- ¼ cup almonds, chopped
- 1 tbsp sesame seeds
- 1 tbsp chia seeds
- 2 tbsp swerve
- 2 tbsp almond butter
- ½ cup coconut oil
- ¼ cup flaxseed meal
- 2 cups shredded coconut
- ¼ tsp salt

Directions:
1. Add all the ingredients into the large mixing bowl and mix until well combined and sticky.
2. Line baking pan with parchment paper and spray with cooking spray.
3. Pour batter into the baking pan and spread evenly. Cover dish with foil and set aside.
4. Pour 2 cups of water into the instant pot then place a trivet in the pot.
5. Place pan on top of the trivet.
6. Seal pot with lid and cook on high for 15 minutes.
7. Release pressure using quick release method than open the lid.
8. Cut into the slices and serve.

Nutritional Value (Amount per Serving):
Calories 381; Fat 36.9 g; Carbohydrates 8.8 g; Sugar 2.4 g; Protein 7.1 g

Choco Almond Pudding

Preparation Time: 10 minutes; Cooking Time: 2 minutes; Serve: 4
Ingredients:
- 1 tsp vanilla
- ½ cup coconut cream

- 1 ¼ cup whipping cream
- 2 tbsp unsweetened chocolate chips
- 2 tbsp unsweetened cocoa powder
- ¼ cup almonds, chopped
- 1 tbsp agar powder
- ¼ cup Swerve
- 1 cup unsweetened almond milk

Directions:
1. Add milk into the instant pot and set the pot on sauté mode.
2. Add swerve, vanilla, coconut cream, and cocoa powder.
3. Stir constantly then add agar powder and cook for 1-2 minutes.
4. Turn off the instant pot.
5. Add almonds and stir well.
6. Transfer instant pot mixture to a large bowl.
7. Add whipping cream and beat using the blender for 2-3 minutes.
8. Allow to cool completely then serve.

Nutritional Value (Amount per Serving):
Calories 282; Fat 27 g; Carbohydrates 8.5 g; Sugar 1.5 g; Protein 4.5 g

Choco Chip Orange Muffins

Preparation Time: 10 minutes; Cooking Time: 30 minutes; Serve: 5
Ingredients:
- 5 eggs
- ¼ tsp cinnamon
- 2 tsp swerve
- 1 tsp orange extract
- ¼ tsp baking soda
- ½ tsp baking powder
- 1 tbsp dark chocolate chips
- 1 tbsp butter
- ½ cup almond milk
- 1 tbsp flaxseed meal
- 1 tbsp chia seeds
- ¼ cup almonds, chopped
- ½ cup almond flour

Directions:
1. In a large bowl, mix together almond flour, baking soda, baking powder, flaxseed meal, chia seeds, and almonds.
2. Add eggs, cinnamon, swerve, orange extract, butter, and almond milk. Beat with a blender until well combined.
3. Pour batter evenly between silicone muffin molds. Top with Chocó chips.
4. Pour 1 cup of water into the instant pot then place a trivet in the pot.
5. Place muffin molds on top of the trivet.
6. Seal pot with lid and cook on high for 30 minutes.
7. Release pressure using quick release method than open the lid.
8. Serve and enjoy.

Nutritional Value (Amount per Serving):
Calories 208; Fat 17.5 g; Carbohydrates 6.2 g; Sugar 2.4 g; Protein 8.4 g

Delicious Vanilla Pudding

Preparation Time: 10 minutes; Cooking Time: 3 minutes; Serve: 3
Ingredients:
- 5 egg yolks
- 5 egg whites
- ¼ tsp nutmeg
- ½ tsp lemon zest
- 1 tsp vanilla
- ½ tsp glucomannan powder
- 3 tsp cocoa powder
- 1 tsp erythritol
- ¼ cup coconut oil
- 1 cup cream cheese

Directions:
1. Add cream cheese into the instant pot and set the pot on sauté mode.
2. Stir in glucomannan powder, coconut oil, erythritol, cocoa, and egg yolks. Stir well and cook for 2-3 minutes.
3. In a large bowl, combine together egg whites, nutmeg, and vanilla and beat using a blender until foamy.
4. Slowly add egg whites into the pot and stir well.
5. Pour mixture into the serving bowl and set aside to cool completely.
6. Place in refrigerator for 1 hour.
7. Serve and enjoy.

Nutritional Value (Amount per Serving):
Calories 554; Fat 53.1 g; Carbohydrates 6.1 g; Sugar 1 g; Protein 16.7 g

Coconut Avocado Pudding

Preparation Time: 10 minutes; Cooking Time: 3 minutes; Serve: 2
Ingredients:
- ½ avocado, cut into cubes
- 2 tsp swerve
- 1 tsp vanilla
- 1 tsp agar powder
- ¼ cup coconut cream
- 1 cup coconut milk

Directions:
1. Add coconut cream and avocado into the food processor and process until smooth. Set aside.
2. In a large bowl, combine together coconut milk, vanilla, swerve, and agar powder. Stir until well combined. Add coconut cream and avocado mixture and stir well.
3. Pour mixture into a heat-safe bowl.
4. Pour one cup of water into the instant pot then place a trivet in the pot.
5. Place bowl on top of the trivet.
6. Seal pot with lid and select steam mode and cook for 3 minutes.
7. Release pressure using quick release method than open the lid.
8. Remove bowl from the pot and set aside to cool completely.
9. Place bowl in refrigerator for 1 hour.

10. Serve and enjoy.

Nutritional Value (Amount per Serving):
Calories 245; Fat 23 g; Carbohydrates 9.9 g; Sugar 1.5 g; Protein 2.4 g

Cinnamon Almond Cheese Cake

Preparation Time: 10 minutes; Cooking Time: 35 minutes; Serve: 8

Ingredients:
- 2 eggs
- ¼ tsp apple pie spice
- ¼ tsp cinnamon
- 1 tbsp unsweetened cocoa powder
- ½ cup cream cheese
- ¼ cup almond butter
- ½ cup Swerve
- ½ cup almond flour
- 1 cup coconut flour
- ½ tsp salt

Directions:
1. In a large bowl, mix together coconut flour, apple pie spice, cinnamon, swerve, almonds, and salt.
2. Slowly add eggs, cream cheese, and butter and beat using a blender until well combined.
3. Pour 1 cup of water into the instant pot then place a trivet in the pot.
4. Spray baking dish with cooking spray.
5. Pour batter into the prepared dish and cover dish with foil.
6. Place dish on top of the trivet.
7. Seal pot with lid and cook on high for 35 minutes.
8. Release pressure using quick release method than open the lid.
9. Serve and enjoy.

Nutritional Value (Amount per Serving):
Calories 89; Fat 7.7 g; Carbohydrates 2.5 g; Sugar 0.3 g; Protein 3.3 g

Yummy Chocolate Truffles

Preparation Time: 10 minutes; Cooking Time: 30 minutes; Serve: 5

Ingredients:
- 3 egg yolks
- ½ tsp stevia
- ¼ tsp cinnamon
- ½ cup whipped cream
- ¼ tsp xanthan gum
- ¼ cup Swerve
- 1 cup heavy cream
- ½ cup dark chocolate chips, melted

Directions:
1. In a large bowl, combine together egg yolks, xanthan gum, and swerve. Using blender blend until well combined.
2. Add heavy cream, stevia, cinnamon, vanilla, and melted chocolate and beat for a minute.
3. Pour batter into the ramekins and cover ramekins with foil. Set aside.
4. Pour 1 cup of water into the instant pot then place a trivet in the pot.
5. Place ramekins on top of the trivet.

6. Seal pot with lid and cook on high for 30 minutes.
7. Allow to release pressure naturally then open the lid.
8. Top with whipped cream and serve.

Nutritional Value (Amount per Serving):
Calories 207; Fat 18.5 g; Carbohydrates 9.8 g; Sugar 6.5 g; Protein 3.2 g

Walnut Pumpkin Mug Cake

Preparation Time: 10 minutes; Cooking Time: 2 minutes; Serve: 2

Ingredients:
- ¼ tsp apple pie spice
- 2 tsp swerve
- 1 tsp baking powder
- 1 tbsp coconut oil, melted
- 1 tbsp pumpkin seeds
- 1 tbsp chia seeds
- 1 tbsp walnuts, chopped
- 1 tbsp almonds, chopped
- ½ cup almond flour
- ¼ tsp salt

Directions:
1. In a large bowl, combine together almond flour, baking powder, pumpkin seeds, chia seeds, walnuts, and almonds.
2. Add apple pie spice, swerve, and coconut oil. Mix well.
3. Pour batter in the heat-safe mug and top with chocolate chips.
4. Pour 1 cup of water into the instant pot then place a trivet in the pot.
5. Place mug on top of the trivet.
6. Seal pot with lid and cook on high for 2 minutes.
7. Release pressure using quick release method than open the lid.
8. Top with pumpkin seeds and serve.

Nutritional Value (Amount per Serving):
Calories 189; Fat 17.3 g; Carbohydrates 7.4 g; Sugar 0.5 g; Protein 4.9 g

Vanilla Coconut Custard

Preparation Time: 10 minutes; Cooking Time: 40 minutes; Serve: 4

Ingredients:
- 5 eggs
- ¼ cup coconut milk
- ¼ tsp cinnamon
- 1 tsp vanilla
- 2 tbsp chia seeds
- ½ tsp agar powder
- 2 tbsp swerve
- 1 cup heavy cream

Directions:
1. In a large bowl, whisk together coconut milk, chia seeds, agar powder, swerve, eggs, and heavy cream. Using blender beat until creamy.
2. Stir in vanilla and beat for a minute.
3. Pour batter into ramekins and cover with foil. Set aside.
4. Pour 1 cup of water into the instant pot then place a trivet in the pot.

5. Place ramekins on top of the trivet.
6. Seal pot with lid and select slow cooker mode and cook for 40 minutes.
7. Release pressure using quick release method than open the lid.
8. Remove ramekins from the pot and set aside to cool completely.
9. Place ramekins in the refrigerator for 1 hour.
10. Serve chilled and enjoy.

Nutritional Value (Amount per Serving):
Calories 240; Fat 21.3 g; Carbohydrates 4.1 g; Sugar 1.1 g; Protein 8.7 g

Vanilla Berry Mousse

Preparation Time: 10 minutes; Cooking Time: 20 minutes; Serve: 4
Ingredients:
- 4 blueberries
- 4 strawberries, sliced
- ½ tsp vanilla
- ¼ cup almond milk
- ½ cup heavy cream
- ¼ cup Swerve
- 2 tbsp water
- 2 egg yolks

Directions:
1. Pour 1 ½ cups of water into the instant pot then place a trivet in the pot.
2. In a small saucepan, add sweetener and water and heat over medium heat until sweetener dissolved.
3. Remove pan from heat and whisk in vanilla, milk, and cream.
4. In a bowl, whisk egg yolks.
5. Slowly add cream mixture and stir into the eggs.
6. Pour mixture into the ramekins and place on top of the trivet.
7. Seal pot with lid and cook on high for 6 minutes.
8. Release pressure using quick release method than open the lid.
9. Remove ramekins from the pot and set aside to cool completely.
10. Place in refrigerator for 1-2 hours.
11. Top with blueberries and sliced strawberries and serve.

Nutritional Value (Amount per Serving):
Calories 125; Fat 7.8 g; Carbohydrates 13 g; Sugar 8.6 g; Protein 2.5 g

Lime Orange Pudding

Preparation Time: 10 minutes; Cooking Time: 3 minutes; Serve: 4
Ingredients:
- 1 tsp lime zest, grated
- 1 tsp orange extract
- 1 tbsp coconut oil
- 1 tbsp swerve
- ¼ cup whipping cream
- ¼ cup coconut cream
- 1 tsp agar powder
- ¼ cup unsweetened coconut milk

Directions:

1. Add coconut oil into the instant pot and set the pot on sauté mode.
2. Add coconut milk, whipping cream, and coconut cream to the pot and stir constantly.
3. Add orange extract, agar powder, and swerve. Stir constantly and cook for 2-3 minutes.
4. Turn off the instant pot and pour pot mixture into the ramekins.
5. Sprinkle lime zest on top of each ramekin.
6. Place ramekins in the refrigerator for 1 hour.
7. Serve and enjoy.

Nutritional Value (Amount per Serving):
Calories 93; Fat 9.6 g; Carbohydrates 2 g; Sugar 0.7 g; Protein 0.5 g

Choco Coconut Truffles

Preparation Time: 10 minutes; Cooking Time: 3 minutes; Serve: 10
Ingredients:
- 1 cup shredded coconut
- 1 tsp lime zest, grated
- 1 tsp vanilla
- ¼ cup unsweetened cocoa powder
- ¼ cup Swerve
- 1 cup heavy cream
- 3 tbsp butter
- 1 cup unsweetened dark chocolate chips

Directions:
1. Add butter into the instant pot and set the pot on sauté mode.
2. Add vanilla, swerve, heavy cream, and chocolate chips. Stir constantly and cook for 3 minutes.
3. Turn off the instant pot.
4. Add coconut and stir well.
5. Transfer pot mixture to the air-tight container and place in refrigerator for 1-2 hours.
6. Using scooper scoop to form the truffles.
7. Serve and enjoy.

Nutritional Value (Amount per Serving):
Calories 267; Fat 23.7 g; Carbohydrates 9.3 g; Sugar 0.6 g; Protein 4.2 g

Delicious Almond Scones

Preparation Time: 10 minutes; Cooking Time: 10 minutes; Serve: 6
Ingredients:
- 2 eggs
- 1 tsp vanilla
- 2 tsp baking powder
- 1 tsp swerve
- ½ cup almond butter, melted
- 1 cup almond flour
- 1 cup fresh strawberries, chopped
- ½ tsp salt

Directions:
1. In a large bowl, combine together all dry ingredients.
2. Add vanilla, almond butter, and eggs and beat using a blender until well combined.

3. Add strawberries and stir well.
4. Make six scones from mixture and place on a baking dish. Set aside.
5. Pour 2 cups of water into the instant pot then place a trivet in the pot.
6. Place dish on top of the trivet.
7. Seal pot with lid and cook on high for 10 minutes.
8. Release pressure using quick release method than open the lid.
9. Remove scones from the pot and set aside to cool completely.
10. Serve and enjoy.

Nutritional Value (Amount per Serving):
Calories 68; Fat 4.6 g; Carbohydrates 4.4 g; Sugar 1.6 g; Protein 3.3 g

Blackberry Cinnamon Brownies

Preparation Time: 10 minutes; Cooking Time: 3 minutes; Serve: 6
Ingredients:
- 1/4 cup almond butter
- ¼ tsp cinnamon
- ½ cup fresh blackberries
- ¼ cup coconut oil
- 3 tbsp swerve
- ¼ cup yogurt
- ¼ cup coconut flour

Directions:
1. Spray baking dish with cooking spray and set aside.
2. Pour 1 cup of water into the instant pot then place a trivet in the pot.
3. Add all ingredients in a large bowl and beat using the blender for 2-3 minutes.
4. Pour batter into the prepared baking dish.
5. Place dish on top of the trivet.
6. Seal pot with lid and cook on high for 3 minutes.
7. Allow to release pressure naturally then open the lid.
8. Serve and enjoy.

Nutritional Value (Amount per Serving):
Calories 100; Fat 9.7 g; Carbohydrates 3.4 g; Sugar 1.4 g; Protein 1 g

Conclusion

In this keto instant pot cookbook, you will find a huge collection of healthy, delicious and nutritious recipes. This book will help people lose their weight and get a healthier lifestyle.

All the recipes are made in instant pot. Instant pot meal is healthier, and its nutrition preserve technology gives your meals with essential nutrients intact including vitamins, minerals, and protein.

Thank you for downloading this book! I really do hope you found the recipes as delicious and mouth-watering as I did.

Happy Cooking!

Manufactured by Amazon.ca
Bolton, ON